Resource Curse and Post-Soviet Eurasia

Resource Curse and Post-Soviet Eurasia

Oil, Gas, and Modernization

Edited by Vladimir Gel'man
and
Otar Marganiya

LEXINGTON BOOKS
A division of
ROWMAN & LITTLEFIELD PUBLISHERS, INC.
Lanham • Boulder • New York • Toronto • Plymouth, UK

Published by Lexington Books
A division of Rowman & Littlefield Publishers, Inc.
A wholly owned subsidiary of The Rowman & Littlefield Publishing Group,
Inc.
4501 Forbes Boulevard, Suite 200, Lanham, Maryland 20706
http://www.lexingtonbooks.com

Estover Road, Plymouth PL6 7PY, United Kingdom

British Library Cataloguing in Publication Information Available

Library of Congress Cataloging-in-Publication Data
Resource curse and post-Soviet Eurasia : oil, gas, and modernization / edited
by Vladimir Gel'man and Otar Marganiya.
   p. cm.
 ISBN 978-0-7391-4373-5 (alk. paper) — ISBN 978-0-7391-4375-9 (electronic)
 1. Petroleum industry and trade—Europe, Eastern. 2. Petroleum industry
and trade—Russia (Federation) 3. Natural resources—Europe, Eastern. 4.
Natural resources—Russia (Federation) 5. Post-communism—Economic
aspects. I. Gel'man, Vladimir, 1965– II. Marganiya, Otar, 1959–
  HD9575.E852R47 2010
  338.2'7280947—dc22   2010010542

Printed in the United States of America

Contents

Figures and Tables

FIGURES

TABLES

Acknowledgments

This book resulted from the research project conducted under the auspices of the Center for Modernization Studies at the European University at St. Petersburg. It could not have been written without the generous assistance and help of many people and institutions. We would like to thank our numerous colleagues and graduate students of the European University at St. Petersburg for their active participation in various discussions and their stimulating comments during the period of the project. Our special thanks go to Simon Patterson for translating the chapters of the book and to Maria Roti for her linguistic assistance. Thanks also to our editors at Lexington Books for their patience and forbearance. Needless to say that those errors of fact and interpretation that remain in the book, as well as statements and views expressed herein, are those of the authors and not necessarily those of any institution.

Introduction

Resource Curse and Post-Soviet Eurasia

Vladimir Gel'man

By the end of the 2000s, the term "resource curse"[1] had become so widespread that it had turned into a kind of magic keyword, not only in the scholarly language of the social sciences, but also in the discourse of politicians, commentators, and analysts all over the world—like the term "modernization" in the early 1960s or "transition" in the early 1990s. In fact, the aggravation of many problems in the global economy and politics, against the background of the rally of oil prices in 2004–2008, became the environment for academic and public debates about the role of natural resources in general and oil and gas in particular, in the development of various societies.[2] The results of numerous studies do not give a clear answer to questions about the nature and mechanisms of the influence of the oil and gas abundance on the economic, political, and social processes in various states and nations. However, the majority of scholars and observers agree that this influence in most of the countries is primarily negative.[3] According to widespread opinion, the "oil curse" gives rise to pathologies of development in various issue areas—ranging from civil wars[4] and corruption[5] to significant restrictions on political and civil rights (including issues that are not closely related to the oil and gas sector—such as media freedom[6] or gender equality[7]). At the same time, individual "success stories" of oil- and gas-rich countries are rather an exception that proves this rule.

The oil curse has and continues to have an ambiguous effect on the political and economic trajectories of various states and nations at various historical periods. The experience of countries of post-Soviet Eurasia, which arose after the collapse of the Soviet Union, was not unique in this respect. Oil-rich countries—Russia, Azerbaijan, and Kazakhstan as well as gas-rich Turkmenistan for almost the last two decades have shown inconsistent trends of their development, which in many ways was also caused by the preceding "legacy" that was established primarily during the Soviet period of their history. Oil abundance became one of the most important factors of post-Communist modernization in these nations.[8] At the same time, while the process of "triple transition" in Eastern Europe included a simultaneous transition from the central planned economy to competitive markets, from one-party regimes to pluralist democracies, and from Communist empire to nation-states,[9] countries of post-Soviet Eurasia transformed in a manner of pendulum-like swings, including under the influence of oil and gas. At the end of the 2000s, the results of two decades of the transformation in oil-rich countries of post-Soviet Eurasia looks rather contradictory. In terms of economic reforms, after a severe and lengthy transformation recession in the 1990s (which in the case of Russia ended with the default in 1998), during the 2000s post-Soviet nations showed an impressive growth, which was in many ways achieved thanks to high world oil prices.[10] However, the global economic crisis of 2008–2009 cast doubts on the prospects of stable economic development of Russia and its post-Soviet oil-rich neighbors, such as Kazakhstan and Azerbaijan. In terms of political changes, in the 1990s Kazakhstan and Central Asian countries established their personalist authoritarian regimes, characterized by internal instability; in the 2000s, Azerbaijan became one of the few cases of successful dynastic leadership succession of an authoritarian regime. Russia, which made an attempt at democratization in the 1990s, in the 2000s showed a tendency for the establishment of a new authoritarianism, although the issue of its prospects so far remains open.[11] At the same time, despite a certain improvement in a number of socioeconomic indicators of development during the 2000s, the quality of governance, indicators of the rule of law, the protection of property rights, and economic freedoms remained in all countries of post-Soviet Eurasia at an extremely low level throughout the entire period of two decades of transformation, against the background of an increase in corruption in these countries.[12]

In light of these assessments and evaluations, we have to say that the oil-rich countries of post-Soviet Eurasia are far from being success stories of post-Communist modernization, but rather stories, if not of their complete collapse, then at least of a kind of sideways trend of economic and political development. But should these processes be connected with oil and gas? To what extent is the oil abundance really a curse rather than a blessing for the countries of post-Soviet Eurasia, or has it only had a side effect against the background of effects of other more fundamental tendencies, or has it not had any fundamental importance at all? What are the mechanisms and consequences of the influence of oil and gas factors on such aspects of their development as state building, democracy, rule of law, property rights, state-business relationships, and foreign policy? How did the global economic crisis of 2008–2009 influence the oil nations of post-Soviet Eurasia, and what are the short-term trends and long-term prospects of their development? This book is also devoted to finding answers to these questions. The authors, specialists in different disciplines of social sciences (economics, political science, international relations), have made it their task to make a critical review of different aspects of economic and political development in Russia and in other post-Soviet nations in the light of the concept of the resource curse. This chapter presents, on the one hand, a survey of approaches of the influence of the oil abundance on the economic and political development of various countries. On the other hand, it summarizes the analysis of answers of countries of post-Soviet Eurasia to the challenges of the resource curse. It also presents the results of studies of different aspects of these problems, which make up the basis of the subsequent chapters of this book.

RESOURCE CURSE: INEVITABLE OR CONDITIONAL, FULL-FLEDGED OR PARTIAL?

Essentially, all the manifestations of negative economic and political effects of the resource curse, in one way or another, are connected with the extraction and distribution of the resource rent[13]—above all, in the oil and gas sector. The technological aspects of the production, delivery, distribution, and sale of oil and gas, caused by the low share of people employed in this sector and the relatively low production costs and concentration of production in a small number of major companies is added to by the fact that the governments of oil nations are capable of setting a highly concentrated rent, the size of which depends on the prices on international markets. As, on the one hand, this process is structurally bounded, and does not depend on the steps made by economic and political actors, and on the other, the governments of oil nations are concerned to stay in power and strive for a maximum oil rent, this constellation of conditions causes a number of important economic and political consequences. Governments of oil nations not only have additional capabilities for corruption, controlling easily lootable resources, but also have incentives to conduct inefficient economic policy.[14] Owing to pressure from special interest groups, the "voracity effect" arises[15]: the state expenditures begin to grow swiftly, faster than the amount of rent, while the revenues from the export of oil and gas are often used by government to implement ambitious investment projects that do not give positive returns (the "white elephants" effect).[16] In its turn, the oil and gas sector becomes the most attractive object for investments, attracting major financial flows that do not reach other sectors of the economy, where a decline begins (the "Dutch disease" effect).[17] Accordingly, this causes a decrease in labor productivity in non–raw material sectors. In general, this developmental trajectory causes economic stagnation rather than growth. Furthermore, the instability of international oil markets causes an unstable development of oil nations, which often go through cyclical changes according to the principle "from boom to bust" and vice versa.[18]

The governments of oil nations are also forced to deal with the citizens of their countries, who are inclined to redistribute the resource rent in their favor. The need to protect their rule causes governments to resort to the use of force, and to look for compromises with various social groups. Thanks to the oil and gas rent, the governments receive the opportunity to purchase the loyalty of the population, both through the low level of individual taxation ("taxation effect"), and personal or group social payments and benefits.[19] Furthermore, they are inclined to expand the scale of the state machinery unjustifiably, and the public sector in general, including the increase of employees who are not employed in the oil and gas sector (which has a small number of personnel), creating additional jobs for some social groups, and isolating others from the labor market (above all women and young people).[20] Thus, incentives not only for an economic but also for a political autonomy of society in general, and of its various social groups in particular, are dramatically undermined. But besides the juicy carrots for their citizens, governments of oil nations are also forced to hold heavy sticks, in order to protect themselves from other rent-seekers. They use the oil and gas rent to increase the size and financing of the coercive apparatus of the state, and thus create additional jobs in the army, police, and security troops (repression effect).[21] To summarize, one should note that the combination of significant amounts of oil and gas rent, and incentives from their inefficient use by governments, often prevents the successful modernization of "oil states."[22] Their governments, and also their citizens, are inclined to spend resources on increasing current consumption, instead of striving for long-term sustainable development: a modernization effect arises, which corrodes states and societies, and undermines incentives for good governance in the long-term perspective.[23]

This sad picture of the negative consequences of the resource curse, however, looks at least incomplete: it puts new issues on the research agenda. Why do some oil-rich countries (such as Norway) manage to minimize these consequences, and the oil and gas abundance serves as the basis for their long-term stable prosperity, while other oil-rich states (such as Nigeria) are unable to break out of the vicious circle of conflicts, inefficiency, and corruption? Why in the same countries do the various negative effects of the resource curse perform differently? Some of them demonstrated a completely destructive influence on the economic and political development of oil states, while the consequences of others have partial effects, or governments of these states are able to combat them more or less successfully. In other words, is the negative influence of the resource curse on various nations and societies conditional, or is it inevitable? And what factors affected this influence in a full-fledged or partial nature?

Above all, the very concept of "oil states" requires rethinking and clarification, as the role of oil and gas in their economies and politics is rather different in a number of important dimensions and parameters. Thad Dunning, in his comparative cross-national study, outlines three gradations of these oil states by the degree of their dependence on the export of natural resources: (1) "resource-abundant" states, which have a fairly significant amount of natural resources that can be exported on the world market; (2) "rentier states," where the share of revenue from export of natural resources is a fairly significant amount of their gross revenue (high resource to revenue ratio); and finally, (3) "resource-dependent" states, where the export of natural resources makes up a fairly significant share of their gross domestic product (high resource to GDP ratio).[24] Some authors propose to examine these parameter characteristics not in absolute terms, but calculated per capita.[25] Examples of each of the gradations of oil states may be, for example, Canada, Norway, and Nigeria. The effects of the resource curse have a fundamentally different effect on the states belonging to each of these gradations. In cases of resource-abundant states, these effects are not of great importance, but in cases of rentier states and resource-dependent states, they differ significantly from one country to another.[26]

Specialists analyzing the resource curse in the comparative perspective link the negative effects of this phenomenon or the lack of them above all with the quality of the institutional environment of various oil and gas states.[27] To put it bluntly, one might say that countries that have created strong and efficient institutions are much better at resisting the effects of the resource curse than countries with weak and inefficient institutions. As not only institutions are affecting the resource curse, but the influence of the resource curse may also weaken institutions, a virtuous circle of successes in the cases of some (few) countries arises, and a vicious circle of failures in many other countries is also visible. In other words, in countries that are hit by the negative effect of the resource curse, the demand for high-quality institutions decreases not only from the side of the governments, but also from the society as a whole: an example of this may be the decline in media freedom in a number of oil states.[28] According to this approach, this conditional negative effect of the resource curse becomes the consequence of the side effects of low-quality institutions,[29] which are incapable of playing the role of a filter that prevents pathologies in the development of oil states.

However, this approach quite logically puts on the agenda the issue of the genesis of the causes and mechanisms of the evolution of the institutions themselves, and a search for answers lies at the heart of the agenda of modern economic and political studies.[30] While some institutions are established and caused by historically grounded and deeply embedded legacy, and their nature is path-dependent, other institutions are created "here and now" during the interaction of domestic and foreign economic and political actors. Their incentives in the process of institution building are primarily driven by the aspiration to utility maximization, which in oil nations corresponds to the tasks of maximization of the resource rent: as Douglass North notes, "Institutions . . . are created to serve the interests of those with the bargaining power to devise new rules."[31] A list of various factors that influence institutions include structural conditions (such as the geopolitical position of the states), cultural issues (such as the values, attitudes, and orientations of the actors),[32] and policy-related aspects. Thus, explanations of the combination of continuity and change of institutions requires a generalization of analysis of combinations of both structural factors and the role of agency: inevitably, they lie outside the actual concept of the resource curse as such, and are of a more universal nature.[33]

In this sense, the argument on the conditional resource curse also requires certain clarification. This means that the negative effect of the resource curse on the political and economic development of oil states manifests itself in combination with the influence of other factors that are not directly connected with oil, such as structural and ac-tor-based factors—from the historically embedded "legacy of the past" to the strategic political and policy decisions of governments. Institutions themselves do not create the resource curse: they only mediate the negative effects of these influences, increasing or hindering them. While strong institutions serve as a kind of barrier to the effects of the resource curse, weak institutions rather serve to aggravate them. Depending on the quality of institutions, they may act as a more or less powerful "filter" in a certain issue area of the economy and/or politics, and thus the resource curse may have either a full-fledged or a partial nature.

This understanding of the logic of the resource curse requires a deeper analysis not only of oil-related factors of the economy and politics of oil states, but also a rethink of the wider context of their development both in the past and the present. This is shown by the "success story" of Norway—a country that the oil curse could not spoil—and the "story of failure" of Nigeria—a country that has become a symbol of everything bad that resource abundance can bring to modern states and societies. It can be said that the long-term prosperity of Norway and the permanent troubles of Nigeria have become the result not only of the oil wealth of these countries as such, but also the logical consequence of the entire trajectory of the previous historical evolution ("petro-states are built on what already exists")[34] and their contemporary dynamics. Thus, a study of the trajectories of development of different oil states involves not only using the schol-arly value of theories, analyzing the effects of the influence of the resource curse, but also an interdisciplinary inclusion of area studies on specific aspects of the political and economic processes in various countries within the theoretical and comparative context. It is this approach that lies at the basis of our studies of various manifestations of the resource curse in the states of post-Soviet Eurasia—Russia and its neighbors.

OIL, GAS, AND POST-SOVIET DEVELOPMENTS

A significant influence of the oil abundance on politics and the economy has been inherent to Russia since the late nineteenth century, when it first joined the club of leading world oil states, as one of the major international oil producers. In the Soviet period, especially during World War II, oil abundance served as one of the cornerstones of the military power of the country. In the 1960s, the discovery of major oil and gas fields in Western Siberia had a dramatic effect on the subsequent trajectory of the development of the Soviet Union.[35] On the one hand, under conditions of an inefficient planned economy, the large flow of revenues from the export of oil and gas to Western Europe enabled the leadership of the country to keep up with the arms race during the Cold War. Export revenues were successfully used for buying food and consumer goods abroad, which allowed the Soviet state to ensure a relatively decent level of consumption for citizens of the country. On the other hand, the presence of an extra source of export revenues allowed the Soviet leadership to keep the status quo in politics and the economy: they simply did not have any incentives to conduct market-oriented economic reforms. On the contrary, the need to get the resource rent "here and now" enabled the "predatory" development of oil fields in the Soviet Union (by the late 1980s, a part of the Siberian fields were on the brink of exhaustion).[36] At the same time, the country that was closed in the political and economic sense, and had become a rentier state, deepened its dependence on the international oil market, and in carrying out an aggressive foreign policy, it proved vulnerable under changing international conditions. Therefore, the drastic drop of world oil prices in 1985–1986, which dealt a serious blow to a number of oil states from Venezuela to Mexico,[37] proved fatal for the Soviet economic and political system. The lack of alternative sources of revenues in the country led not only to the freezing of many investment projects and a drop in the population's living standards, but also to a complete destruction of the economic mechanism on which the Soviet system had rested over the previous two decades. Attempts to overcome the economic crisis by partial and inconsistent political and economic liberalization in the late 1980s and early 1990s put an end to the very existence of the Soviet Union, which in 1991 was dissolved by the agreement of the leaders of its republics.[38]

Post-Communist Russia, like other oil states established in the ruins of the Soviet Union (above all, Kazakhstan and Azerbaijan) faced a complex legacy of the past in the 1990s, which was formed as a consequence of the Soviet economic policy and inherited trends of political and economic development. In general, the post-Soviet oil states, like their predecessor, the Soviet Union, proved to be structurally doomed to the role of rentier states: export of oil and gas by the beginning of the 2000s made up to half of the total amount of their exports.[39] However, they did not turn into resource-dependent states like Nigeria or Saudi Arabia—the share of the oil and gas sector throughout the 2000s in Russia did not exceed 25 percent of GDP.[40] But just like the Soviet Union, the post-Soviet oil states were unable to avoid the negative effects of the resource curse completely. During the market reforms of the 1990s, post-Soviet countries not only experienced a transformation recession, but also encountered problems of building new institutions against the background of a decline in state capacity that affected the processes of state building.[41] The Soviet past of these countries not only served as a counterproductive basis for the establishment of efficient institutions, but in many ways was the catalyst of rent-seeking behavior of political and economic actors, who shared the former Soviet assets between them.[42] Unsurprisingly, post-Soviet institution building led to a partial and low-level equilibrium of the "rules of the game."[43] These difficulties were intensified not only by the military conflict in Nagorny Karabakh (in the case of Azerbaijan) and in Chechnya (in the case of Russia), but also by the turbulent conflicts of the political and economic elites of post-Soviet states, which were among many other things focused around the redistribution of resource rents.[44] Finally, the 1990s period was characterized by low oil prices on world markets, and the cheap oil, along with other factors, made a considerable contribution to the 1998 crisis, which dealt a severe blow to the economies of post-Soviet states.

In contrast with the stormy period of the 1990s, in the 2000s, Russia and other post-Soviet countries, after the transformation recession, saw a relatively prosperous period of economic growth and political stability, against the background of high oil prices on world markets, up until the beginning of the global financial crisis in 2008. Some analysts, following specialists from Goldman Sachs investment bank, saw Russia optimistically among the BRIC countries (Brazil, Russia, India, China), which could lay claim to global leadership by the mid-twenty-first century. However, it should be noted that the dependence of Russia and its neighbors on the resource abundance in the 2000s grew swiftly, and the intentions of governments to diversify the economies of these countries and reduce their dependence on the situation of world oil markets were not put into practice. By 2005, the export of hydrocarbons (raw materials) accounted for 59 percent of all Russian exports, and by 2008 it exceeded 63 percent, while the oil and gas sector provided for over 30 percent of all budget revenues in the country.[45] The subsoil use tax alone and export duties on oil in 2004 came to almost 40 percent of the Russian federal budget, and in the following three years this share fluctuated from 49 percent to 56 percent.[46] The fluctuations of oil prices on the world market—from the rally of 2004–2008, which reached a historic maximum of $147 per barrel, to the record drop of 2008–2009, when prices reached $35 per barrel in January 2009 and then turned back to roughly $80 in

December 2009—caused uncertainty for the prospects of the oil states of post-Soviet Eurasia. During the global economic crisis of 2008–2009, the extent of the output decline of the Russian economy proved to be much greater than in other G20 countries; serious economic losses during this period were also suffered by other post-Soviet states. It is hard to say how long and successful their recovery will be. However, the end of the period of the "oil boom" of the 2000s may serve as a useful point of departure for rethinking the experience of the political and economic development of the oil states of post-Soviet Eurasia, in the light of the concept of the resource curse.

Did the post-Soviet oil states, during the period of the oil boom of the 2000s, overcome the pathologies of the resource curse, or at least avoid a worsening of them? The authors of this book, like most other observers, give a primarily negative answer to this question. Furthermore, in the 1990s, many negative effects of the resource curse (from a high level of corruption to inefficient economic policy conducted under the strong pressure of special interest groups) may to a certain extent have been seen as a side effect of inevitable troubles of the post-Communist transformation.[47] However, in the 2000s, the pathologies of the resource curse were observed in "purer" form, not caused by the features of the context of the transitional period, and affected much broader issue areas of economic and political development of the oil states of post-Soviet Eurasia.[48] The turbulent and frequently unjustified growth of state expenditures against the background of an increase in the size of the state apparatus as a whole and the repressive apparatus in particular; the rise of corruption encompassing the economy, politics, and governance; the failure of the rule of law—these are just a few trends that were seen in these countries in the 2000s. But the answer to the question as to whether the contribution of the resource curse as such to these pathologies is decisive and unavoidable, or whether the resource curse is of a conditional nature and only damages the economy and society in combination with the influence of other factors, looks unclear at best—at least for post-Soviet states.

In fact, Russia, Kazakhstan, and Azerbaijan (not to mention Turkmenistan) have not become—at least not yet—the equivalents of both post-Soviet Norway and post-Soviet Nigeria. Concerning the trends of their political and economic development in the 1990s and 2000s, the thesis of a "normal country," which was put forward by Andrei Shleifer and Daniel Tresiman regarding Russia, seems very appropriate.[49] Some pathologies of the resource curse (for example, the corruption effect)[50] in these countries are visible to a greater extent than others (for example, the Dutch disease effect).[51] Some negative tendencies (for example, the decline of democratic institutions and the rule of law)[52] merely depend on the previous trajectories of development of oil states of post-Soviet Eurasia, while others, on the contrary, could be slowed down or weakened using successful economic policies (for example, by the Stabilization Fund that was created during the boom period of the 2000s in Russia, designed to stabilize oil and gas extra revenues).[53] Although the very picture of the consequences of the post-Soviet resource curse looks rather gloomy and unpredictable, to paint it exclusively in black shades would not only be factually incorrect, but also fruitless in scholarly terms. Between the success stories and stories of failure, between the rare Norways and the numerous Nigerias, there are many intermediary cases, which are not so much black or white, but represent different shades of gray. In our view, Russia and other oil states of post-Soviet Eurasia are located in this underexplored and undertheorized "gray zone." Our book, among other things, is designed to penetrate this gray zone and make a contribution to the analysis of conditions of the effect of the resource curse on the politics and economy of post-Soviet countries.

OUTLINE OF THE BOOK

The chapters of this book lie along the lines of the above-mentioned approach, according to the logic of the conditional resource curse applied to an analysis of the trends of political and economic development of countries of post-Soviet Eurasia. At the same time, unlike in a number of other edited volumes, the authors of these chapters were not bounded by common theoretical framework and methodological schemes: rather, we offer a kind of multicolored and multifaceted patchwork, which is not only designed to sew interdisciplinary scholarly pluralism into a coherent picture, but also to stimulate cross-fertilization aimed to supplement the research contribution of each of the chapters presented below.

In the second chapter, "Resource Curse: Rethinking the Soviet Experience," Dmitry Travin and Otar Marganiya analyze in detail the effect that resource abundance has had on the historical trajectories of economic development of Russia and the Soviet Union, starting from the end of the nineteenth century. The authors show that the discovery of oil fields and the expansion of oil export enabled the integration of the country into the world economy (in the pre-Soviet and Soviet periods of its history), while the economic autarchy of the Soviet Union and its system of centralized planned economy hindered the progress of the oil and gas sector for a long time, and the economic development of the country as a whole. However, the Soviet economy changed over time, and its drive from the orientation toward military and strategic goals to satisfaction of demands of mass consumption, which came at the same time as the discovery of the oil and gas fields of Western Siberia in the 1950s and 1960s, played a fundamental role in the subsequent development of the country. On the one hand, this drive was the result of the strategic choice of the leaders of the Soviet state, which made it possible to solve at least partially the deepening problems of the Soviet economy for a certain period of time. On the other hand, it caused an increasing dependency of the entire Soviet economy on the export of natural resources, not to mention the growing costs of the production and transportation of oil and gas. So it should be no cause for surprise that the inefficient Soviet economy found it increasingly difficult to cope not only with major problems, but also with the challenges of the international environment: this constellation, as the authors demonstrate, enabled the collapse of the Soviet system in the late 1980s and early 1990s. At the same time, Travin and Marganiya dispute the widespread opinion that the collapse of the Soviet Union was primarily caused by the consequences of the oil shock.[54] The resource curse was rather just one of the factors, albeit a very important one, in the collapse of the Soviet economic system—along with the increasing technological backwardness of the Soviet Union and the reaction to these challenges by a new generation of Soviet leaders, and also the inability of the Soviet elite to pursue economic reforms under the conditions of political repressions. Travin and Marganiya claim that paradoxically, oil abundance, thanks to which the Soviet Union achieved relative prosperity in the 1970s and early 1980s, greatly contributed to the collapse of the Soviet system. Thus, their analysis, in spite of historical institutionalism,[55] confirms the well-known argument of Douglass North: "history matters."[56]

The negative effect of the resource curse on the political development of oil states is analyzed by Andrey Scherbak in the third chapter, "The Impact of the Oil Shock on the Post-Soviet Regime Changes," which is devoted to the causes for the rise of authoritarianism in post-Soviet countries. Using data from post-Soviet countries, it statistically tests hypotheses on the causal link between the dependence of states on the export of natural resources and the decline of their democratic institutions, which Michael Ross advanced in comparative cross-national studies.[57] The regression analysis presented in this chapter demonstrates very convincingly that the most significant mechanism by which the resource curse makes governments of post-Soviet oil states hinder the democratic development of these countries is the repression effect. The governments of Russia and its neighbors are capable of investing some revenues from export of oil and gas into increasing the size of the coercive apparatus, and, to a much smaller degree, in increasing the costs for maintaining it. Owing to this, they are able not only to crush the opposition systematically, but also to recruit more employees in the apparatus, ensuring their jobs and political loyalty. It is noteworthy that this negative effect of the resource curse on political regimes is caused by the export of hydrocarbons, while export of metals and minerals besides oil and gas, as Scherbak shows, does not have such great significance in this respect. It was also discovered in the analysis that another important antidemocratic mechanism of the resource curse, the taxation effect, connected with an increase in the level of state expenditures and a decrease in the level of taxation in oil states, is also statistically insignificant, at least for post-Soviet countries.[58] At the same time, Scherbak notes another important factor that accompanies the antidemocratic effect of the resource curse on the political development of post-Soviet states—the increase in socioeconomic inequality, which in its turn increases as a result of the elites of oil states taking the resource rent in an undemocratic government.[59] As a result, a number of post-Soviet countries, including Russia, fall into a kind of "vicious circle" of authoritarianism. Even the global economic crisis of 2008–2009, which was accompanied by a drop in world oil prices, could not bring down the authoritarian regimes in post-Soviet countries, at least not in the short-term perspective. Thus, Scherbak demonstrates the lock-in effect of the resource curse in post-Soviet politics.

How significant is another effect of the resource curse, connected with a decline in the rule of law and property rights? Andrey Zaostrovtsev devotes the fourth chapter to an answer to this question: "Oil Boom: Is It Devastating to Property Rights and the Rule of Law?" In analyzing comparative data on a large group of countries and fifteen states that export oil and gas (including Russia, Kazakhstan, and Azerbaijan), Zaostrovtsev convincingly demonstrates that in an average oil state in the comparative perspective, property rights look no worse than in the non-oil states. Furthermore, within this group of oil states, such significant differences are seen that they cannot be explained exclusively from the viewpoint of the theory of the resource curse without using other—additional or alternative—explanations. The situation of the rule of law is somewhat different, where the indicators of oil states on average are significantly lower than for the non-oil states. However, under these parameters, the group of oil states is rather diverse and the differences between them cannot be explained by one single factor. As Zaostrovtsev notes, failed democracies (including not only post-Soviet states, but also Venezuela and Bolivia) in international comparisons look much worse than the long-standing autocracies of the oil states of the Persian Gulf. This comparison leads Zaostrovtsev to make the conclusion that the negative influence of the resource curse on property rights is no more than a hypothesis that requires additional testing. At the same time, he believes, in a search for explanations for the decline of the rule of law, it is necessary to analyze the historical developmental paths and the political-economic trends of various oil states. In particular, in discussing the peculiarities of Russia, which throughout the 2000s demonstrated a significant decline of indicators of the rule of law and property rights, Zaostrovtsev connects these tendencies not only with the resource curse, but also with other factors—the values and orientations of Russian citizens. In particular, he notes in this connection not only the hostility to privatization and the private property created during the period of market reforms (it is typical for many post-Communist countries), but also the extremely low demand for democratic institutions, separation of powers, and the control of society over the state. Thus, based on Russian data, Zaostrovtsev develops the argument that "culture matters" for the determining influence of values and attitudes in economic development, which is advanced in the edited volume by Lawrence Harrison and Samuel Huntington.[60]

The fifth chapter, "The Logic of Crony Capitalism: Big Oil, Big Politics, and Big Business in Russia," is devoted to an analysis of the interactions of the state and economic actors in the Russian oil and gas sector. These dynamics over the last two decades in many ways resembled pendulum-like swings: from the complete dominance of centralized state control, the country moved in the 1990s to "state capture" by "oligarchs," representatives of big business, including and above all in the oil and gas sector. In the 2000s, the redistribution of property rights in Russia led to the partial restoration of the Soviet model of state ownership with control[61] and the rise of a predatory state, which led to the policy of business capture. As shown in this chapter, inefficient political institutions, partially inherited from the Soviet period and partially established in the 1990s (and especially in the 2000s), played the key role in these trends, which were responsible for the logic of the development of crony capitalism[62] in Russia. While the pathology of state capture in Russia in the 1990s had the nature of continuing "growing pains," the tendencies of business capture and the formation of the predatory state seen in the 2000s should be considered as dangerous symptoms of chronic diseases in the Russian economy and politics, if the current low-level equilibrium of state-business relationships will be preserved in the long term. Thus, the conclusion of this chapter is not only that the resource curse has a negative effect on political institutions, but also that the inefficient political institutions under conditions of authoritarianism, as Russia's experience shows, may exacerbate this effect. They drag the country into a vicious circle of political monopolism and a statist economic policy, thus imposing a high barrier to further economic and political reforms. Although the answer to the question "Do institutions matter?"[63] is clearly affirmative in the Russian case, the political and economic effects of these institutions prove to be primarily negative.

In the sixth chapter, "Oil Boom and Government Finance in Russia: Stabilization Fund and Its Fate," Andrey Zaostrovtsev analyzes the budgetary policy of the Russian government, which in the 2000s faced the problem of sterilization of budget super-revenues from oil and gas export in a situation when prices on world oil markets rallied. The establishing of a special financial reserve, and then the Stabilization Fund, allowed the Russian government to avoid bursts of inflation and not to fall into the temptation of populist fiscal policy, avoiding the threat of the Dutch disease. Furthermore, a large amount of funds from the Stabilization Fund were spent on paying the country's foreign debt and other high-priority needs. This budgetary policy, based on the successful experience of several oil states (such as Norway) became possible in Russia among other things under the influence of lessons taken from the experience of economic reforms of the 1990s, when the government had to fight unsuccessfully against high inflation and faced the financial crisis of 1998. However, Zaostrovtsev notes that under conditions of the sharp rise of oil and gas revenues in Russia, the Stabilization Fund can still not fulfill all the tasks it faces, also because of the pressure that is put on the government by lobbyists of special interest groups: Russia has encountered relatively high inflation and the threat of macroeconomic populism. Shortly before the start of the macroeconomic crisis of 2008, the Stabilization Fund was practically replaced by the Reserve Fund, and the Fund of National Prosperity, which was designed to carry out the same functions as its predecessor. However, as Zaostrovtsev shows, due to the severe economic decline, a significant portion of the money accumulated in these funds was directed toward "filling in gaps" in 2009 and 2010—that is, to cover the current deficit of the Russian federal budget, on the one hand, and the current costs of the country's pension fund, on the other. Thus, although the Stabilization Fund did play the role of a kind of "insurance policy," which prevented the fiscal crisis of the Russian state during the global economic crisis, the further possibilities of supplementing the budget with oil and gas revenues, as Zaostrovstev demonstrates, are now in many ways exhausted, and not just because of the situation in world oil markets. The author comes to the conclusion that the era of financial abundance in Russia is in the past, and that this will have long-term consequences for the development of the country.

In the seventh chapter, "Oil, Gas, Transit, and Boundaries: Problems of the Transport Curse," Nikolay Dobronravin examines the influence that the geopolitical position has on the development of oil states of post-Soviet Eurasia. He notes that the three post-Soviet oil states (Azerbaijan, Kazakhstan, and Turkmenistan) have since the collapse of the Soviet Union joined the LLDC group (Landlocked Developing Countries), which means that the possibilities for their oil and gas export have been restricted by the conditions for transport of hydrocarbon raw materials through the territory of transit countries. In general, the high dependency of LLDCs on gateway countries poses serious challenges to their economic and political development. The responses of post-Soviet states to these challenges have been different, not only as the result of the geographical configuration, but also under the influence of the transport infrastructure, partially inherited from the Soviet period, and also the foreign policy carried out by their governments. Throughout the post-Soviet period, Kazakhstan has quite successfully shown an aspiration toward diversification of export routes of oil and gas, trying to escape from the pipeline dependence on Russia, on the one hand, and increasing its ties with China, on the other. This flexible policy has allowed Kazakhstan, if not to overcome the effect of the transport curse, then at least to weaken it to some degree. On the contrary, Turkmenistan has become the hostage of its unfavorable geographic location in the beltway of transit countries, which is worsened by the deterioration of the old pipelines, and also the economic and political autarchy, especially during the rule of Saparmurat Niyazov (Turkmenbashi), who was the head of the country until his death in 2006. Therefore, at the moment, Turkmenistan, despite its significant potential, has not been able to overcome the negative effects of the transport curse. Finally, Azerbaijan has tried to move most actively not only on the path of diversifying deliveries of oil to European markets (through the Baku-Tbilisi-Ceyhan pipeline, and participation in the promising Nabucco gas pipeline project), but also in turning the country into a transit state on the route of export of hydrocarbons from countries of Central Asia. Thus, according to Dobronravin, against the background of an expected increase in export of oil deliveries of South and East Asia (primarily China), the prospects for overcoming the transport curse for Azerbaijan do not look obvious at least in the short term. In other words, as it follows from this chapter, "geography matters,"[64] including in relation to the effects of the resource curse.

In the context of an analysis of the effect of the resource curse on the development of countries of post-Soviet Eurasia, special attention should be paid to a rethinking of the experience of oil states of the Third World, which is presented in chapter 8, "Oil, Gas, and Modernization of Global South: African Lessons for Post-Soviet States." As Nikolay Dobronravin shows, attempts at nationalization of the oil and gas sector and the battle with transnational corporations in African countries that were under the influence of the Soviet Union brought the oil states of this continent into an economic and political dead end. Examples of this kind are the Congo and Angola, where pro-Soviet governments were in power for a long time. At the same time, the destructive effects of the resource curse could also not be avoided by countries that tried to orient themselves toward Western models of political and economic development: they faced similar problems, and among the oil states Nigeria became a symbol of corruption, separatism, ethnic conflicts, and inefficient governance. But nevertheless, Dobronravin believes, the orientation of a number of African countries toward a socialist model of development had the most dramatic consequences, while in such countries as Nigeria and Gabon, the negative political influence of the resource curse was less catastrophic. On the whole, however, the oil and gas sector in African (and non-African) countries of the Third World may become a "state within the state," existing autonomously from the development of societies and capturing the resources required for their modernization.[65] The future will show whether Russia and other post-Soviet countries are able to avoid this developmental trap.

Dmitry Travin, in chapter 9, "Conclusion: Oil, Gas, Russia, and the 2008–2009 Economic Crisis," summarizes the analysis of the effect of the resource curse on the economic development of Russia, which became clear during the recent global economic crisis. Travin notes that directly or indirectly benefits from the revenues from the export of oil and gas were received by practically all citizens of Russia, and thus they became heavily dependent on the trends of world oil markets. As a result, the country, which benefited to a greater extent than other developed nations on the growth of world oil prices, lost out more than others during the crisis from the fall in prices. The severe decline in late 2008 and 2009 was in many ways objectively caused by the structure of the Russian export-oriented economy, but was aggravated to a large degree by the lost opportunities for its diversification. The consequences of the crisis in Russia were partially alleviated: the very existence of the Reserve Fund allowed Russia (unlike a number of other nations) to avoid the sharp drop in the living standard of employees of the public sector and pensioners, and a reasonable macroeconomic policy made it possible to avoid a rise in inflation. But in general, Travin shows that because of the effects of the resource curse, the prospects for the Russian economy today look rather uncertain, even against the background of overcoming the global economic crisis. The issue as to what lessons the governments of oil states in post-Soviet Eurasia can learn from this experience remains open.

At the same time, rethinking of the experience of Russia and other post-Soviet oil states, which is the focus of this book, may be beneficial for a study of the effects of the resource curse on political and economic processes in the broader theoretical and comparative perspective. Of course, we have not tried to answer all the questions, or make a final diagnosis in intensive discussions on the causes, mechanisms, and consequences of the resource curse in general and in post-Soviet countries in particular. This task, in our opinion, may only be solved as a result of collective efforts by scholars of different research approaches within the interdisciplinary and international academic community. Our goal was more modest—to analyze different aspects of the resource curse in countries of post-Soviet Eurasia against the background of factors of their development (from history and politics to geography and culture). As we believe, this book is one of the steps in this direction, and we hope that following it we and our colleagues in various countries will make other steps. To be continued?

NOTES

1. Richard Auti, *Sustaining Development in Mineral Economies: The Resource Curse Thesis* (London: Routledge, 1993); Jeffrey Sachs and Andrew Warner, "Natural Resource Abundance and Economic Growth," *NBER Working Papers*, no. 5398 (1995); Jeffrey Sachs and Andrew Warner, "The Curse of Natural Resources," *European Economic Review*, 45, no. 5–6 (2001), 827–38.

2. Terry Lynn Karl, *The Paradox of Plenty: Oil Booms and Petro-States* (Berkeley: University of California Press, 1997); Michael Ross, "The Political Economy of the Resource Curse," *World Politics*, 51, no. 2 (1999), 297–322; Daniel Lederman and William F. Mahoney, eds., *Natural Resources: Neither Curse Nor Destiny* (Washington, D.C.: The World Bank, 2007); Macartan

Humphreys, Jeffrey Sachs, and Joseph E. Stiglitz, eds., *Escaping the Resource Curse* (New York: Columbia University Press, 2007); Mary Caldor, Terry Lynn Karl, and Yahya Said, eds., *Oil Wars* (London: Pluto Press, 2007); Thad Dunning, *Crude Democracy: Natural Resource Wealth and Political Regimes* (New York: Cambridge University Press, 2008).

3. Paul Stevens, "Resource Impact: Curse or Blessing? A Literature Survey," *Journal of Energy Literature*, 9, no. 1 (2003), 3–42.

4. Michael Ross, "A Closer Look at Oil, Diamonds, and Civil Wars," *Annual Review of Political Science*, 9 (2006), 265–300.

5. Carlos Leite and Jens Weidmann, "Does Mother Nature Corrupt? Natural Resources, Corruption, and Economic Growth," *IMF Working Papers*, WP/99/85 (1999).

6. Georgy Egorov, Sergei Guriev, and Konstantin Sonin, "Why Resource-Poor Dictators Allow Freer Media: A Theory and Evidence from Panel Data," *American Political Science Review*, 103, no. 4 (2009), 645–68.

7. Michael Ross, "Oil, Islam, and Women," *American Political Science Review*, 102, no. 1 (2008), 107–23.

8. David Lane, ed., *The Political Economy of Russian Oil* (Lanham, Md.: Rowman and Littlefield, 1999); Pauline Jones Luong and Erika Weinthal, "Prelude to the Resource Curse: Explaining Energy Development Strategies in Soviet Successor States and Beyond," *Comparative Political Studies*, 34, no. 4 (2001), 367–99; Younkyoo Kim, *The Resource Curse in a Post-Communist Regime: Russia in Comparative Perspective* (Burlington, Vt.: Ashgate, 2003); Marshall Goldman, *Petrostate: Putin, Power, and the New Russia* (New York: Oxford University Press, 2008).

9. Claus Offe, "Capitalism by Democratic Design? Democratic Theory Facing the Triple Transition in East Central Europe," *Social Research*, 58, no. 4 (1991), 865–92.

10. Peter Rutland, "Putin's Economic Record: Is the Oil Boom Sustainable?" *Europe-Asia Studies*, 60, no. 6 (2008), 1051–72; Hillary Appel, "Is it Putin or Is it Oil? Explaining Russia's Fiscal Recovery," *Post-Soviet Affairs*, 24, no. 4 (2008), 301–23.

11. Henry Hale, "Regime Cycles: Democracy, Autocracy, and Revolutions in Post-Soviet Eurasia," *World Politics*, 58, no. 1 (2005), 133–65.

12. *Governance Matters 2009: Worldwide Governance Indicators, 1996–2008*, http://info.worldbank.org/governance/wgi/index.asp (accessed 17 November 2009); Andrei Zaostrovtsev, "Modernizatsiya i instituty: Podkhody k kolichestvennomu izmereniyu," *European University at St. Petersburg, M-Center Working Papers*, no. 4 (2009), www.eu.spb.ru/images/M_center/zaostrovtsev_modern_inst.pdf (accessed 17 November 2009).

13. Ross, "The Political Economy of the Resource Curse."

14. Leite and Weidmann, "Does Mother Nature Corrupt?"; M. Steven Fish, *Democracy Derailed in Russia: The Failure of Open Politics* (New York: Cambridge University Press, 2005), 114–38.

15. Aaron Tornell and Philip Lane, "The Voracity Effect," *American Economic Review*, 89, no. 1 (1999), 22–46.

16. James A. Robinson and Ragnar Torvik, "White Elephants," *Journal of Public Economics*, 89, no. 2–3 (2005), 197–210.

17. See chapter 6 in this volume.

18. Karl, *The Paradox of Plenty*, 161–85.

19. Michael Ross, "Does Oil Hinder Democracy?" *World Politics*, 53, no. 2 (2001), 325–61.

20. Ross, "Oil, Islam, and Women."

21. Ross, "Does Oil Hinder Democracy?"; see also chapter 3 in this volume.

22. Nikolay Dobronravin and Otar Marganiya, eds., *Neft', Gaz, Modernizatsiya Obshchestva* (St. Petersburg: Ekonomicheskaya Shkola, 2008).

23. Ross, "Does Oil Hinder Democracy?"

24. Dunning, *Crude Democracy*, 15–20.

25. Vladimir Milov, "Mozhet li Rossiya stat' neftyanym raem?" *Pro et Contra*, 10, no. 2–3 (2006), 9–13.

26. Dunning, *Crude Democracy*.

27. Halvor Mehlum, Karl Ove Moene, and Ragnar Torvik, "Institutions and the Resource Curse," *Economic Journal*, 116, no. 1 (2006), 1–20; Halvor Mehlum, Karl Ove Moene, and Ragnar Torvik, "Cursed by Resources or Institutions?" *World Economy*, 29, no. 8 (2006), 1117–31.

28. Egorov, Guriev, and Sonin, "Why Resource-Poor Dictators Allow Freer Media."

29. See chapter 4 in this volume.

30. Lee Alston, Thrainn Eggertson, and Douglass North, eds., *Empirical Studies in Institutional Changes* (New York: Cambridge University Press, 1996); R. A. W. Rhodes, Sarah Binder, and Bert Rockman, eds., *The Oxford Handbook of Political Institutions* (New York: Oxford University Press, 2006).

31. Douglass North, *Institutions, Institutional Change, and Economic Performance* (New York: Cambridge University Press, 1990), 16.

32. Douglass North, "Institutions and Credible Commitments," *Journal of Institutional and Theoretical Economics*, 149 (1993), 11–23.

33. See chapters 4 and 5 in this volume.

34. Karl, *The Paradox of Plenty*, 74.

35. Yegor Gaidar, *Collapse of an Empire: Lessons for Modern Russia* (Washington, D.C.: Brookings Institution Press, 2007); see also chapter 2 in this volume.

36. Thane Gustafson, *Crisis Amid Plenty: The Politics of Soviet Energy under Brezhnev and Gorbachev* (Princeton, N.J.: Princeton University Press, 1989); Maria Slavkina, *Triumf i Tragediya: Razvitie Neftegazovogo Kompleksa SSSR v 1960–1980-e Gody* (Moscow: Nauka, 2002).

37. Karl, *The Paradox of Plenty*; Vladimir Gel'man, "Venesuela i Meksika: Neft', avtoritarizm, i populism," in Nikolay Dobronravin and Otar Marganiya, eds., *Neft', Gaz, Modernizatsiya Obshchestva* (St. Petersburg: Ekonomicheskaya Shkola, 2008), 165–220.

38. Gaidar, *Collapse of an Empire*.

39. Kim, *The Resource Curse*, 21–37.

40. See chapter 6 in this volume.

41. Vadim Volkov, *Violent Entrepreneurs: The Role of Force in the Making of Russian Capitalism* (Ithaca, N.Y.: Cornell University Press, 2002); Timothy Colton and Stephen Holmes, eds., *The State After Communism: Governance in the New Russia* (Lanham, Md.: Rowman and Littlefield, 2006); Gerald Easter, "The Russian State in the Time of Putin," *Post-Soviet Affairs*, 24, no. 3 (2008), 199–230.

42. See chapter 5 in this volume.

43. Joel Hellman, "Winners Take All: The Politics of Partial Reforms in Post-Communist Transitions," *World Politics*, 50, no. 2 (1998), 203–34; Clifford Gaddy and Barry Ickes, *Russia's Virtual Economy* (Washington, D.C.: Brookings Institution Press, 2002); Vladimir Gel'man, "The Unrule of Law in the Making: The Politics of Informal Institution Building in Russia," *Europe-Asia Studies*, 56, no. 7 (2004), 1021–40.

44. Chrystia Freeland, *Sale of the Century: Russia's Wild Rule from Communism to Capitalism* (New York: Crown Publishers, 2000); Paul Khlebnikov, *Godfather of the Kremlin: Boris Berezovsky and the Looting of Russia* (New York: Harvest Books, 2001); David Hoffman, *Oligarchs: Wealth and Power in the New Russia* (New York: Public Affairs Books, 2002); Richard Sakwa, *The Quality of Freedom: Khodorkovsky, Putin, and the Yukos Affair* (New York: Oxford University Press, 2009).

45. Valerii Kryukov and Anatolii Tokarev, *Neftegaovye resursy v transformiruemoi ekonomike* (Novosibirsk: Nauka-Tsentr, 2007), 10.

46. See chapter 6 in this volume.

47. Anders Aslund, *How Russia Became a Market Economy* (Washington, D.C.: Brookings Institution Press, 1995); Andrei Shleifer and Daniel Treisman, *Without a Map: Political Tactics and Economic Reform in Russia* (Cambridge, Mass.: MIT Press, 2000); Stefanie Harter and Gerald Easter, eds., *Shaping the Economic Space in Russia* (Burlington, Vt.: Ashgate, 2000).

48. Peter Baker and Susan Glasser, *Kremlin's Rising: Vladimir Putin's Russia and the End of Revolution* (New York: Scribner, 2005); William Tompson, "The Political Implications of Russia's Resource-Based Economy," *Post-Soviet Affairs*, 21, no. 4 (2005), 335–59; Anders Aslund, *Russia's Capitalist Revolution: Why Market Reforms Succeeded and Democracy Failed* (Washington, D.C.: Peterson Institute for International Economics, 2007).

49. Andrei Shleifer and Daniel Treisman, "A Normal Country," *Foreign Affairs*, 83, no. 2 (2004), 20–38; Andrei Shleifer, *A Normal Country: Russia After Communism* (Cambridge, Mass.: Harvard University Press, 2005).

50. Fish, *Democracy Derailed in Russia.*

51. See chapter 6 in this volume.

52. See chapters 3 and 4 in this volume.

53. See chapter 6 in this volume.

54. Gaidar, *Collapse of an Empire.*

55. Sven Steinmo, Kathleen Thelen, and Frank Longstreth, eds., *Structuring Politics: Historical Institutionalism in Comparative Analysis* (New York: Cambridge University Press, 1992).

56. North, *Institutions, Institutional Change, and Economic Performance,* 3.

57. Ross, "Does Oil Hinder Democracy?"

58. Ross, "Does Oil Hinder Democracy?" 332–35, 347–49.

59. Dunning, *Crude Democracy.*

60. Lawrence Harrison and Samuel Huntington, eds. *Culture Matters: How Values Shape Human Progress* (New York: Basic Books, 2002); Lawrence Harrison, *The Central Liberal Truth: How Politics Can Change a Culture and Save It from Itself* (New York: Oxford University Press, 2008).

61. Pauline Jones Luong and Erika Weinthal, "Rethinking the Resource Curse: Ownership Structure, Institutional Capacity, and Domestic Constraints," *Annual Review of Political Science,* 9 (2006), 241–63.

62. David Kang, *Crony Capitalism: Corruption and Development in South Korea and the Philippines* (New York: Cambridge University Press, 2002).

63. Kent Weaver and Bert Rockman, eds., *Do Institutions Matter? Government Capabilities in the United States and Abroad* (Washington, D.C.: Brookings Institution Press, 1993).

64. Beth Mitchnek, "Geography Matters: Discerning the Importance of Local Context," *Slavic Review,* 64, no. 3 (2005), 491–516.

65. Douglas Yates, *The Rentier State in Africa: Oil Rent Dependency and Neocolonialism in the Republic of Gabon* (Trenton, N.J.: Africa World Press, 1996); Ian Gary and Terry Lynn Karl, *Bottom of the Barrel: Africa's Oil Boom and the Poor* (Baltimore, Md.: Catholic Relief Services, 2003), www.earth.columbia.edu/cgsd/STP/documents/Bottom_of_the_Barrel_English_PDF.pdf (accessed 17 November 2009).

2

Resource Curse

Rethinking the Soviet Experience

Dmitry Travin and Otar Marganiya

EARLY STEPS: THE OIL EMPIRE OF THE NOBELS

In contemporary Russia, oil and gas play an enormously overwhelming role, but in the nineteenth century, when the oil industry was born, it was difficult to imagine this future. At that time Russia entered the European market as a leading exporter of grain. The Russian Empire, rich in fertile lands and with major ports on both the Black Sea and the Baltic Sea, had obvious comparative advantages in producing and trading grain. At the same time, Russian industry noticeably lagged behind the industry of leading European nations and the United States. The major source of energy for enterprises was coal, large deposits of which developed in the eastern regions of Ukraine (Donbass). Among oil products in those years, kerosene was of major importance, which was used to light houses with special kerosene lamps. Prospects for development of the oil business were extremely problematic, even when the Russian economy began to develop swiftly. Until the 1930s, cars were not manufactured in the country. The traffic roads were in terrible condition.[1] Millions of houses did not use any other source of energy but logs. And nevertheless, the development of oil fields in the Russian Empire began.

The major source of oil at that time was Azerbaijan. Today this is an independent state, but in the second half of the nineteenth century, Azerbaijan was a distant corner of the Russian Empire. However, despite its remoteness, it was easier to discover and develop oil deposits there than in Siberia, which was practically unexplored at the time, but which has now become the major source of Russian energy resources. Also, the Caucasus, unlike Siberia, was densely populated, with an ancient culture and direct and relatively short distance access to the sea, which was important for transporting cargo.

Peter the Great, who captured Azerbaijan from Persia, gave the order to mine for oil here, and transport it on boats up the Volga River. However, neither at that time nor one century later did oil have any importance for the economy. This is what was said during these years about oil development on the shores of the Caspian Sea: "On the Apsheron peninsula, there is a natural form of kerosene, which is white, and more liquid than ordinary oil. The Russians drink it! They say it helps with internal diseases. And you can also use it to get stains out of silk—but it stinks afterwards."[2] The first oil processing enterprise was built in 1857, to the north of Baku—the largest city in Azerbaijan, and now the capital of the independent country. However, in the 1860s, the development of industry was held back by the state monopoly on oil. Only after 1873, when the privatization of land plots began, were oil deposits officially sold at auction to private enterprises. By 1878, there were 301 oil wells functioning in the Baku region.[3]

There were quite a lot of private businesses in this sector, but the leading role in the development of the oil industry from this moment until the Russian revolution of 1917 was played by the Swedish Nobel family. The importance of the business that was founded by the Nobel brothers (Robert, Ludwig, and Alfred) lay in the fact that they were the first to bring major foreign capital and modern technologies of that time to the oil processing industry. Russia did not have either of these before the foreign investors arrived (at least not in sufficient quantity). In the area where the Nobels settled, there were already 120 small oil distilleries working, but outdated methods of production and processing of oil were used. They could not seriously compete with the Swedish investors for two reasons. First, the industrial empire of the Nobels by that time was already a large and efficient company, specializing in the field of military production. The owners could quite easily use the money received from the sale of rifles, cannons, and dynamites for producing and processing oil. The Nobels were immediately capable to organize large-scale production and transportation of oil and oil products.[4] Second, Robert Nobel who was a good chemist by his training, improved the oil production process himself, and also invited advanced foreign specialists to the Baku oil fields. European science of that time immediately began to work actively for the development of the Russian oil industry (and to this day the use of foreign capital and technology has great importance for the development of Russian oil fields). This is what Ludwig

Nobel wrote about his brother: "Robert achieved truly wonderful results, as unlike the 30 percent of oil products that were normal for Baku, and also heavy and of poor quality, from the same raw materials he gets 40 percent of excellent light kerosene, which is in all ways no worse than the most excellent American products. Thus, we can enter the market with a commodity which will ensure the company has an outstanding reputation."[5]

Over time, as the Russian economy developed, the importance of kerosene began to decrease. The major product of the Nobels' company became black oil, which was actively used by various enterprises. The Nobels' company was the largest in the Caucasus, but not the only one. Several major manufacturers together produced around half of the Baku oil, while the other half was produced by small businesses. However, not everything went smoothly. Difficulties in business development in these years were in many ways determined by opposition from the local authorities. Certainly, as is also the custom in Russia today, they tried to receive bribes. For example, the Baku authorities refused the Nobels permission to lay a pipeline through the territory of the city. They were only able to resolve the issue through the imperial capital, St. Petersburg, after its top-down pressure on Baku officials. As a result, the money invested in the pipelines brought profits to the Nobels in one year. Subsequently, the Nobel brothers established an entire fleet of tankers to transport oil and kerosene across the Caspian Sea and farther (on barges) along the Volga to Russia.[6] After some time, for the development of their business in Russia the Nobels also developed special railway cistern wagons, in which kerosene was transported all over the country. Russian traders received the product at railway stations.

On the European market, oil products were first transported by English tankers from Russia with the financial assistance of capital from the Rothschild family in the mid-1880s. They were transported through the Black Sea port of Batum (now Batumi, Georgia). The Nobels transported kerosene to northern Europe mainly by railway. Thus, for the first time Russia began to receive export turnover from the export of oil, although it did not yet have the importance that it has today. By the beginning of the twentieth century, the Nobels' company played one of the leading roles on the oil market of Europe. The Baku oil that was produced by the Nobels and their competitors, according to some estimates, accounted for around 10 percent of the world production of this type of fuel.[7] However, further developments of Russian politics undermined the Nobels' position and then completely eliminated their empire.

The revolutionary movements and the strikes of oil workers struck a harsh blow to the company. In 1903, during the Baku rebellion, thirty-six of the Nobels' oil derricks were destroyed, the company office was looted, and the apartments of managers were damaged. All over the city, burned-down houses were observed, and bloody corpses lay in the streets. But this was just the beginning of the tragedy. The Russian revolution of 1905–1907 once more struck a blow to the oil business: the Nobels' company suffered both material and human losses. During this period, bandits killed and injured engineers and managers from time to time. According to some assessments, the Nobels were not able to restore the position they lost as a result of the revolution and return to the level of 1904 until right before World War I.[8] This war assisted the development of the oil business in Russia for a short time, as it increased the demand for fuel for the military. However, the main consequence of the war was the new revolution in Russia. In 1917, power in the country was seized by the Bolsheviks, who nationalized industrial enterprises in 1918. The Nobels' empire, which had done so much for the development of the Russian oil industry, ceased to exist.

SOVIET OIL AND THE "SECOND BAKU"

After the 1917 revolution, Russia ceased for a long time to be a major player on the world oil markets. Initially the country had to overcome the devastating consequences of the revolution and the civil war, and then (around the late 1920s and early 1930s), the political leadership headed by Joseph Stalin followed a policy of industrialization and comprehensive strengthening of military power. Major factories, plants, railways, and power stations were built. Grain was exported abroad in large quantities, and money received from its export was spent on equipment necessary for industrialization. The limited oil resources of the Soviet Union were used primarily for the country's rising domestic consumption: in particular, automobiles and tanks possessed by the Red Army had to have a sufficient amount of fuel. Also, foreign capital that could have been invested in development, production, and processing of oil as well as into its export to the world market was driven out of the Soviet economy. All industry went into the hands of the state and developed according to centralized planning directives approved by the top political leadership of the Communist Party.

At the same time, the geological project conducted in the vast area between the Volga River and the Urals mountain chain led to a discovery of major oil fields. The issue arose about developing them. Soviet scholars and industrialists began to talk of the establishment of a "second Baku" in this region. In the 1930s, a small amount of oil was first produced in Bashkiria (Ishimbaevo field), and then in the Orenburg Oblast.[9] However, only in 1939, that is, after more than two decades after the 1917 Bolshevik revolution, did a congress of the Communist Party make the decision to launch major development of oil fields in the area between the Volga and the Urals.[10] In other words, postrevolutionary political cataclysms and a breakdown of ties with the world economy held up the economic development of the Soviet Union for a long time. Furthermore, the start of World War II, and especially the attack of Nazi Germany on the Soviet Union in June 1941, did not allow implementation of the project to establish the "second Baku" until the beginning of the 1950s.

The oil issue had a serious effect on world history during the period of World War II. The German forces, which entered deep into Russia, attempted to reach the Caucasus and the Baku oil fields in order to provide themselves with stable deliveries of fuel. The Romanian oil fields were no longer sufficient for the huge number of German tanks and automobiles. Especially, the Soviet army was concerned with the Wehrmacht's attempt to reach the banks of the Volga River. If it had succeeded, then essentially the only convenient transport route for Baku oil to the center of Russia would have been cut off, that is, to the main theater of military actions. In these conditions, the Soviet army would have been left without fuel. This development of events would have been truly tragic for the Soviet Union, even if the defenders of the Caucasus had been able to defend the Baku region for a long time. If the Wehrmacht had been able to drive the Soviet troops from the banks of the Volga, then things would probably have ended sadly for the defenders of the Caucasus as well. However, the lengthy and bloody battle of Stalingrad (now Volgograd) ended in victory for the Red Army. The German troops were surrounded, and the Caucasian oil fields remained under the control of Moscow. The battle of Stalingrad signified a major breakthrough in World War II on the Eastern front. In Soviet historiography, the Stalingrad battle is considered to be the most important of all the events of World War II. In fact, it was essentially a battle for control of oil and the transport corridor by which oil from Baku was delivered to the center of Russia.

After World War II, the oil of the second Baku gradually began to play a serious role in the Soviet economy. As foreign capital was still not involved in the development of the Soviet oil industry, many specialists from the Caucasus came to this region. Azerbaijani managers and engineers made an enormous contribution to the development of oil fields and processing enterprises that were located far away from Azerbaijan. In the early 1950s, the development of major oil fields between the Volga and the Urals began. Soon after that, the structure of consumption of energy resources in the Soviet Union underwent considerable changes. In 1950, 66.1 percent of fuel was coal. Oil accounted for 17.4 percent, and gas for just 2.3 percent[11] (the rest was turf, shale, and wood). By 1960, the share of coal had declined to 53.9 percent. The share of oil grew to 30.5 percent, and the share of gas to 7.9 percent. But by 1965, the shares of oil and gas combined significantly exceeded the share of coal (35.8 percent, 15.5 percent, and 42.7 percent, respectively).[12]

Nevertheless, even the active development of the second Baku can still not be considered a sign of truly fundamental changes in the oil and gas sector of the Soviet economy. The major rise of the oil and gas industry in Russia is determined by major changes that took place somewhat later. In order to understand the reasons for the subsequent changes, one should look into the nature of the Soviet economy, and the evolution of economic policy and governance that took place in the 1950s. The conscious elimination of private business by the Bolsheviks gradually led to an emergence of the centralized hierarchical system of governance, where the major economic decisions were concentrated in the center. Directive plans were issued to state enterprises from Moscow, and directors of these enterprises were merely to implement them obediently, while the spirit of entrepreneurship was not welcomed, and in most cases it was harshly punished. Increasing labor productivity, reducing expenses, or developing new production was not considered to be an achievement of the enterprise if it did not fulfill the directive plan on volume of production; if directors were unsuccessful during the Stalin years they could be simply sent to the Gulag. Thus, the structure of the Soviet economy depended on political decisions that were taken by the leaders of the Communist Party, and primarily by Stalin himself. And for Stalin, the major economic goal was the production of arms, and all the things that provided for this industry—metal, coal, electricity, and various kinds of cargo transport. After several decades, the Soviet economy completely lost its capacity to satisfy consumers. Enterprises that did not focus on market demand could not accordingly pay the labor of their employees: the level of payment at various enterprises was approximately the same (in Soviet economic slang this was called "leveling"), which led to a situation where the quality of labor of the majority of Soviet skilled workers, engineers, and scientists had been diminished and distorted. To put it bluntly, the Soviet economy gradually lost the ability to produce any competitive goods that could enter the world market. Even if the Communist leaders in Moscow suddenly set the task of trade with Western countries in order to earn foreign currency, Soviet enterprises could not have done this. The only exception was the sector of natural resources. Production of grain, wood, ferrous and nonferrous metals, and also oil and gas depended little on the entrepreneurial spirit of directors of enterprises and on the quality of labor of their subordinates. Accordingly, the only chance to enter the world market to earn currency was selling natural resources, and with a low level of processing, which did not require modern technologies and high-level skills by personnel of enterprises.

For some time after World War II, the Soviet economy did not change at all: it was focused on strengthening the defensive capability and continuing the industrialization project that was launched in the late 1920s and early 1930s. However, after the death of Stalin (1953), a fundamentally important transformation began. The leaders who replaced the fierce dictator believed that the well-being of the population should be improved to a certain extent. The new policy began to be followed during the years of rule of the Soviet government of Georgy Malenkov (1953–1955), and when all power was concentrated in the hands of Nikita Khrushchev (in the second half of the 1950s to 1964), the aspiration to feed and clothe Soviet people only increased. Further development of the oil and gas sector was in many ways determined by this strategic policy change of Kremlin leaders. Khrushchev launched mass housing construction, and welcomed the production of domestic equipment, fabrics, and clothes. He launched the development of virgin lands of Kazakhstan in order to resolve the problem of food supply for urbanized populations: when it turned out that there was still not enough food, the Soviet Union began to import grain from abroad. In order to purchase food and other consumer goods, the Soviet Union required foreign currency. The major issue was the need to find sources for this money. As the Soviet ruble was not a convertible currency at the time, and as was shown above the Soviet economy was incapable of providing any competition on the world market of industrial production, it was only possible to receive currency by exporting raw materials.[13] It is not surprising that Soviet leaders began to think about the need for a significant expansion of the oil and gas sector not only to provide for domestic consumption, but also to export these natural resources. The need for expansion of production, fortunately for the Soviet Union, coincided with possibilities.

Throughout the 1950s and 1960s in Western Siberia there were active geological projects to expand territories that until recently had not been developed at all, where small backward ethnic groups lived in severe natural conditions—Khants, Mansy, and so on. The living conditions in the enormous territory were so severe that in the mid-1960s, there were only twelve thousand members of the Khanty people and four thousand Mansy.[14] However, from 1953 to 1965, twenty-nine oil fields and twenty-six gas fields were discovered in this region—80 percent of them were in the territory of the Tyumen Oblast of the Soviet Union.[15] Soon, it became clear that the country had much richer natural resources than was believed until recently. If from the nineteenth century to the mid-twentieth century, Russia's specialization in the international system of division of labor was believed to be grain production, now oil and gas began to come to the fore. This breakthrough in the 1950s and early 1960s was important for the further developmental trajectory of Russia even after the collapse of the Soviet Union. The reserves of the oil fields situated between the Volga and the Urals were not sufficient for the expansion on the world market of oil and gas that was conducted by the Soviet Union in the 1970s. The development of oil production in the second Baku only proceeded actively until the mid-1970s. In 1975, production reached its peak, and then began to decline. In 1990 it fell to the level that existed in 1960.[16] Without the development of Western Siberian oil fields, the Soviet Union could not have entered the world market of energy resources as a major exporter.

THE "THIRD BAKU" AND THE ROLE OF ALEXEI KOSYGIN

In the 1960s the active development of rich oil and gas fields of Western Siberia, which according to a tradition among oil men began to be called the "third Baku," had been launched. And the goal of this enormous expensive campaign this time was not so much to strengthen industry and the military power of the country, but to assist the growth of the prosperity of the population. The fact that petrodollar revenues in many ways served as a tool to gratify millions of citizens, and thus preserve social stability in the diminishing ideological attractiveness of the Communist regime, to a large degree determined the problems of the perestroika era, which began in the mid-1980s when Mikhail Gorbachev came to power.

The first oil in Western Siberia was produced in 1960. It is interesting that the radiogram on this event was reported from the oil field in Tyumen to the management in the Azeri language. Many oil workers of Siberia were from the Baku region. So that information about the important event did not spread prematurely, they communicated in a language that they knew well, but which the vast majority of the citizens of the Soviet Union naturally did not know at all.[17]

How did the development of the new oil producing region begin? The Soviet legend about the beginning of large-scale developments of oil in Western Siberia goes as follows. The first secretary of the Tyumen Oblast Communist Party Committee and the head of a major geological research institution once came to the chairman of the Gosplan (the major central state agency in charge of planning). They proposed to organize production of oil in Tyumen, of approximately ten to fifteen million tons per year. The chairman of the Gosplan called his deputy, who was in charge of issues related to oil processing. The deputy, without even looking at the geological maps on the table, announced that the "enormous supplies of oil and gas that the people from Tyumen talk about are nothing more than the fruit of a provincial sick mind." And he concluded, "We must stop fooling everyone and get on with our business." This type of reaction was quite typical for high-ranking Soviet officials, given the fact that neither the top managers of the Gosplan nor the directors of enterprises could have a share of the profits received from developing new oil-bearing regions. However, even in the Soviet system some incentives sometimes began to work. Some managers and directors wanted to increase their personal political weight, showing the Moscow Communist leadership that they were able to achieve an important result. Some were filled with enthusiasm, and so tried to achieve progress regardless of the amount of money received from the project. Evidently, one of these factors had an effect in this situation. The Siberians got angry and were about to leave, saying, "We thought we had come to Soviet state officials, but it turns out that this is a bureaucratic Tsarist service of 100 years ago. There is nothing for us to do here." However, the chairman of the Gosplan proved to be a sensible person. He proposed to listen to the Siberians' arguments. In the end, a proposal was prepared on the start of a project in Western Siberia.[18]

This legend probably reflects reality, although it certainly simplifies the situation somewhat. In the Soviet Union, stories like that were extremely popular (including fictional ones from novels and films) about the battle between selfish or ignorant bureaucrats and smart party members who were convinced of the truth of the Communist idea. Nevertheless, it cannot be denied that a solution to the problem depended in many ways on the relationships of power-holders at the very top of the Soviet bureaucratic hierarchy. A very high-ranking official had to be found who would take on the initiative and risk of launching the major investment of resources in developing the oil and gas sector. And this person was indeed found. The major initiator of the development of Siberian oil and gas fields in the 1960s and 1970s was in the end the head of the Soviet government, Alexei Kosygin. This political figure played a major role in Soviet history. He was not just a high-ranked bureaucrat or even an ordinary prime minister. People link the name of Kosygin with the first attempts at implementing economic reforms directed toward serious expansion of the independence of enterprises from central planning, and the provision of material incentives for their workers and managers. The Kosygin reform that was proposed in the mid-1960s had a great deal in common with the Hungarian economic reform that was started by Janos Kadar in 1968. However, unlike Hungary, in the Soviet Union the reform was soon stopped, above all for political reasons. The Soviet leadership was afraid that economic changes would be followed by a major drive to political changes, like in the Prague spring of 1968, when the Czechoslovakian Communists aspired at the same time to build market socialism and democratize the socialist system that was imposed on them from Moscow. Kosygin was unable to reform the Soviet economic system and raise the level of prosperity of citizens, and so as a result he concentrated his efforts on increasing oil and gas production, which was supposed to bring into the country export revenues necessary for its own production and to buy consumer goods abroad.

Kosygin was directly in charge of all the major projects in the oil and gas sector, and even determined how and how not to build pipelines. Kosygin personally rang (including on weekends) major Soviet top managers responsible for developing oil fields and asked them how work was processing. According to Nikolay Baibakov, who knew the head of the Soviet government quite well, Kosygin kept many details in his head—technical data of compressors, diameters of pipes, length of planned gas pipelines, and remembered the names of dozens of surveyors, builders and assemblers, drilling masters, and knew the names of all manufacturing factories.[19] As there were no private enterprises in the Soviet Union, all the work connected with developing Siberian oil and gas fields was taken on by the state. Kosygin even established a special ministry for building enterprises of the oil and gas industry headed by Alexei Kortunov. In the Tyumen region, the experienced economic executive Viktor Muravlenko was in charge of managing the production of oil and gas.

Gas production was launched in the major west Siberian fields (in 1972, the Medvezhe field began to operate, in 1978 Urgenoi, and in

1986 Yamburg). At the same time, the oil industry was expanded intensively—Samotlor, Fyodorovka, Kholmogory. Approximately fifteen to twenty major oil fields were put into operation over the 1970s and 1980s.[20] Siberian oil and gas fields were developed under extremely harsh natural conditions. The average temperature in January in the areas of the major oil and gas fields was –22C, while the absolute minimum temperature recorded was –55C.[21] Construction equipment often could not withstand these temperatures. Lift arms and chain tracks of cranes shattered like glass, and engines broke down. As a result, to protect expensive equipment, the management ordered construction work to be stopped when the temperature was below –35C.[22] Difficulties were not only caused by the severe Siberian frosts, but by the nature of the location. Up to 70 percent of the territory of Western Siberia is totally impassable swamps, where equipment sinks and it is practically impossible to organize normal living conditions.[23] It seems that if it were not for the technical capabilities that appeared in the second half of the twentieth century, the Western Siberian region would remain undeveloped. The difficulties of developing fields were incomparable with those in Azerbaijan and in the region between the Volga and the Urals. In the first Baku and second Baku, people lived and did various types of businesses that were unrelated with oil production. In the third Baku, practically nothing can exist apart from oil and gas production. Indigenous people of the north, who are located in this region, remained at the economic, social, and cultural levels of development of centuries long past until the twentieth century.

These undeveloped conditions of Western Siberia determined the peculiarities of the oil and gas sector in this area. Oil and gas men had to move construction equipment over extremely large distances, where there were no villages at all.[24] During the summer, transportation of goods across the territory of Western Siberia was somewhat easier than during winter. With a lack of normal roads, the major transportation routes were rivers, which mainly flow from the south to the north. Along these rivers, construction materials, equipment, and food were transported from the more developed southern part of Siberia to the north, where the major oil and gas fields are located. All Siberian rivers are covered with a thick layer of ice during winter, and it is impossible to use them during this period; only in summer does the navigation season begin. Almost everything was delivered in this way over many kilometers to northern destinations, including such basic construction materials as sand, break stone, and gravel, which are virtually nonexistent in the swampy area of Western Siberia.[25] These harsh conditions caused major difficulties in establishing towns and villages where oil and gas workers could reside.[26] It is clear that conditions for developing the oil and gas fields of Siberia were not only extremely difficult, but frequently intolerable.

It proved to be difficult to attract people to this work. Nevertheless, they still came and worked under these conditions. To a certain degree, the role of the enthusiasm of builders of Communism cultivated by Soviet propaganda played a minor role, and also the romanticism of mastering distant spaces that was a feature for the generation of Soviet young people in the 1960s and 1970s. However, by the time that the territories of Western Siberia were developed, belief in Communism was already seriously undermined, and so material incentives came to the fore. By Soviet standards, oil and gas workers were paid extremely well. In the late 1970s, the average wage in the oil and gas sector in Western Siberia was more than three times the average wage in the country.[27] At the same time, for the Soviet Union with its administrative economy, differentiation of wages was not typical at all. The gap in the salary of skilled and nonskilled workers was insignificant. Only the extreme importance of developing oil and gas fields forced the Soviet leadership to use such major material incentives in Western Siberia.

In the 1970s, production of Tyumen oil came to just 31 million tons. Five years later it had already reached 148 million. And in 1980, the amount of oil production achieved 313 million tons. Production increased tenfold in a decade.[28] Besides oil and gas developments in Western Siberia, the pipeline network also had to be developed actively. If oil could be transported by rail and roads from the first Baku and second Baku, then in the third Baku, there was no alternative at all to the pipelines. Furthermore, the need to develop the pipeline network was also determined by the increasing role of gas production, so gigantic gas pipelines had to be built. If before the Bolshevik revolution of 1917, the total length of pipelines in Russia came to just 1,200 km, by 1980 it was fifty times more.[29] According to Baibakov, the development of the oil and gas industry played an enormous role in providing everyday goods for Soviet citizens: in fact, oil and gas of Western Siberia not only became a reliable basis of the energy supply for the Soviet Union and Communist countries of Eastern Europe, but also were a major source of export hard currency revenues for the purchase of food and necessary equipment for major industrial enterprises. During these years in total, export revenues were used for purchasing equipment for more than fifty enterprises of various kinds.[30]

A golden age for the Soviet economy came after the oil shock of 1973: at this time there was a drastic increase in revenues from the export of oil to Western Europe. If in 1970 the Soviet Union received $0.87 billion from the export of energy resources, ten years later, in 1980, it received $12.97 billion: in other words, this was almost fifteen times growth.[31] It is not surprising that the Kremlin used these revenues to ensure the needs of Soviet citizens with imported goods. Statistics of this time recorded a drastic growth in the import of grain and meat in the mid-1970s. The balance of grain trade became negative for the Soviet Union as early as 1964. Yet, in the second half of the 1960s, the export of grain once again exceeded the import, but since 1972, the balance went to negative figures; in 1973 it increased by almost two times, and in 1975 by two times again. And subsequently, the Soviet Union continued to purchase an increasing amount of grain abroad. In 1981, the negative balance on grain trade came to $7,712 million.[32] This amount of foreign currency could only be obtained by exporting oil and gas.

Not everything that was purchased abroad was used effectively, however. The extremely low retail prices on bread that were set up by the state led to major losses, to irrational use of products (including use for animal feed). However, even despite some failures due to the nature of the Soviet planning system, the importance of the oil factor in providing goods for the people was undoubtedly extremely high. The problem was that the Soviet economy soon became heavily dependent upon export revenues not only for development but also for covering everyday needs, thus the negative effects of the "resource curse" (such as the major increase of state expenditures) and the "Dutch disease" hit the Soviet Union—even harder than many other petrostates, which nevertheless were market economies. Thus, the oil-induced short-term success of the Soviet Union in the 1970s brought in major failures in the late 1980s.

Top managers in the oil and gas sector of the Soviet period recalled that Kosygin not only persuaded rank and file managers to increase the amount of oil production, but also pressured the major officials of the entire oil and gas sector. For example, he often said to Viktor Muravlenko, the head of the oil industry in the key Tyumen Oblast, "The situation with bread is bad—give us three million tons [of oil] above of the plan."[33] The need to increase the production of Siberian oil was so high that the leadership of the country not only persuaded enterprises, but ordered this to be done, despite the lack of capacities to do so. In the Soviet economy, Communist Party bosses and the government often dictated to enterprises what to do and how, and sometimes this led to catastrophes like those in Western Siberia in August 1973. Oil workers were asked to increase the daily production of oil to ten thousand tons at the request of top Communist Party leaders. The local manager who well understood the danger of this incompetent order refused to fulfill this request and was dismissed from his position. The bosses who replaced him opened the valves at the boreholes of the field that were ready for operation and began to pump gas, but the workers began to suffocate from the gas, and finally there was a sudden explosion. Everything around turned into an enormous fire: a large number of innocent people were killed, and irreparable damage was done to oil production.[34]

Nevertheless, despite the accidents and the major difficulties, the development of the "third Baku" continued. Along with the significant expansion of the export of oil, a new project was oriented toward delivery of Soviet natural gas from Siberian fields to Western Europe. However, as the Soviet economy itself did not manufacture appropriate pipes for gas pipelines, the contract involved a barter exchange: Moscow acquired pipes in West Germany and paid for them by deliveries of gas. This deal, known as "gas for pipes," was initially proposed in the early 1960s. However, because of the Cuban missile crisis, relationships between the Soviet Union and NATO were drastically spoiled, and so it was not possible to bring the project to implementation. The chancellor of West Germany, Konrad Adenaur, refused to make the deal with Nikita Khrushchev. And the president of the Italian oil and gas company ENI Enrico Mattei, who was a big enthusiast of cooperation with the Soviet Union, died under mysterious circumstances in a helicopter crash shortly after his meeting with Khrushchev. There were rumors that Mattei was killed, and the reason for this was his agreement with the Soviet side. However, no one was able to ascertain to what extent these suspicions corresponded to reality. The contract between the Soviet Union and West Germany was only signed in 1970 by Soviet leader Leonid Brezhnev and West German chancellor Willy Brandt. West Germany began to deliver large diameter pipes to the Soviets, and the German company Ruhrgas began to buy Soviet gas. On 1 October 1973, gas was delivered from the Soviet Union to Western Europe for the first time.[35]

Thus, as one can see, in the 1970s and 1980s, a close mutual link was established in the Soviet Union between the export of oil and gas and the provision of basic goods to the population at large, for both food and everyday consumption items. Fundamentally new developments, which were different from previous decades, affected the entire nature of the Soviet economy. But what seems to be a plausible solution for the Soviet Union for some period of time proved to be a source of major troubles when oil markets crashed in the 1980s. These troubles also contributed to the Soviet collapse in 1991.

CRISIS OF THE MID-1980S AND COLLAPSE OF THE SOVIET UNION

The major dependence of the Soviet economy on the oil and gas export revenues in many ways determined the course of further events. Now, in order to maintain the living standards of the Soviet people, there was a constant need to increase production and export of oil and gas to Western Europe. The inefficient Soviet economy performed badly, so the entire country in fact depended on the oil and gas industry alone. However, its possibilities were limited, and so some time after the golden age of the 1970s, the period of crisis began. The amount of oil produced in Western Siberia increased swiftly until 1984. But then the very opportunities for further growth proved to be exhausted. New fields were not developed, and, as a result, the oil and gas sector stagnated, which continued almost until the very moment of the Soviet collapse.[36]

The fall of the oil production in the second Baku and the stagnation in the third Baku together caused a major decline in production in the oil and gas industry, thus inevitably causing a reduction in export. The Soviet leadership refused to reduce deliveries of subsided gas to countries of the Soviet economic bloc of Eastern Europe for purely political reasons: the states that were dependent on Moscow had to be kept in the orbit of its influence somehow. Accordingly, export of oil and gas to the West had to be reduced. In 1984 this export came to 44.0 million tons, in 1985 it declined to 33.3 million, and in 1986 its growth was rather insignificant—to 37.6 million tons.[37] The fall of oil and gas export limited the possibilities of import for deliveries of food. This hit the consumer market of the Soviet Union very hard, and by the end of the 1980s, the increasing money emission and the sudden rise of inflation unbalanced the economy.

At this time, the new Soviet leader, Mikhail Gorbachev, who announced perestroika in the Soviet Union, launched some economic changes that were rather unsuccessful. Enterprises finally received the chance to earn money in accordance with the revenue that they received from sale of production, but at the same time the state was unable to reduce the enormous irrational expenditures, especially due to the heavy military burden. A budget deficit began to grow, which was covered by money emission. At a certain point, the Soviet leadership de facto lost control over this process. They filled all the gaps that appeared in the economy with cash, no longer worrying if the amount of the money emission matched whether the economy produced a sufficient amount of goods that consumers could acquire. No wonder that Soviet citizens found themselves with large amounts of cash, and tried to spend it on food and consumer goods. But the shortage of goods, which had also previously been the Achilles' heel of the Soviet economy, naturally dramatically increased in these years. Even the goods and products that were relatively easy to buy under Brezhnev became inaccessible for ordinary people in the last years of Gorbachev's years in power.

The exhaustion of already developed oil and gas fields was not the only problem that the oil and gas sector, and thus the entire Soviet economy, faced. The low labor productivity, the lack of technological breakthroughs, and the lack of serious material incentives for work also affected the oil and gas industry. For example, according to an assessment by the renowned Soviet economist Valentin Kudrov, labor productivity in the oil processing industry of the Soviet Union came to just 50–60 percent of the labor productivity in the equivalent American industry in 1987.[38]

The problems of the Soviet economy would perhaps not have had such catastrophic consequences if it weren't for the unfavorable situation on the world oil markets in the 1980s. The decline in oil production coincided with a major decline in prices. By March 1983, the Organization of the Petroleum Exporting Countries (OPEC) decided to reduce the official oil price from $34 to $29 per barrel. And since early 1985 (exactly at the time when Gorbachev announced perestroika in the Soviet Union), "the decline in oil prices becomes a clear fact that determines the development of the world economy," according to the major Russian economic reformer Yegor Gaidar.[39] In 1986, the average oil price was as low as $19.90 per barrel; the next year it increased to $24.90, but then it fell once more to $19.50. In 1989, the oil price was $22.80 on average, in 1990—$28.20, and in 1991—$22.90 per barrel.[40] With this low level of oil prices, the Soviet leadership was unable to deal with the severe economic problems of an oil exporting country: "A major money overhang had already emerged in the country by this time. . . . Soviet citizens who did not have the ability to buy goods that were in demand had accumulated savings. Even when it decided to conduct a large-scale price increase, the Soviet leadership would have been forced to deal with the . . . shortage of basic consuming goods. The threats to stability of the regime due to implementation of such policy seemed unavoidable in the mid-1980s."[41] The consequences of the economic policy that was conducted against the background of a lack of petrodollars were truly catastrophic for the Soviet Union. In the early 1990s, the popularity of Gorbachev was almost zero. If in the first years of perestroika, Soviet citizens believed that the improvement of socialism proclaimed by the new leader would really improve their lives, on the eve of the Soviet collapse they at best considered Gorbachev to be a deceiver and demagogue who was only capable of chattering, but incapable of doing anything practical.

In 1990, the Soviet leader was forced to abandon the proposal of economic changes and the program of market reforms initiated by the group of young economists led by Grigory Yavlinsky. Gorbachev, evidently, did not risk carrying out radical steps when his previous popular support had been lost. As a result, the situation involving food and other consumer goods in the Soviet Union got completely out of hand. Sugar, meat, alcohol, soap, and some other goods began to be allocated by coupons, and the state did not have enough reserves even to satisfy requirements according to the established norms. No wonder that a large number of Russians completely abandoned their support of Gorbachev and shifted their sympathies to the opposition politician, Boris Yeltsin, who in 1991 became the president of Russia. If many people in the West continue to respect Gorbachev to this day, as a person who put an end to the Cold War, in Russia only a few people have kept their trust in him due to his inability to feed the people and ensure a decent economic performance. Perestroika ended in August 1991 when a group of top Soviet officials staged a coup in Moscow, removing Gorbachev from power and attempting to arrest Yeltsin. The Russian president headed the resistance to the putschists, and eventually won. However, Gorbachev could no longer return to power, and finally, in December 1991, the Soviet Union was dissolved by agreement of the Russian, Ukrainian, and Belarussian leaders. The notoriously inefficient Soviet economy discredited the Communist system once and for all. At the time, people hoped that the leaders of republics that had gained independence since the Soviet collapse would be able to conduct economic reforms more successfully than the leaders of the Soviet Union.

So, the collapse of the Soviet Union occurred in 1991 against the background of the major crisis in the oil and gas sector, which for a long time had provided the state with the capacity to feed the people with imported food and basic goods. But here a question arises: should we, taking into account everything that has been said above, say that the collapse of the Soviet Union was primarily because of a major decline in oil prices and a lack of foreign currency to provide the Soviet population with basic consumer goods?

RETHINKING THE SOVIET COLLAPSE

This interpretation of the developments of Gorbachev's perestroika is very popular in Russia today. If many nationalists believe that the collapse of the Soviet Union was the consequence of betrayal on Gorbachev's part and a conspiracy organized by the American secret services, many liberals pay attention primarily to the economic background of the events. They believe that the attempt to reform the Soviet economic system in order to increase its efficiency was a consequence of the increasing shortage of goods, primarily food. And all the subsequent political changes were caused by the unsuccessful conduct of economic reforms. However, it seems that the answers to the question on the causes of the Soviet collapse and on the impact of the resource curse cannot be so straightforward. In fact, there was a combination of a number of factors in the Soviet collapse.

There are no doubts that problems with the import of grain and other goods really were an important factor that caused market reform in the Soviet Union. The Soviet political leadership really should have thought about how to feed the population. At the very beginning of the 1980s, it initiated a development of a special food program to increase production of food, but the implementation of this program failed completely, and accordingly the shortage of foreign currency (and declining import capability) should have led to extremely serious difficulties in this respect. Gaidar quotes Gorbachev's speech at a meeting at the Central Committee of the Communist Party on 23 August 1986. The Soviet leader said that "in connection with the existing situation in the production of oil and gas condensate, our export resources, and accordingly the possibilities of import in 1986 have declined significantly. And this seriously complicates for us the problem of balancing not only the export plan, but also the economy in general. Under these conditions, the issue of the use of currency is extremely important. We of course spend a lot of currency on purchasing agricultural products—grain, meat, other products. We purchase more than 9 million tons of steel, and steel pipes for 3 billion, is a large amount of raw materials . . . for chemistry, non-ferrous metallurgy, light industry etc. In general all of this is necessary. We buy because we cannot live without this."[42] Gorbachev continued to demonstrate his serious concern with problems caused by the major decline in oil prices. If in 1986 he still enjoyed high popularity among the people, after two to three years the Soviet leaders already needed to strengthen their political positions in some way. And to do so they needed to feed the population of the country. The state's incapability to provide material support to large groups of the population could not help the leader of the country.

Thus, it can be said that the entire developmental trajectory of the Soviet economy, starting from Kosygin's initiatives on developing the third Baku, led the Soviet Union to a severe social crisis, which was determined by a strong dependence of the living standards of the population on the inflow of petrodollars. And still, there is no reason to believe that the oil factor alone strictly determined the beginning and the further dead end of perestroika. Along with the oil, there were a number of other important factors in operation, and their contribution to the developments of the country could even have been more significant. This conclusion, in our opinion, can be confirmed both by historical comparisons, and by an analysis of the course of events in the second half of the 1980s.

It is well known that the Soviet Union, even before the beginning of Gorbachev's perestroika, experienced serious troubles with the food supply on a number of occasions, but they never led to the fall of the Communist regime. At a difficult moment, the Soviet leaders could always increase terror and repressions and ensure the obedience of the population. For example, this was the situation in the early 1930s, when the farmers who were forcibly driven in collective farms had grain confiscated from them in large quantities, in order to export it, and the money received was used to buy equipment required for the extensive construction of the industrialization period. According to a number of assessments, millions of farmers (primarily in Ukraine) died of starvation during this time, but the Soviet regime endured, and was later even able to oppose Nazi Germany during World War II. In the 1930s, some foreign observers believed that the peasants would revolt because of the intolerable difficulties of life and overthrow the inhuman Bolshevik regime. But nothing of the kind actually happened. Yet another example of the cruelties of the regime in solving the problem of a food shortage was Stalin's repressions in the second half of the 1940s. The catastrophic destruction of the war and the human losses at the front drastically reduced even those low living standards of the Soviet people that were reached in the 1930s. However, instead of putting the existing modest resources into producing food and consumer goods, after World War II Stalin actively developed new weapons. Despite the difficulties that people experienced at the time, many Soviet citizens were prepared to accept deprivations for the sake of strengthening the country's defense capability. Many of them genuinely believed that they would thus avoid a greater danger—to be conquered by capitalist aggressors. One very typical statement was made in 1960 by a very old woman who had lived through World War II: "I'm prepared to eat potato peel and dry bread with salt and water, so that there is no war."[43] The food difficulties that the Soviet Union encountered in the second half of the 1980s because of the effect of the oil factor were undoubtedly not unprecedented. Furthermore, the scope and scale of these difficulties were clearly not as great as those in the 1930s and 1940s.

If during Gorbachev's perestroika other changes had not taken place in the Soviet Union apart from the drastic reduction in the flow of petrodollars, the Soviet leaders could have ensured the survival of the Communist regime even with low oil prices and a decline in grain import. However, judging from historical experience, they did not want a further development of the country with the use of repressions, and so they tried to solve economic problems by economic reforms. In this sense, we may say that the oil factor did affect the development of the country, but did not determine it strictly. If one browses through voluminous memoirs and historical literature about how the perestroika began and collapsed in the second half of the 1980s, there is no clear proof that the Soviet leaders were worried primarily by the problems of petrodollars and the troubles connected with this in providing the population with various types of goods. Rather, Soviet leaders of the time emphasized the priority of more general problems of the Soviet economy, which at that time demonstrated inefficiency of enterprises and the lack of major independence material incentives to make workers work. There was also the major discussion of the development of socialist democracy, of perestroika in the system of international relations. But all these discourses and arguments were based on the need for a major improvement of the entire socialist system as a whole, and there was not much concern about those severe difficulties caused by the shortage of petrodollars.

Gorbachev's speech at the Twenty-Seventh Congress of the Communist Party of the Soviet Union is typical in this sense. This speech was made in February 1986—that is, less than a year after Gorbachev came to power, and six months before the meeting where the Soviet leader complained about the decline in the import capabilities of the country. According to the strong Soviet tradition, the speech by the party leader at the congress (they were held once every five years) had to address major programmatic statements and provide guidelines to the entire country for the next five years. Gorbachev drew the attention of the entire country, not only pointing out achievements, as Brezhnev always did, but also major flaws and unsolved tasks. He noted that "in the 1970s, difficulties began to increase in the national economy. The rates of economic growth declined noticeably. As a result, the tasks for developing the economy set by the Communist Party program were not implemented. . . . The social program that was set for these years was also not implemented in full. The material basis of science and education, public health and the culture . . . were allowed to lag behind. Of course, the state of affairs was also affected by several factors that did not depend on us. But they were not decisive. The main thing is that we did not make a political assessment on time of the change of the economic situation, did not recognize the seriousness and urgency of the transition of the economy to intensive methods of development, and the active use in the national economy of achievements of scientific and technical progress. There were numerous appeals and discussions about this, but things practically remained unchanged. Out of inertia, the economy . . . focused on bringing additional labor and material resources into production. As a consequence, there was a serious decline in growth rates of labor productivity, and several other indicators of efficiency. Attempts to fix matters by new construction worsened the problem of balance. The national economy, which possessed enormous resources, faced a lack of them."[44] This programmatic statement by Gorbachev shows that the political leadership of the Soviet Union in early 1986 already had a general idea of the nature of the major economic problems that the country had encountered. He quite rightly pointed out the inability of the Soviet economy to make use of the achievements of science and technology, and the divide between the needs of the population and the level of production. Gorbachev realized that the problem did not only lie in the fact that petrodollars were missing, thus causing the urgent need to cover the largest holes. The problem was that the Soviet Union lagged behind the developed nations of the West.

Unlike the previous generation of Soviet leaders, who did not know or want to know how people lived abroad, the new generation of leaders had a fully adequate perception of the situation. Gorbachev had traveled extensively around the world before he became a leader of the Soviet Union. His closest ally, Alexander Yakovlev, served in Canada for ten years as the Soviet ambassador. Foreign Minister Eduard Shevardnadze was very interested in the way of life in the West. Yakovlev discusses in detail in his book of memoirs and analysis about how his mind-set was transformed before perestroika, and how he began to doubt the policy that had been followed since the times of Lenin and Stalin. He clearly demonstrates that people like him had the need to reform the country regardless of the oil prices.[45] Of course, we cannot rule out the fact that the real motivations for perestroika did not coincide with those officially declared statements. And still, it seems that if the oil factor had determined the strategy of perestroika, this would be found in some way or another in numerous publications that told us about this time.

It is much more sensible to assume that in the mid-1980s, regardless of the oil market, the Soviet leadership had agreed about the need to significant changes in the country. This was determined primarily in the generation changes in the political establishment of the Soviet Union. In the first half of the 1980s, the vast majority of leaders whose political biography went back to Stalinist times passed away. The worldview of Gorbachev and his associates was developed to a large degree in the 1950s, under the influence of the Khrushchev thaw. Also, the new generation of Soviet leaders was not tied down by old dogma and was not tainted with the blood of mass repressions of the Stalinist era. These people had a more elaborate understanding of the modern world than their predecessors. It is unlikely that they seriously dreamed about a market economy and democracy of the Western type at this time, but they did indeed aspire to bring the Soviet Union closer to the developed world. These aspirations, in their turn, had two major consequences: First, for people of Gorbachev's type, it was impossible by their very nature to launch brutal attacks toward the people who were angry with the lack of necessary goods. And so the shortage of petrodollars and the troubles of importing grain must have made political leaders think about the need of radical economic and political changes. Second, these radical changes themselves, regardless of the oil market, were part of the ideas of the political leaders of the Soviet Union about how the country should be run during the perestroika era. Yet it seems likely that if the situation on the oil markets had been favorable, there would have been more declarations in their policies and fewer real actions. Furthermore, in this case, the Gorbachev period would probably have lasted longer, and the collapse of the Soviet Union would have occurred much later than it actually did. But a fundamental transformation of the country would still have taken place, as the elite and even broad segments of the mass public truly wanted these major changes.

Thus, we come to the conclusion that the impact of "resource curse" for the Soviet system was of a rather conditional nature. The dependence on Soviet politics and policymaking on the inflow of petrodollars was quite high at that time. The revenues from oil and gas export provided opportunities that in many ways allowed the Soviet Union to maintain the living standards of its population in the 1970s through the first half of the 1980s. However, it cannot be said that in this period the petrodollars, by providing a kind of conditional abundance of material benefits, slowed down changes. In fact, the living standards of the population were low, despite the import of certain goods. People suffered from a shortage of food, clothing, and housing. But the political leadership that formed around Brezhnev was not interested in serious changes to the system, merely because of the nature of its mentality. When Gorbachev and his allies came to power, the mood for change finally appeared, and the decline of prices on the oil market hastened the need for transformations. Furthermore, as these changes were unsuccessful for the Soviet economy, the lack of foreign currency exacerbated the economic crisis and hastened the fall of Gorbachev. And together with his fall, it also hastened the collapse of the Soviet Union.

NOTES

1. A famous Russian proverb goes, "Our country has two problems—fools and roads."

2. Brita Asbrink, *Imperiya Nobelei: Istoriya o znemenitykh shvedakh, bakinskoi nefti I revolyutsii v Rossii* (Moscow: Tekst, 2003), 24.

3. Nikolay Baibakov, *Delo zhizni. Zapiski neftyanika* (Moscow: Sovetskaya Rossiya, 1984), 15.

4. Asbrink, *Imperiya Nobelei*, 30.

5. Asbrink, *Imperiya Nobelei*, 32.

6. Asbrink, *Imperiya Nobelei*, 48.

7. Asbrink, *Imperiya Nobelei*, 201.

8. Asbrink, *Imperiya Nobelei*, 191, 196, 212, 216, 218, 220.

9. Baibakov, *Delo zhizni*, 175, 240.

10. Maria Slavkina, *Triumf i tragediya: Razvitie neftegazovogo kompleksa SSSR v 1960–1980-e gody* (Moscow: Nauka, 2002), 19.

11. It should be noted that unlike oil, which until the revolution was a well-developed business, the gas sector was almost nonexistent in the first decades of Soviet history. For example, in 1940 the Soviet Union produced 3.2 billion cubic meters of gas, while the United States produced 77 billion, that is, twenty-four times more. Viktor Andriyanov, *Kosygin* (Moscow: Molodaya Gvardiya, 2003), 27. The entire gas transportation network in the country appeared after World War II. Slavkina, *Triumf i tragediya*, 32.

12. Slavkina, *Triumf i tragediya*, 13.

13. In principle, the Soviet Union could have significantly increased the export of metals, but this was unacceptable for the Communist leadership. It still

gave a lot of attention to strengthening the defensive capability of the country, and so metal was used for weapons production. Furthermore, the inability of the Soviet planning system to optimize the production led to the machine-building industry manufacturing an enormous amount of unnecessary tractors, combines, and machines, and this used the metal that could otherwise have been exported.

14. Alexander Trapeznikov, *Viktor Muravlenko* (Moscow: Molodaya Gvardiya, 2007), 161.

15. Slavkina, *Triumf i tragediya*, 42.

16. Slavkina, *Triumf i tragediya*, 53.

17. Trapeznikov, *Viktor Muravlenko*, 185.

18. Andriyanov, *Kosygin*, 238–39.

19. Tom Fetisov, ed., *Prem'er izvestnyi i neizvestnyi: Vospominaniya o A.N.Kosygine* (Moscow: Respublika, 1997), 136.

20. Andriyanov, *Kosygin*, 237.

21. Viktor Muravlenko, ed., *Neft' Sibiri* (Moscow: Nedra, 1973), 37.

22. Andriyanov, *Kosygin*, 233, 243. Kosygin once flew in a helicopter with the chairman of the Gosplan, Nikolay Baibakov, in order to supervise progress at one oil field under development. They had to walk 200–250 meters into a biting frosty wind. Kosygin's cheek froze, and Baibakov's ears froze; they had to rub them with snow. Fetisov, *Perm'er izvestnyi i neizvestnyi*, 135.

23. Slavkina, *Triumf i tragediya*, 45.

24. Muravlenko, *Neft' Sibiri*, 155.

25. Trapeznikov, *Viktor Muravlenko*, 190, 200.

26. Initially workers resided in small wooden houses, which had rooms with beds, kitchens for cooking food, and other facilities However, what is good for the European part of Russia (especially for southern regions) is not quite appropriate for Western Siberia. People who lived in these houses had to respond to the challenge of nature in temperatures that reached –30C, and even lower. Slavkina, *Triumf i tragediya*, 102.

27. Slavkina, *Triumf i tragediya*, 98–99.

28. Andriyanov, *Kosygin*, 253.

29. Baibakov, *Delo zhizni*, 42.

30. Fetisov, *Prem'er izvestnyi i neizvsetnyi*, 134–35.

31. Slavkina, *Triumf i tragediya*, 124–25, 128.

32. Yegor Gaidar, *Gibel' imperii: Uroki dlya sovremennoi Rossii* (Moscow: ROSSPEN, 2006), 172.

33. Slavkina, *Triumf i tragediya*, 143.

34. Trapeznikov, *Viktor Muravlenko*, 212–13.

35. Valerii Panyushkin and Mikhail Zygar', *Gazprom: Novoe russkoe oruzhie* (Moscow: Zakharov, 2008), 5–6.

36. Slavkina, *Triumf i tragediya*, 68–69.

37. Gaidar, *Gibel' imperii*, 193.

38. Valentin Kudrov, *Sovetskaya ekonomika v restrospektive: Opyt pereosmysleniya* (Moscow: Nauka, 2003), 300–301.

39. Gaidar, *Gibel' imperii*, 116.

40. Gaidar, *Gibel' imperii*, 118.

41. Gaidar, *Gibel' imperii*, 221.

42. Quoted in Gaidar, *Gibel' imperii*, 234.

43. Boris Grushin, *Chetyre zhizni Rossii v zerkale obshchestvenno mneniya: Ocherki massovogo soznaniya rossiyan vremen Khrushcheva, Brezhneva, Gorbacheva i Yeltsina* (four volumes), vol.1, Epokha Khrushcheva (Moscow: Progress-Traditisiya, 2001), 75.

44. Mikhail Gorbachev, *Politicheskii doklad Tsentral'nogo komiteta KPSS XXVII s'ezdu Kommunisticheskoi partii Sovetskogo Soyuza: Stenograficheskii otchet* (Moscow: Politzdat, 1986), 43–44.

45. Alexander Yakovlev, *Sumerki* (Moscow: Materik, 2003), 373–79.

3

The Impact of the Oil Shock on the Post-Soviet Regime Changes

Andrey Scherbak

Several scholarly approaches have been elaborated in political science to explain the failure of democratization in Russia and some other countries of the former Soviet Union, for example, the cultural approach (which focuses on illiberal and antidemocratic values and attitudes of citizens and elites of these states), the institutional approach (with an emphasis on the "perils of presidentialism"), and the path-dependency approach (which paid major attention to the authoritarian "legacies of the past"). The aim of this chapter is to propose an alternative political-economic explanation of the return of authoritarianism in a number of countries of the former Soviet Union. The explanation is based on the "resource curse" theory, which argues for the negative influence of large amounts of natural resources, in particular oil, on the economic and political development of countries with respective resources. The analysis used the data from 1996 to 2008, which covered the "oil shock" period of 2003–2008. This chapter demonstrates the negative impact between the amount of natural resources (especially oil and gas), which is measured by the export of mineral resources as a share of GDP, and the level of democracy. I also test two causal mechanisms that may explain this influence—the negative effect of oil rent on the public activism and citizen participation (rentier effect) and the use of oil rent to strengthen a coercive apparatus (repression effect). I advance the proposal that the inequality effect is increasingly significant for political development, which might be considered a side effect of the increase of the resource rent in oil-rich countries. Rulers of authoritarian political regimes destroy democratic institutions, aiming to maximize their control over rents and their distribution.

The structure of the chapter looks as follows. The first part presents an overview of the different aspects of the theory of the resource curse, mainly concerning the political consequences of this phenomenon. In this section I discuss the mutual dependency of regimes, revenues, and inequality. The second part is devoted to the data and methodology. The third part presents the results of analysis and their interpretation. Then, the application of the resource curse theory to Russia's political developments is discussed. Preliminary conclusions are outlined in the end of the chapter.

RESOURCE WEALTH—CURSE FOR DEMOCRACY?

The literature devoted to analysis of the effects of large amounts of natural resources on the political and economic developments of various states and nations is extensive.[1] Below are some of the most popular explanations:

- The negative influence of export of natural resources on the economic development—the *"Dutch disease" effect*. The growth of revenues in the resource sector leads to a huge inflow of labor and capital from the production sector into the resource sector and the nontradable goods sector. This leads to a decline in labor productivity, and, as a consequence, to the economic stagnation.[2]
- The negative influence of export of natural resources on the economic development—the *rent-seeking effect* and the *voracity effect*. Economic agents in the resource-dependent economy (oriented toward an export of natural resources) experience a drastic increase in export rents and move from production sectors of economy to the parasitic rent-seeking. This sector is not involved in the production of goods or services, but grabs from the production sector, using coercive methods, and often with the use of violence. As a result, the greater the revenue from the coercive extraction of rents, the lower the revenue from the production sector, which leads to economic stagnation.[3] The "voracity effect" means that the increase in state expenditures grows more quickly that the increase of revenues from rent, in many ways because of aggressive pressure from special interest groups oriented toward rent-seeking.[4]

- The negative influence of export of natural resources on the political development of countries—the increase in likelihood of the *initiation of violent conflicts* (including civil wars), and also the encouragement to continue these conflicts. In many developing countries, control over sources of natural resources is the cause of the outbreak of violent conflicts (including civil wars). Also, the revenues from the sale of easily lootable resources are the major source of financing for the rebellious and separatist groups. Often in these conflicts, the means and the ends are mixed up; the fact is that an abundance of natural resources increases the risk of civil wars and violent political conflicts.[5]
- The negative influence of the export of natural resources on the political development of countries—*weakening of political institutions, decline of incentives for democratization, and the rise of authoritarian trends*, which contribute to preservation of political control over resource rents.[6]

This chapter will be focused on the last effect, that is, the mutual influence of the export of natural resources and the degree and quality of democracy and authoritarianism. Scholars proposed a number of arguments about the nature of the influence of export of natural resources on political regimes. First, when governments derive major revenues from the oil exports, they are likely to tax their populations lightly or not at all, and the public in turn will be less likely to demand accountability from—and representation in—their governments. Why collect taxes if it is easier and more advantageous to receive revenues from exports? Taxation issues are one of the most important incentives for citizens to participate in politics; thus, the interest of individual involvement in politics and as an influence on the political process declines in oil states. One might recall the famous slogan: "No taxation without representation." However, the opposite is also true: no representation without taxation.

Second, oil wealth may lead rulers to greater spending on mass patronage, which in turn dampens open and latent bottom-up pressures for democratization. Extra revenues allow the government to increase social payments, pensions, and benefits, and thus buy the political loyalty of citizens, providing them a showcase of economic efficiency and prosperity.

Third, revenues from export of natural resources encourages a weakening of democratic institutions thus undermining political accountability. The government aims to maximize its control over resource rent and distribution of revenues, and is interested to make this process as nontransparent as possible.

Fourth, the government is inclined to spend more on the state machinery of coercion. This is caused by two reasons: (1) increase of its control over the political developments, because of fears of losing control over resource rent in case of losing political power, and (2) providing additional jobs in the respective agencies such as police and security apparatus because of the poor development of other sectors of the economy, thus averting social tensions.

Fifth, the government expands the state machinery (not just the law enforcement agencies) and the public sector as a whole in order to co-opt potential autonomous social groups and prevent dissenting individuals from political disloyalty and oppositional activism. Oil revenues provide a government with enough money; the government will use this opportunity to prevent the formation of organizations that are operated independently from the state and hence that may be inclined to demand political rights.

Sixth, resource-based economic growth as such may not lead to the process of modernization, which presumed fundamental social, cultural, and political changes. The lack of sociocultural shifts in resource-rich countries contributed to postponing of the modernization project, while export revenues were used merely for the increase in consumption and other current needs. Scholars also acknowledge that the export of different natural resources may have a different influence on these effects.[7]

One of the most seminal studies in this field is the article by Michael Ross, "Does Oil Hinder Democracy?,"[8] where he analyzed the linkage between political regimes and oil export in Europe, the Middle East, Africa, and Latin America. Ross included in his analysis 113 countries for the period between 1971 and 1997. The major conclusion is that there is a negative correlation between the export of oil and minerals and transitions to democracy. Ross proposed three causal mechanisms to explain this phenomenon. The first causal mechanism is the "rentier effect," that is, the low dependence of the government upon tax collection and upon state expenditures. Ross found both these factors as statistically significant for political regimes in oil-exporting states. The second causal mechanism, the "repression effect," involves the argument of coercion, that is, the influence of extra revenues from export of oil on the level of state expenditures on the military and law enforcement apparatus, and the number of employees in this sector. The level of expenditures on military, police, and security apparatus of the state was statistically insignificant, but the number of military and law enforcement officers and servants demonstrated a strong significance: the degree of democratization is negatively correlated with the size of the coercive apparatus of the state. The third causal mechanism, the "modernization effect," proved to be of little statistical significance.

In his study, Ross did not make a special emphasis on countries of the former Soviet Union. This chapter aims to fill this gap. The idea of the analysis is to test the assumption on the dependence between the large amounts of natural resources and the level of democracy in post-Soviet countries. I will try to test the hypotheses advanced by Michael Ross based on the post-Soviet experiences. Indeed, the political paths of post-Soviet countries have diverged widely: from Estonia, Latvia, and Lithuania that were accepted into the European Union to the authoritarian patrimonial Turkmenistan. In the early 1990s, the initial political conditions in all countries were rather similar, while their economic conditions were different. After almost two decades, the political and economic trajectories of all the countries seriously differ. There are countries that are not much involved in the export of natural resources, and there are countries that primarily live due to their resources rents. Does this diversity affect democratization and authoritarianism in the post-Soviet world?

In the early study, the influence of natural resource wealth on the change of post-Soviet regimes has been analyzed.[9] I took data for the fifteen post-Soviet countries for the period of 1996–2004 and tested hypotheses proposed by Ross. An analysis demonstrated a negative link between large amounts of natural resources (especially oil and gas), which was calculated as a share of export in GDP, and the level of democracy. Among the causal mechanisms proposed by Ross, the repression effect was confirmed; the rise of authoritarian tendencies in post-Soviet countries can be explained by an increase in the size of the coercive apparatus of the state. For this chapter, I included in analysis the data for 2005–2008, the "oil shock" period, and test the same hypotheses. Furthermore, I make a special emphasis on the influence of the rise of inequality under the period of economic growth.

There is an alternative assumption that the resource abundance may also have a positive effect on democratization, although not a clear one. In Thad Dunning's recent book, *Crude Democracy*,[10] the argument is advanced that in a number of cases resource rent may be used to mitigate the class conflict, which is often a major hindrance for elites to commit themselves to democracy. When elites come to power in new democracies, they often pursue a populist redistributive policy. In this case, revenues from the export of natural resources may be viewed as an alternative source of funding social programs directed toward improving the living standards of the major part of the population.[11]

The standard socioeconomic approach to democracy states that democracies, as a rule, are wealthier than authoritarian regimes.[12] This also mean that for democracy a certain level of socioeconomic development is required, and increasing the median income of the population is a prerequisite for establishing democracy. However, as part of the theory of the resource curse, increasing incomes in resource-rich countries does not always lead to an advance in the process of democratization. This clearly follows from the "rentier effect" proposed by Ross: increasing revenues from resource rents increases incentives for maximization of appropriation (or reclaiming) of rent by the ruling elites, which in their turn are interested in a weakening of mechanisms of political control and accountability. As a result, democratic institutions are eroded and inequality grows over time.

I propose that the success of democratization does not depend on an increase of the level of state revenues, but that its failure may be caused by an increase in export of natural resources and flow of petrodollars. To put it differently, democratization is caused in many ways by merely political factors, and not just socioeconomic factors. An increase in the individual income and well-being of the population during the oil shock period, a decline in poverty, and the rise of an urban middle class does not cause an increasing demand for expansion of political rights. Inequality seems to negatively affect democratization in the post-Soviet countries and elsewhere. With a high degree of inequality, the ruling elites are inclined to fear providing full-fledged political rights to impoverished citizens of their respective countries. Data on inequality is presented in table 3.1.

I focus on two causal mechanisms proposed by Ross: (1) the negative influence of export of natural resources on democratization through effects of taxation and social expenditures that hinder the degree of mass political participation, and (2) the negative influence of export of natural resources on democratization through a strengthening of the coercive apparatus of the state. In order to test these proposals, the following hypotheses are put forward:

1. An increase in export of natural resources (oil, gas, and minerals) leads to a decline in the level of democracy.
2. An increase in export of natural resources (oil, gas, and minerals) leads to a decline or, at least, stagnation in the share of

Table 3.1.   GINI Index in Post-Soviet Countries in 1994 and 2006

Country	GINI in 1994	GINI in 2006
Russia	44.1	45.1
Ukraine	47.4 (1995)	41
Belarus	37.3 (1995)	32.1
Moldova	37.9	32.7
Estonia	36	33
Latvia	32.5	39
Lithuania	39	39
Armenia	32.1	37
Azerbaijan	42.8	50.8 (2002)
Georgia	49.9	43.9
Kazakhstan	31.6	41.4
Kyrgyzstan	44.3	46
Tajikistan	44.3	39.7
Turkmenistan	N/A	N/A
Uzbekistan	31	39.7

Sources: TransMONEE Database, 2008; World Income Inequality Database, 2008; World Bank, 2008[13]

taxes in the state revenues and an increase in social expenditures.
3. An increase in export of natural resources (oil, gas, and minerals) leads to an increase in expenditures on the coercive apparatus of the state and to an increase in the number of officers and servants in this apparatus.

DATA AND METHODOLOGY

In this study, I use the multiple logistic regression analysis for testing hypotheses. I took a sample of the fifteen countries of the former Soviet Union, in a period from 1996 to 2008. The dependent variable will be the political regime for the corresponding year in a given country. The years from 1996 to 1998 were the period of a low international oil market, and from 1999 to 2000, a swift growth of world oil prices began. The choice of this period of time will allow testing the assumption about the positive influence of the fall of oil prices on democratization. For this variable, I will use annual data from Freedom House reports. The assessment of the political regime in the Freedom House ratings of political rights and civil freedoms may vary from 1.0 to 7.0, where 1.0 is the highest value (developed democracy with full-scale

Table 3.2.   Freedom House Ratings for Countries of the Former Soviet Union (2003 and 2008)

Country	2003	2008	↑↓
Armenia	4	5	↑
Azerbaijan	5.5	5.5	
Belarus	6	6.5	↑
Georgia	4	4	
Kazakhstan	5.5	5.5	
Kyrgyzstan	5.5	4.5	↓
Latvia	1.5	1.5	
Lithuania	1.5	1	↓
Moldova	3.5	4	↑
Russia	5	5.5	↑
Tajikistan	5.5	5.5	
Turkmenistan	7	7	
Ukraine	4	2.5	↓
Uzbekistan	6.5	7	↑
Estonia	1.5	1	↓

Source: Freedom House, 2009 (free countries are in italics, non-free countries are bold)[14]

political rights and civil freedoms), and 7.0 is the lowest position (total lack of democracy).

From 2004 to 2008, several regime changes occur in the post-Soviet space. The data about these changes is presented in table 3.2.

The table shows that the freedom in the post-Soviet area in 2003–2008 did not decrease in general: the decline of democracy in five countries (Armenia, Moldova, Belarus, Russia, and Uzbekistan) was "compensated" for by an increase in freedom in four countries. It is interesting that two of these countries are Baltic States (this should be explained by the influence of the European Union), and in two other countries "color revolutions" took place in 2004–2005 (Ukraine and Kyrgyzstan).

The oil shock that began in 2004 increased the share of export of natural resources (and, therefore, revenues of exporting countries) in comparison with the period of 1999–2004. The data is presented in table 3.3.

As an independent variable for measuring the dependence of the country on oil, I took the share of oil export in GDP. By "oil," I understand products that meet the classification of the UN statistics division *SITC Rev.3* in section 3 (petroleum, petroleum products, natural gas, and electric current). I borrowed this data from the World Bank, UN Comtrade Database, and the Russian Federal State Statistics Ser-

Table 3.3.   Change in the Average Indicators of Export of Natural Resources for Countries of the Former Soviet Union

	1996–2003	1996–2008
Percentage of export of resources in GDP	8.3%	11.4%
Percentage of export of oil in GDP	7.5%	8.5%
Percentage of export of minerals in GDP	2.1%	2.3%

Sources: UN Comtrade Database, 2009; World Bank, 2008[15]

vice.[16] As an indicator of the country's dependence on the export of Minerals, I similarly took the share of export of minerals in GDP. By minerals, I understand goods that come under the classification *SITC Rev.3*, section 27 (crude fertilizers, crude minerals), section 28 (metalliferous ores and metal scrap), and section 68 (non-ferrous metals). I also borrowed this data from the World Bank, UN Comtrade Database, the Russian Federal State Statistics Service, and the Interstate Statistical Committee of the Commonwealth of Independent States.[17] As an independent variable Resources, I took the share of export of natural resources in GDP. This data is calculated by combining the export of oil and minerals.

As a control variable, I use Regime$_{(t-5)}$, which reflects the political regime in the country in the five years before the selected year. This will enable tracing of the trajectory of regime changes, which in many ways depend on the logic of the previous political development of the country. This path-dependency effect prevents major regime changes depending on the current oil prices: a democratic regime cannot suddenly become authoritarian because of oil, or vice versa.

The indicator for the importance of taxation for governments is the variable Taxes, which is the share of government revenues raised through taxes on goods, services, income, profits, and capital gains. I borrowed this data from the World Bank, the Russian Federal State Statistics Service, and the Interstate Statistical Committee of the Commonwealth of Independent States.[18] The variable Government Consumption is measured as a share of GDP and includes all current expenditures for purchases of goods and services by all levels of government, excluding state-owned enterprises. It also includes capital expenditures on national defense and security. I borrowed this data from the World Bank.[19] For the variable that shows Military Expenditures, I took expenditures of the national budget on the military as a share of GDP. I borrowed this data from the World Bank.[20] The variable showing Military Personnel measures the size of the military as a share of the labor force; it includes some paramilitary forces "if those forces resemble regular units in their organization, equipment, training, or mission." Another name for this variable is *siloviki* (literally, "men of force" in Russian). I borrowed this data from the World Bank.[21] As control variable I took Income, measured as the natural log of per capita GDP corrected for purchasing power parity (PPP), in current international dollars. The data is obtained from the World Bank.[22] As the Gini variable, the Gini coefficient, one of the most widespread indicators of inequality, is used. This data is received from the Trans-MONEE Database, the World Bank, and the World Income Inequality Database.[23]

In order to record the specific regional features, I included two control dummy variables—the Baltic States and Central Asia. The Baltic States took a path toward European integration from the time of gaining their independence, and in 2004 joined the European Union; this factor had a positive influence on democratization. Central Asia has its own developmental trajectory, affected by several cultural and historical factors, including the predominance of Islam. Belonging to this region, I suspect, should have had a negative influence on democratization.

For all independent variables, I use a two-year lag (i.e., the Regime for 2004 will correspond to the value of all independent and control variables for 2002, etc.). While Ross used a five-year lag in his article, the time range of post-Soviet period does not allow me to use such a huge lag; post-Soviet politics is notable by its considerable dynamics, and I assume that less time is required between the event and its effect. I only took a five-year lag for the variable Regime$_{(t-5)}$. All regressions are calculated with dummy variables for each year, in order to record the peculiarities of the selected years in each of post-Soviet countries.

RESULTS AND EXPLANATIONS

Before testing the main hypotheses, let's have a look at which factors influence Income. As a dependent variable, I will take Income, and as independent and control variables, I will take Resources, Oil, Minerals, Regime$_{(t-5)}$, Gini, Baltic States, and Central Asia. Model 1 includes the variable Resources, and model 2 includes the variables Oil and Minerals (see table 3.4).

Results of the regression analysis demonstrated that an increase in income is determined by the growth of export of natural resources, while model 2 demonstrated that export of oil plays a dominant

Table 3.4. Influence of Export of Natural Resources on Income (dependent variable—Income)

	Model 1	Model 2
	Standardized Beta-coefficients	
Baltic States	0,483**	0,398**
Central Asia	−0,348**	−0,253**
Regime$_{(t-5)}$	−0,139	−0,267*
Resources	0,434**	—
Oil	—	−0,520**
Minerals	—	−0,025
Gini	−0,174**	−0,185**
R-square	0,602	0,681
Adjusted R-square	0,587	0,667
Observations	135	136

* significant at the 0.05 level
** significant at the 0.01 level

role here. Inequality has a negative value—the higher the income of citizens of a country, the lower the level of inequality. Furthermore, model 2 shows that the political regime as such is of little importance for the level of income, but the existence of a democratic regime has a positive influence on the growth of income of residents of post-Soviet countries. The goal of this chapter is not to analyze the factors that explain the growth of incomes in the post-Soviet area, but it is important that incomes depend strongly on the export of natural resources (particularly oil), with the partial exception of the Baltic States. Thus, one might suggest that oil-exporting countries could demonstrate higher incomes, if they had more democratic regimes and could solve the problem of inequality.

The basic regression model for further analysis is the following:

$$Regime_{i,t} = a_i + b_1(Regime_{i,t-5}) + b_3(Resources_{i,t-2}) + b_3(Oil_{i,t-2})$$
$$+ b_4(Minerals_{i,t-2}) + b_5(Gini_{i,t-2}) + b_6(Baltic\ States_{i,t}) + b_7$$
$$(Central\ Asia_{i,t}) + b_8(Year_1) + \ldots + b_{21}(Year_{13})$$

Model 1 includes the variable Resources, and model 2 includes the variables Oil and Minerals separately (see table 3.5).

These results confirm the hypotheses that were previously tested on the data from 1996 to 2004.[24] A regression analysis shows that the export of natural resources has an antidemocratic influence in the post-Soviet area. Model 1, which shows their effect as a whole,

Table 3.5. Influence of Export of Natural
Resources on Political Regimes in the Post-
Soviet Area (dependent variable—Regime)

	Model 1	Model 2
	Standardized Beta-coefficients	
Resources	0,113**	—
Oil	—	0,144**
Minerals	—	−0,020
Regime$_{(t-5)}$	0,543**	0,501**
Gini	−0,072*	−0,078*
Baltic States	−0,364**	−0,395**
Central Asia	0,059	0,088*
R-square	0,910	0,917
Adjusted R-square	0,897	0,905
Observations	135	136

* significant at the 0.05 level
** significant at the 0.01 level

demonstrates that with a large number of control variables included
in the model, Resources remain significant as a major factor of influence on the political regime. When these natural resources are divided
into oil and minerals, it turns out that the major factor responsible for
the trend toward authoritarianism is oil, which is unsurprising given
the extremely high oil prices in 2004–2008. At the same time, mineral
wealth under conditions of the oil shock does not have a significant
influence on the political regime. How can this be explained? Perhaps
this is because the amount of revenues from export of minerals is
incomparable in its effect to the export of oil. At the same time, it is
clear that a major role is also played by the regional breakdown—belonging to the Baltic States has a strong democratic effect, and belonging to Central Asia has a weak antidemocratic effect. When the
Income variable is included in the analysis, both models prove to be
insignificant. Inequality in both models has a weak but statistically
significant negative influence on democratization in the post-Soviet
region. We explain this by the fact that elites are not much interested
in preserving elements of democratic control over the distribution of
revenues from export of natural resources. As a result, appropriation of
rent, while democratic institutions are destroyed or don't exist at all,
leads to a rise of the level of inequality.

How can we interpret the negative effect of natural resources on
political regime changes in the post-Soviet area? I will try to test two
causal mechanisms proposed by Ross. The first mechanism explains

the antidemocratic nature of the influence of natural wealth through the "rentier effect": first, the state spends extra revenues from exportation of natural resources on social programs (increase of state expenditures to GDP) aimed at buying the loyalty of the subjects, and second, the state, which receives its major revenues from export of natural resources, is not interested in taxing its citizens and nonexport sectors of the economy (individual income taxes and corporate profit taxes). Even though fiscal agencies exist in these states, their major function is not fiscal, but rather punitive. As citizens are relatively free from major tax burden, they are not much interested in political control over the government. I introduce two independent variables and include them into the model: Government Consumption/ GDP, and Taxes. I expect that government expenditures will influence democratization negatively, and taxes positively. The results of the analysis are presented in table 3.6.

As in the analysis of 1996–2004 data, the hypotheses based on the rentier effect in fact have not been confirmed. This causal mechanism does not work. Only in model 1 was the growth of government expenditures to GDP statistically significant. But with a division of resources into oil and minerals, government expenditures no longer prove significant. The insignificance of the Taxes variable may indirectly show that post-Soviet countries are covering their budgets not only with revenues from oil export, but by collecting taxes from their companies and citizens. Belonging to the Baltic States is still statisti-

Table 3.6. "Rentier Effect" (dependent variable—Regime)

	Model 1[1]	Model 2
	Standardized Beta-coefficients	
Resources	0,130*	—
Oil	—	0,186**
Minerals	—	−0,026
Regime$_{(t-5)}$	0,524**	0,469**
Gini	−0,046	−0,068
Government consumption/GDP	0,101*	0,075
Taxes	0,031	−0,016
Baltic States	−0,427**	−0,448**
Central Asia	0,052	0,083
R-square	0,901	0,908
Adjusted R-square	0,880	0,888
Observations	105	106

1. Model is significant at the 0.05 level
* significant at the 0.05 level
** significant at the 0.01 level

cally significant, but not to Central Asia. Inequality proves to be an insignificant variable after all.

The other causal mechanism that attempts to explain the authoritarian influence of the wealth of mineral resources is the "repression effect." It is stated that the governments fear even the hypothetical possibility of losing power—and, as a consequence, their control over the distribution of extra revenues from export of natural resources. The ruling elite starts to spend extra revenues on preserving the status quo of the authoritarian regime, which first means increasing expenses on the military and security apparatus, in order to guarantee the loyalty of the *siloviki* in the case of a possible political crisis, and second, increasing the number of *siloviki*—in order to maintain control over the political developments in the country, and in order to create jobs for those who do not join the ranks of dissidents. In order to test this effect, I added two variables—Military Personnel, and Military Expenditures/GDP. It is expected that an increase of expenditures on *siloviki* and an increase of their number will have an antidemocratic effect. The results of the analysis are presented in table 3.7.

The results of the test demonstrate that the repression effect may serve as one of the key explanatory mechanisms of the negative influence of natural resource wealth on democratization in the post-Soviet area. In both models, with preservation of the value of all control and independent variables, the size of the military and security apparatus

Table 3.7. "Repression Effect" (dependent variable— Regime)

	Model 1	Model 2
	Standardized Beta-coefficients	
Resources	0,088*	—
Oil	—	0,124**
Minerals	—	−0,034
Regime$_{(t-5)}$	0,389**	0,366**
Gini	−0,072*	−0,078**
Military expenditures/GDP	0,037	0,037
Military personnel	0,197**	0,178**
Baltic States	−0,386**	−0,412**
Central Asia	0,193**	0,201**
R-square	0,932	0,938
Adjusted R-square	0,921	0,927
Observations	132	133

* significant at the 0.05 level
** significant at the 0.01 level

proves significant. In both models, Military Expenditures/GDP proves rather insignificant, though. Model 2 demonstrates that the major antidemocratic contribution belongs to oil. One should note that Minerals once again proves to be a statistically insignificant variable.

How should these results be interpreted? Regimes that enjoy extra revenues from oil export increase the size of the military and security without major increases in expenditures in these sectors. Roughly speaking, as a result these countries got numerous cheap "soldiers," who guard the oil wells, and the premises of the owners of these wells. Low financing of the military and security apparatus will mean a low professional quality of these "soldiers" and as a result numerous violations of law and abuse of power by the military and security officers and servants. Violations of human rights could initiate a conflict in which the government will be forced to protect its guards, and it will put more pressure on existing political institutions such as courts and the media. Furthermore, the large size of the military and security apparatus may be explained by the need to resolve the issue of employment. Since the oil-based economy does not provide everyone with a sufficient amount of highly paid jobs,[25] young unemployed people in these countries often face a dilemma—to join criminal gangs (often as the only option for a highly paid job beyond the government) or to join the soldiers; the government faces the same problem—to deal with a large number of bandits or soldiers? In choosing soldiers, the government contributed to the undermining of the possibilities of democratization.

The analysis has shown that a wealth of natural resources has an antidemocratic influence on post-Soviet political regimes. The abundance of natural resources, namely oil (not minerals!), which are regarded by both elites and the masses as a boon, have a rather contradictory influence on the development of the resource-rich countries. Economists talk of the pernicious influence of oil on economic development, claiming that oil export distorts the structure of the economy and even undermines prospects for economic growth (the Dutch disease). Our political analysis strengthens this argument: resource abundance does harm not only economic growth, but also political developments. Resource-abundant post-Soviet states become more authoritarian, which has a pernicious effect on the elites and the mass public in terms of their participation and political contestation. Export of minerals does not have such apparent effects, at least not in post-Soviet countries. Our analysis has also shown that natural resource wealth is linked not only with the rise of authoritarian trends, but also with the rise of inequality, which might be caused by the aspiration of ruling elites to maximize the appropriation of resource rent.

Inequality seems to have a negative effect on democratization in the post-Soviet area and elsewhere in the world. One cannot say with certainty that the rise of inequality is a consequence of the "oil curse." Statistical data show that in the mid-1990s in most of the post-Soviet countries, the Gini index was quite high; however, in resource-rich countries in the late 1990s it increased even more but decreased in resource-poor countries. Perhaps the inequality, and not income, is the socioeconomic variable that explains the failure of democratization in resource-rich countries; this issue is worth further analysis. The contribution of revenues from the export of natural resources to the increase of individual income of the population in resource-rich countries is not so obvious. This is probably an addition to the argument of M. Steven Fish[26] on corruption in oil-rich states: if export revenues are not converted into income, then rents simply do not reach the ordinary people and disappear. To summarize: ruling elites of a number of oil-rich states aspire, first, to preserve their control over rents, and second, to maximize their share of the rent. In many ways, this is what leads to the rise of authoritarian trends in the post-Soviet area.

All the successful antiregime "color revolutions" in the post-Soviet area took place between 2003 and 2005 in the resource-poor countries (Georgia, Ukraine, and Kyrgyzstan). On the contrary, in oil-rich countries—Azerbaijan, Kazakhstan, Turkmenistan, and Russia—color revolutions either failed or did not take place at all. In these countries the governments have something more to lose if they lose power, especially with the rally of oil prices on world markets.

RUSSIAN "OIL BURDEN"?

My analysis included all post-Soviet countries, but the Russian case is the focus of this section. The period of 2003–2008 was the time of unprecedented growth of oil prices on world markets, and the extra revenues from oil export began flowing into Russia. There is every reason to assume that Russia may unfortunately become a textbook example of the negative influence of the resource curse. These assumptions are based on major changes in Russian politics in 2003–2008 in terms of state-business relations, the (lack of) rule of law, political institutions (including elections), and regional politics. The penetration of the oil and gas wealth into the flesh and blood of Russian society proved so important that according to a Public Opinion Foundation (FOM) survey of 2009, the young people of Russia regarded working at Gazprom as the most attractive job in the country.[27]

Economists were the first to sound the alarm, for example, Andrei Illarionov, the former economic advisor to Vladimir Putin who claimed that the inflow of revenues from the oil export would damage economic growth—through the Dutch disease effect.[28] Rents in the oil industry are higher than anywhere else, so entrepreneurs are not interested in investments in other sectors than oil. The labor productivity in nonexport sectors is falling, the competitive advantage of Russian goods is declining, and the sector of nontradable goods is increasing. In recent years, official statistics have begun to show a swift growth of import: 2004—$97.4 billion, 2005—$125.4 billion, 2006—$164.3 billion, 2007—$223.5 billion, 2008—$292 billion.[29] This data, at least, can indirectly confirm the argument of the Dutch disease effect, when the sector of nontradable goods grows sharply, and the market of tradable goods shrinks because of the increase of import.

If under President Boris Yeltsin, the overwhelming influence of large businesses (not least oil companies) on politics was widely criticized, under Putin the concept of "equal distancing of the state from oligarchs" was proclaimed. An informal agreement between Putin and major business leaders was reached on the nonencroachment of business into politics and on recognition (and nonrevision) of the results of privatization by the state. However, for a number of reasons this informal agreement was broken in 2003. On the eve of 2003 parliamentary elections, the Kremlin initiated a "war on oligarchs," which resulted in the Yukos affair. The Kremlin was afraid that business would try to convert its oil revenues into political influence. Yukos, the largest Russian private oil company, seemed to be the most suitable candidate for capture, especially because of the deep involvement of its top managers into political activism. After this, the trend for the gradual nationalization of the oil industry in Russia became clear. Yukos found itself on the verge of bankruptcy, and was deprived of its most important assets. Furthermore, Gazprom, the major state-owned company in Russia, acquired Sibneft assets in 2005. After this, most of the Russian oil industry came under state ownership.[30] Also, the process of nationalization of the Russian oil industry through major revisions of property rights had a dramatically negative impact for the rule of law like in the cases of Yukos[31] and Russneft, the private oil company acquired in 2007 by entrepreneur Oleg Deripaska, who is close to the Kremlin.[32] And this is not the only evidence of the erosion of major political and legal institutions under the influence of oil rents.

In 2004, the Russian government established the Stabilization Fund (SF), for sterilization of extra revenues from oil export. By January 2008, the SF had at least $160 billion.[33] Naturally, the faster that the volume of the SF grows, the more demands there will be to spend this money on "long-term investment projects." At the end of 2005, the government decided to take some of the money from the fund, creating a special Investment Fund. This is very similar to the "white elephants" model.[34] According to this model governments of oil-exporting countries strive to invest the majority of extra revenues from the export of natural resources into their economic develop-ment. However, due to the lack of strong political institutions, the major target of investment is not achieving the officially proclaimed economic efficiency, but purchasing political loyalty. As a result, rulers of these countries could stay in power permanently, but their economies stagnate. For example, following the Arab embargo of October 1973 the sharp increase in oil prices produced huge gains to oil exporters. The bulk of the oil rents were invested in large-scale projects but with no growth payoff (for OPEC countries as a whole GDP per capita on average decreased by 1.3 percent each year from 1965 to 1998).[35] In Russia, especially before the federal elections of 2007–2008, it becomes very likely that "long-term investment proj-ects" will not be aimed at economic efficiency, but at ensuring the political loyalty of elites and the mass public. One should note that public discussions on the Russian economic policy of 2005–2008 in many ways focused on debates about the need to spend and/or invest money of the SF in certain projects.[36]

By controlling revenues from oil rent, the Kremlin uses it to strengthen its political influence. This can partially explain the results of the parliamentary elections of 2003. One of the main components in the victory of the major progovernment party, United Russia, was the dependency of the regional authorities on federal financial aid.[37] The source of this financial aid is extra revenues from oil export. Also, a certain increase in social expenditures using oil rent allows the Krem-lin to reduce the influence of left-wing parties thus hindering political competition.

As early as the beginning of the 1990s, the abundance of natural resources had a negative influence on Russian regions and center-pe-riphery relations. One of the most important problems of the Russian politics then was the separatist activism in a number of ethnic-based republics. In many cases, the economic basis for these trends was the abundance of natural resources in these republics, especially oil, as in Tatarstan and Bashkiria. In exchange for recognition of Moscow's rule,

these republics received the legal right to keep regional oil companies—Tatneft and Bashneft, respectively—under their control through
"republican ownership." The reason for the separatist moods in the
Sakha-Yakutia republic in the early 1990s was the demand to put the
diamond industry under the control of the regional authorities. Oil in
Chechnya was also one of the factors of the violent conflict, and still
one of the hot issues causing tensions between Moscow and pro-Rus-
sian Grozny authorities due to the permanent demand by the leadership of the republic (former president Akhmad Kadyrov, and then his
son Ramzan Kadyrov) to place the oil industry in Chechnya—Groz-
neftegaz company—under the control of republican government. Furthermore, the key point in the bilateral agreement between Chechnya
and the federal center, proposed by republican leadership, was the
transfer of control over the entire oil and gas sector to the republican
government for a minimum of ten years.[38] The battle for control over
Chechen oil may aggravate the already complicated relations between
Moscow and Grozny.

A test of the political and economic system built in Russia was
the international financial and economic crisis of 2008–2009. After the
record $147 per barrel of oil, a sharp decline began, and the Russian
economy faced a partial devaluation of the national currency, a drop
in export revenues, and accordingly budgetary problems. For the first
time in several years, the Russian budget showed a deficit, partially
covered by the Stabilization Fund.[39] In 2009, a decline in GDP reached
almost 8.5 percent, and there were suggestions that Russia could leave
the BRIC group based on the consequences of the crisis.[40] The crisis
demonstrated that the economic system that was built during the
years of the oil shock was vulnerable, and all the calls of the government and expert community to diversify the Russian economy did not
progress beyond the discussion stage.

The rich natural resources are slowly but irrevocably eroding
already weak political institutions in Russia. One gets the impres-
sion that at the beginning of the 2000s, the oil and gas sector was
mentioned in the discourse of Russia's rulers as a source of funding
for large-scale modernization, as a source of investment in other sectors of the economy, and for social development, but more recently,
especially after the record rise of oil prices on international markets,
the control over the energy sector is the major item on the Kremlin's
political and policy agenda. This will practically lead to the fact that
Russia's domestic and foreign policies concentrated almost exclusively on taking measures to keep control over oil wells ("preemptive
counterrevolution"),[41] or on spending extra revenues from oil rents

("national projects"), or on projects of new gas and oil pipelines. It is unlikely that this corresponds to the tasks that are faced by the Russian state and society.

CONCLUSION

The analysis in this chapter generally confirmed the results of the previous study about the negative influence of the resource curse on regime changes in countries of the former Soviet Union. Inclusion of the new data for 2005–2008 in the analysis, and the introduction of new variables, allows us to take a closer look at the effect caused by the oil abundance on the political and economic development of post-Soviet countries.

The oil shock of 2003–2008 led to a noticeable increase in income of the post-Soviet oil-rich countries and their citizens, which was however accompanied by a growth of inequality. The analysis shows that these factors influence the growth of authoritarian trends in the post-Soviet region. It should be noted that reverse causality is so far incorrect. The economic crisis, which in many ways was caused by the fall in oil prices, did not lead to any drive to democratization in the post-Soviet area, at least in the short-term perspective. Yet its clear consequences are the fall of GDP, the decline of revenues and income of the population, and the rise of unemployment. Perhaps an indirect democratic effect of the resource curse in a period of crisis is that elites of oil-rich countries are forced to demonstrate their governance skills. If the level of these skills is low, then in the future a major split in the ruling elites is possible, which may be a necessary condition for democratization.

NOTES

1. Michael Ross, "The Political Economy of the Resource Curse," *World Politics*, 51, no. 2 (1999), 297–322; Paul Collier and Anna Hoeffler, "Greed and Grievance in Civil War," *Oxford Economic Papers*, no. 56 (2004), 563–95; James A. Robinson, Ragnar Torvik, and Thierry Verdier, "Political Foundations of the Resource Curse," *Journal of Developmental Economics*, 79, no. 2 (2006), 447–68; Michael Ross, "A Closer Look at Diamonds, Oil and Civil War," *Annual Review of Political Science*, 9 (2006), 265–300; Halvor Mehlum, Karl Ove Moene, and Ragnar Torvik, "Cursed by Resources or Institutions?" *World Economy*, 29, no. 8 (2006), 1117–31; Thad Dunning, *Crude Democracy: Natural Resource Wealth and Political Regimes* (New York: Cambridge Uni-

versity Press, 2008); Yegor Gaidar, *Gibel' imperii: Uroki dlya sovremennoi Rossii* (Moscow: ROSSPEN, 2006).

2. Ragnar Torvik, "Learning by Doing and the Dutch Decease," *European Economic Review*, 45 (2001), 285–306.

3. Ragnar Torvik, "Natural Resources, Rent Seeking and Welfare," *Journal of Development Economics*, 67 (2002), 455–70; Halvor Mehlum, Karl Ove Moene, and Ragnar Torvik, "Parasites," in Samuel Bowles, Steven N. Durlauf, and Karla Hoff, eds., *Poverty Traps* (Princeton, N.J.: Princeton University Press, 2003), 79–94.

4. Aaron Tornell and Philip Lane, "The Voracity Effect," *American Economic Review*, 89, no. 1 (1999), 22–46.

5. James D. Fearon, "Primary Commodities Exports and Civil War," *Journal of Conflict Resolution*, 49, no. 4 (2005), 483–507; Michael Ross, "What Do We Know about Natural Resources and Civil War?" *Journal of Peace Research*, 41, no. 3 (2004), 337–56.

6. Michael Ross, "Does Oil Hinder Democracy?" *World Politics*, 53, no. 2 (2001), 325–61; Halvor Mehlum, Karl Ove Moene, and Ragnar Torvik, "Institutions and the Resource Curse," *Economic Journal*, 116, no. 1 (2006), 1–20.

7. Ross, "Does Oil Hinder Democracy?" 336.

8. Ross, "Does Oil Hinder Democracy?"

9. Andrey Scherbak, "'Neftyanoie proklyatie' i post-sovetskie rezhimy," *Obshchestvennyie nauki i sovremennost'*, no. 1 (2007), 47–56.

10. Dunning, *Crude Democracy.*

11. Dunning, *Crude Democracy.*

12. Seymour M. Lipset, "Some Social Requisites of Democracy: Economic Development and Political Legitimacy," *American Political Science Review*, 53, no. 1 (1959), 69–105.

13. TransMONEE Database, 2008, www.unicef-irc.org/databases/transmonee/#TransMONEE (accessed 20 October 2009); World Income Inequality Database, 2008, www.wider.unu.edu/research/Database/en_GB/wiid/ (accessed 20 October 2009); World Bank, 2008, *World Development Indicators*, go.worldbank.org/U0FSM7AQ40 (accessed 20 October 2009).

14. Freedom House. Freedom in the World. Country ratings, www.freedomhouse.org/template.cfm?page=439 (accessed 20 October 2009).

15. UN Comtrade, 2008, United Nations Commodity Trade Statistics Database, comtrade.un.org/db/ (accessed 20 October 2009); World Bank, 2008.

16. UN Comtrade, 2008; World Bank, 2008; Russian Federal State Statistics Service, www.gks.ru/wps/portal/english (accessed 20 October 2009).

17. UN Comtrade, 2008; World Bank, 2008; Russian Federal State Statistics Service; Interstate Statistical Committee of the Commonwealth of Independent States, www.cisstat.com/eng/index.htm (accessed 20 October 2009).

18. UN Comtrade, 2008; World Bank, 2008; Russian Federal State Statistics Service; Interstate Statistical Committee of the Commonwealth of Independent States.

19. World Bank, 2008.

20. World Bank, 2008.

21. World Bank, 2008.

22. World Bank, 2008.

23. TransMONEE Database, 2008; World Income Inequality Database, 2008; World Bank, 2008.

24. Scherbak, "'Neftyanoie proklyatie' i post-sovetskie rezhimy."

25. Pedro D. Bo and Ernesto D. Bo, "Workers, Warriors and Criminals: Social Conflict in General Equilibrium," Brown University, Department of Economics Working Paper no. 2004–11 (2004), www.brown.edu/Departments/Economics/Papers/2004/2004–11_paper.pdf (accessed 20 October 2009).

26. M. Steven Fish, *Democracy Derailed in Russia: The Failure of Open Politics* (New York: Cambridge University Press, 2005).

27. *Newsru.Com*, "Opros: rossiiskaya molodezh' bol'she vsego zhelaiet rabotat' v 'Gazprome'" (27 March 2009), www.newsru.com/finance/27mar2009/fom_opros.html (accessed 20 October 2009).

28. Igor Veletminskii, "Vse bolezni v odnom flakone," *Rossiiskaia gazeta*, no. 3787 (3 June 2005).

29. Russian Federal State Statistic Service, Foreign Trade of Russian Federation, www.gks.ru/bgd/regl/b09_12/IssWWW.exe/stg/d02/26–02.htm (accessed 20 October 2009).

30. See chapter 5 in this volume.

31. Andrey Gromov, "Protsess," *Expert*, no. 2 (2005), 80–82.

32. Lenta.ru, *Ukhod Guzirieva iz "Russnefti" i biznesa*, 2007, lenta.ru/story/russneft (accessed 20 October 2009).

33. Rossbalt, "Profitsit byudzheta RF v 1 polugodii prevysil 1,3 trln rublei" (9 July 2008), www.rosbalt.biz/2008/07/09/502376.html (20 October 2009).

34. James A. Robinson and Ragnar Torvik, "White Elephants," *Journal of Public Economics*, 89, no. 1 (2004), 197–210.

35. Robinson and Torvik, "White Elephants," note 2.

36. See chapter 6 in this volume.

37. Andrey Scherbak, "Ekonomicheskii rost i itogi dumskikh vyborov 2003 goda," *Politicheskaia nauka*, no. 2 (2005), 105–23.

38. Vedomosti, "Alkhanov: Peredacha 'Grozneftegazu' litsenzii na dobychu nefti reshit problem" (5 October 2005), www.vedomosti.ru/newsline/news/2005/10/05/183663 (accessed 20 October 2009); *Moskovskii komsomolets*, "Ramzana ozolotyat po-chernomu" (23 August 2005); Polit.Ru, "Gossovet Chechni nastaivaet na peredache kontrol'nogo paketa aktsii 'Grozneftegaza' v sobstvennost' respubliki" (27 April 2004), www.polit.ru/monitor/2004/04/27/1.html (accessed 20 October 2009).

39. Lenta.Ru, "Rezervnii fond za mesyats sokratilsya eshchyo na 146 milliardov rublei" (3 August 2009), lenta.ru/news/2009/08/03/minfin/ (accessed 20 October 2009).

40. Newsru.Com, "Iz-za padeniia VVP v 2009 godu Rossiia mozhet vyletet' iz BRIC, a po itogam 2008 analitiki konstatiruiut polnomasshtabnuiu retsessiiu" (27 January 2009), www.newsru.com/finance/27jan2009/recession.html (accessed 20 October 2009).

41. Andrey Ryabov, "Moskva prinimaiet vyzov 'tsvetnykh' revolyutsii," *Pro et Contra*, 9, no. 1 (2005), 18–27; Alexander Etkind and Andrey Scherbak, "The Double Monopoly and Its Technologists: The Russian Preemptive Counterrevolution," *Demokratizatsiya: The Journal of Post-Soviet Democratization*, 16, no. 3 (2008), 229–39.

4

Oil Boom

Is It Devastating to Property Rights and the Rule of Law?

Andrey Zaostrovtsev

The international and Russian experience in the 1990s and in Putin's era (from 2000 onward) provides plenty of evidence to attempt to find an answer to the question outlined in the title of this chapter. The devastation of property rights and the rule of the law are usually seen as one of the most pernicious effects of the resource curse that was examined in the preceding chapters. However, is this decay of basic institutions of the market economy in a number of countries that export hydrocarbons truly caused by their high world prices, and the revenues of these countries that correspond to these prices? And if so, then are there any other more powerful or at least no less significant factors that lead to the same outcomes?

To find a solution to this puzzle, I will first look at the picture that demonstrated varieties of property rights and the rule of law in oil- and gas-exporting countries, including Russia and several countries of post-Soviet Eurasia. A closer look at the data raised certain doubts in the universal conclusions of the argument of the resource curse in terms of the negative influence of resource wealth on property rights and the rule of law. As one can see, for a number of oil- and gas-exporting countries, a prolonged growth of prices on exported resources has not spoiled the conditions of property rights, and in some cases they have even become better protected and consolidated. Things are somewhat worse with the conditions of the rule of law, but here, too, resource abundance does not always result in institutional failure in this respect. In the conclusion, I examine and briefly discuss approaches of Russian economists to the resource curse and its negative influence on institutions. Their major conclusion is that

the causes for the decline in property rights and the rule of law in
Russia may be connected not only with the hostility to privatization of major enterprises, but also to shared mental models that are
deeply embedded among Russians, who demonstrated low demand
for government accountability, separation of power, and electoral
rights of citizens. These attitudes allowed the Russian ruling elites
to make a hostile takeover of major private assets in the oil industry
without major resistance.

OIL- AND GAS-EXPORTING COUNTRIES AND PROPERTY RIGHTS: INTERNATIONAL COMPARISONS

The comparative data of the state of property rights are elaborated
in the International Property Rights Index (IPRI) developed by the
Property Rights Alliance (PRA). In 2007 the PRA presented for the
first time the IPRI produced under the Hernando de Soto Fellowship
program. The 2009 IPRI stands as the most comprehensive effort at
creating an international gauge of private property rights throughout
the world covering 115 countries.[1] The following three core components are considered essential to the strengthening and protecting of a
country's private property system:

1. Legal and Political Environment (LP)
2. Physical Property Rights (PPR)
3. Intellectual Property Rights (IPR)

"The Legal and Political Environment (LP) component represents
the fundamental essence of a free environment in which judicial independence and the rule of law bestows on individuals the right to
benefit from the existence of a strong private property rights system. A
positive combination of judicial independence, the rule of law, political stability and the control of corruption creates an environment con-
ducive for the growth of the economy through a system which upholds
the protection of property rights."[2] In general the structure of the IPRI
includes ten variables, which are divided into the above-mentioned
three main components:

1. *Legal and Political Environment*
   • Judicial Independence
   • Rule of Law

- Political Stability
- Control of Corruption
2. *Physical Property Rights*
   - Protection of Physical Property Rights
   - Registering Property
   - Access to Loans
3. *Intellectual Property Rights*
   - Protection of Intellectual Property Rights
   - Patent Protection
   - Copyright Piracy

The overall grading scale of the IPRI ranges from 0 to 10, with 10 representing the strongest level of property rights protection and 0 reflecting the nonexistence of secure property rights in a country. Similarly, each component and variable is placed on the same 0 to 10 scale. For the calculation of the final index score, the variables within each component are averaged to derive the score for each of the three components. The final overall IPRI score is itself the average of the component scores.

Without going into more detail about the methodological arrangement of the IPRI and its components, one should note that unfortunately the project launched relatively recently, and only the *2009 Report* and *2008 Report* provide sufficient coverage of oil- and gas-exporting countries.[3] Furthermore, this means that it is impossible to make any cross-temporal comparisons based on this data. However, it is clear from table 4.1 that the fifteen leading international oil and gas exporters covered by the project differ significantly by the values of IPRI and its major components.

The picture presented in table 4.1 supplements figure 4.1, from which it can be seen that four countries have a higher IPRI value than the median value (for 115 countries). For these four countries, it is also higher than the average value (5.4). If one analyzes the individual components of IPRI, we may see that the four leading countries exceed the average (5.2) and median (4.6) value of LP, the average (5.9) and median (5.7) value of PPR. As for intellectual property rights, here the average (5.1) and median (4.9) values are exceeded by three countries (United Arab Emirates, Qatar, Bahrain).

Of the fifteen oil and gas exporting countries presented in table 4.1 and figure 4.1, only the UAE is in the top quintile, with three countries in the second quintile (Qatar and Bahrain), three in the third (Kuwait, Trinidad and Tobago, and Mexico), four in the fourth

Table 4.1.   International Property Rights Index and Its Components (Report 2009)

Countries	IPRI	LP	PPR	IPR
1. UAE	6.9 (23)*	6.6 (27-30)	7.7 (16)	6.4 (29)
2. Qatar	6.5 (29–32)	7.0 (24)	6.8 (33–35)	5.6 (40)
3. Bahrain	5.7 (44)	5.5 (49–50)	6.5 (41)	5.2 (47–48)
4. Kuwait	5.6 (46–49)	6.3 (32–35)	6.9 (31–32)	3.7 (88–91)
5. Trinidad & Tobago	5.1 (57–59)	4.7 (55)	5.1 (78–80)	5.5 (41–44)
6. Mexico	4.8 (62–67)	4.1 (73–75)	5.4 (71–72)	4.9 (55–59)
7. Kazakhstan	4.1 (87–89)	3.8 (81–83)	5.6 (59–68)	3.0 (102–3)
8. Russia	4.1 (87–89)	3.1 (99–102)	4.8 (87–89)	4.3 (71–74)
9. Algeria	4.0 (90–93)	3.7 (84–88)	5.0 (81–84)	3.7 (88–91)
10. Ecuador	4.0 (90–93)	2.7 (108–10)	4.6 (94–98)	4.6 (66–68)
11. Bolivia	3.6 (100_103)	3.1 (99–102)	4.2 (106-109)	3.4 (94–96)
12. Nigeria	3.5 (104–6)	2.6 (111)	4.3 (105)	3.6 (92–93)
13. Azerbaijan	3.4 (107)	3.2 (98)	5.0 (81–84)	2.1 (111–13)
14. Venezuela	3.2 (109–13)	2.0 (113–14)	4.5 (99–102)	3.2 (99)
15. Angola	2.8 (114)	3.0 (103–6)	3.0 (114)	2.4 (109)

* Ranks in brackets.
Source: International Property Rights Index (IPRI) 2009 Report.

(Kazakhstan, Russia, Algeria, and Ecuador), and the remaining five countries in the bottom fifth quintile (Bolivia, Nigeria, Azerbaijan, Venezuela, and Angola).

It would seem that the fact that the majority of these countries (nine out of fifteen) are in the fourth or fifth quintile, and that ten of

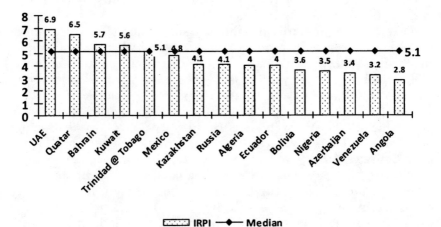

Figure 4.1.   IPRI by Countries and Its Median Meaning

them do not reach the average and median values of IPRI is consistent with the resource curse argument and illustrates the negative influence of the export of oil and gas on property rights and on institutions in general. However, if one excludes the twenty-nine member countries of the Organisation for Economic Co-operation and Development (OECD) from this list of 115 countries,[4] it will be clear that the divide between the countries examined and the rest of the world is not large enough to support claims to universality of the resource curse argument alone. The average IPRI value for the fifteen oil and gas exporting countries is 4.5, while for all other countries after the exclusion of the OECD member states it is 4.7. Its median value on the curtailed list of eighty-six countries is 4.6 (4.1 for the fifteen countries). In other words, six out of fifteen, or 40 percent, of major oil and gas exporters have individual IPRI figures that exceed the median.

A closer look at the individual components of IPRI demonstrated the following approximate picture. The average LP for the fifteen major oil and gas exporters is 4.1; for all other countries after the exclusion of the twenty-nine OECD member states, it is 4.4. The respective median values are 3.7 and 4.2. And here, for six of the fifteen oil and gas exporters, the individual LP values exceed the median values. The examination of the PPR component reveals a similar picture. Of the curtailed list of eighty-six countries, its average value is 5.5, and the median value is 5.5. The equivalent figures for the fifteen oil and gas exporters are 5.3 and 4.8 respectively. In this respect, for seven major oil and gas exporters the individual values of PPR exceed the median values. And finally, the last component, IPR, is also not awfully low in oil- and gas-exporting states. For eighty-six countries its average value is 4.3, and for oil and gas exporters it is 4.1; the median values are 4.3 and 3.7 respectively. For six oil- and gas-exporting countries, individual IPR is higher than the median value, and for one it coincides with the median value. The results are summarized in table 4.2 for convenience.

Table 4.2.   International Property Rights Index and Its Components (Mean and Median)

	IPRI		LP		PPR		IPR	
	Mean	Med.*	Mean	Med.	Mean	Med.	Mean	Med.
86 countries	4.7	4.6	4.4	4.2	5.5	5.5	4.3	4.3
15 oil and gas exporters	4.5	4.1	4.1	3.7	5.3	4.8	4.1	3.7

* Median
Source: International Property Rights Index (IPRI) 2009 Report.

An analysis of the data in table 4.2 combined with the exceeded average and median values of IPRI and its components noted above and respective indicators in oil- and gas-exporting countries does not demonstrate that the export of oil and gas has a particularly destructive influence on property rights. However, the greatest doubts as to the decisive role of a high share of revenues from the export of oil and gas in the total amount of export or GDP in weak guarantees of property rights is in the countries that are not rich in oil and gas (and not even exporters of other natural resources) and located in the last ten positions in IPRI ranking. For example, the 104th position for IPRI, together with Nigeria, is shared by Albania and Paraguay. Bosnia-Herzegovina is in 108th position. Burundi shares 109th position with oil-rich Venezuela, yet Zimbabwe and Guyana also share this position. And while the last two countries export their natural resources (but not oil and gas), Bangladesh that occupies the very last position in the ranking receives approximately 80 percent of export revenues from the sale of readymade garments.[5] Thus, the economists that claim there is a direct connection between a poor protection of property rights with the high level of revenues from export of oil and gas should take into account that in fact the protection of property rights there is just as bad in other countries where the export of natural resources either does not play a significant role, or is entirely lacking.

One of the well-known attempts to link insecurity of property rights with the effects of the resource curse was made by Karla Hoff and Joseph Stiglitz.[6] They divided the countries of Central and Eastern Europe, and also the former Soviet Union, into three groups: with low natural resource exports (< 10 percent of total exports), with moderate natural resource exports (≥ 10 percent of total exports and ≤ 20) and high natural resource exports (> 20 percent of total exports). According to their analysis, the protection of property rights was relatively high in the first group of countries and poorest in the third. At the same time, they did not include in the examination such countries of the post-Soviet area that are deprived of natural resources (and in particular oil and gas) such as Armenia, Belarus, Georgia, Tajikistan, and Ukraine, which do not receive a high position in international ratings of property rights.[7] One could also add Serbia, which was not part of the examination (and shares 100–103th position in IPRI with Nicaragua, Bolivia, and Moldova), and the above-mentioned Albania and Bosnia-Herzegovina. In the classification of countries by Hoff and Stiglitz, Moldova is justly classified as a country with a low resource endowment, and at the same time it is a country with one of the poorest protection of property rights (almost on the level of countries that are deprived of them in the third group). However, the authors do not give any explanation of this phenomenon, which does not fit into the resource curse argument.

A further analysis of the validity of the claims on the negative influence of the inflow of revenue from the export of oil and gas on property rights requires a cross-temporal evaluation. Here the two sources that are available for a closer look at several countries demonstrated contradictory results. Above all, the study of Economic Freedom of the World (EFW), which is carried out annually by the Frazer Institute (Canada), evaluates five components of economic freedom, including legal structure and security of property rights. The key ingredients of a legal system consistent with economic freedom are rule of law, security of property rights, an independent judiciary, and an impartial court system. The following seven components are evaluated in the section on legal structure and security of property rights:

- Judicial independence
- Impartial courts
- Protection of property rights
- Military interference in rule of law and the political process
- Integrity of the legal system
- Legal enforcement of contracts
- Regulatory restrictions on the sale of real property[8]

In table 4.3, the indicators of the EFW Index are presented in terms of the legal structure and security of property rights (the higher the

Table 4.3.   EFW Index (Legal Structure and Security of Property Rights)

	2000	2001	2002	2003	2004	2005	2006	2007
Algeria	2.9	2.9	2.7	2.7	3.1	5.3	5.1	4.6
Azerbaijan	n/a	n/a	n/a	n/a	4.6	5.6	5.7	6.2
Bahrain	5.9	5.9	5.9	6.0	5.5	5.6	6.1	6.5
Bolivia	3.4	3.0	2.8	3.1	3.2	4.3	4.1	3.9
Ecuador	3.3	2.5	2.9	2.7	2.4	4.1	4.1	3.9
Kuwait	6.9	6.9	6.9	6.8	6.8	7.4	7.4	7.4
Mexico	4.2	3.6	4.2	3.9	4.5	5.7	5.5	5.3
Nigeria	3.7	3.1	3.4	3.4	3.5	3.0	4.0	4.3
Russia	4.4	3.8	4.4	4.7	4.3	5.5	5.7	5.8
Trinidad & Tobago	5.9	6.5	5.8	5.4	4.8	5.7	5.5	4.9
UAE	6.6	6.6	6.6	6.8	6.2	6.9	7.0	7.0
Venezuela	3.7	1.9	1.6	1.4	1.8	3.3	3.1	2.9

Source: Economic Freedom of the World: 2009 Annual Report. 2009 dataset, www.freetheworld.com/release .html (17 November 2009).

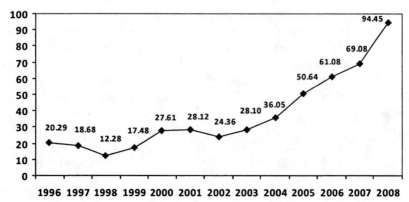

Figure 4.2.   Yearly Average Oil Price (OPEC basket, U.S. dollars/barrel)

value of the indicator, the better the state of affairs). It contains the oil and gas exporting countries that were in table 4.1, excluding Angola and Kazakhstan, which have yet to be evaluated in the study.

The data in table 4.3 show that the protection of property rights in a number of examined oil-exporting countries is not declining despite the growth of world oil prices (see figure 4.2), as is often typically claimed by proponents of the resource curse argument.

It is not difficult to notice that even if one takes the indicators for 2005–2007 (they demonstrated the dynamics of the process more correctly, as only from 2005 all the seven above-listed components of legal structure and security of property rights began to be assessed), only in half of the countries (six out of twelve) were the evaluations of 2007 less than those for 2005. In Azerbaijan and Bahrain, there was considerable progress, and even the situation in Russia also improved somewhat.

Yet another analysis of property rights is conducted on an annual basis by the Heritage Foundation as part of their Index of Economic Freedom project. The *2009 Index of Economic Freedom* also encompasses 2008 data. Each country's property rights are graded according to the following criteria (commentary for value 80 is omitted, as it is not mentioned in table 4.4):

90—Private property is guaranteed by the government. The court system enforces contracts efficiently. The justice system punishes those who unlawfully confiscate private property. Corruption is nearly nonexistent, and expropriation is highly unlikely.

70—Private property is guaranteed by the government. The court system is subject to delays and is lax in enforcing contracts. Corruption is possible but rare, and expropriation is unlikely.

60—Enforcement of property rights is lax and subject to delays. Corruption is possible but rare, and the judiciary may be influenced by other branches of government. Expropriation is unlikely.

50—The court system is inefficient and subject to delays. Corruption may be present, and the judiciary may be influenced by other branches of government. Expropriation is possible but rare.

40—The court system is highly inefficient, and delays are so long that they deter the use of the court system. Corruption is present, and the judiciary is influenced by other branches of government. Expropriation is possible.

30—Property ownership is weakly protected. The court system is highly inefficient. Corruption is extensive, and the judiciary is strongly influenced by other branches of government. Expropriation is possible.

20—Private property is weakly protected. The court system is so inefficient and corrupt that outside settlement and arbitration is the norm. Property rights are difficult to enforce. Judicial corruption is extensive. Expropriation is common.

10—Private property is rarely protected, and almost all property belongs to the state. The country is in such chaos (for example, because of ongoing war) that protection of property is almost impossible to enforce. The judiciary is so corrupt that property is not protected effectively. Expropriation is common.

 0—Private property is outlawed, and all property belongs to the state. People do not have the right to sue others and do not have access to the courts. Corruption is endemic.[9]

As the project has been conducted for fifteen years, it gave an opportunity for cross-temporal evaluations in many oil- and gas-exporting countries. Saudi Arabia and Turkmenistan are added in table 4.4 to the list given in table 4.1. Based on the data presented in table 4.4, one would come to a conclusion about the effects of the oil and gas curse on protection of property rights. Guarantees of property rights in 2008 (the time lag is a year in table 4.4) declined in almost all countries compared to previous years (the only exception is Qatar, where

Table 4.4. Heritage Foundation: Index of Economic Freedom (Property Rights)

	1995	1996	1999	2000	2001	2002	2003	2004	2005	2006	2007	2008	2009
Algeria	50	50	50	50	30	30	30	30	30	30	30	30	30
Azerbaijan	n/a	n/a	30	30	30	30	30	30	30	30	30	30	30
Bahrain	60	60	60	60	60	60	70	60	70	70	60	60	60
Bolivia	50	50	50	50	30	30	30	30	30	30	30	25	20
Ecuador	50	50	50	50	30	30	30	30	30	30	30	30	25
Kuwait	n/a	90	90	90	90	70	70	50	50	50	50	55	50
Mexico	70	50	50	50	50	50	50	50	50	50	50	50	50
Nigeria	60	50	50	50	50	30	30	30	30	30	30	30	30
Qatar	n/a	n/a	50	50	50	50	50	50	50	50	50	50	50
Russia	50	50	50	50	50	30	30	30	30	30	30	30	25
Saudi Arabia	n/a	90	70	50	50	50	50	50	50	50	50	50	40
Trinidad & Tobago	n/a	90	90	90	70	70	70	70	70	70	70	65	60
Turkmenistan	n/a	n/a	30	30	30	30	30	30	30	10	10	10	10
UAE	n/a	90	90	90	90	70	70	70	50	50	40	40	40
Venezuela	50	50	50	50	30	30	30	30	30	30	30	10	5

Source: *2009 Index of Economic Freedom*, www.heritage.org/index/excel/Downloadrawdata.xls (20 July 2009).

the index did not change). Nevertheless, the question remains: what caused a similar trend of decline of guarantees of property rights in a number of other countries that are very poor in natural resources? Is it possible to expect that the reasons for this trend in these countries are fundamentally different than for the oil and gas exporters?

These claims might be examined in comparison with two countries of the post-Soviet Eurasia that are lacking natural resources: Armenia and Belarus. According to the data of the Heritage Foundation, in Armenia, the property rights score in reports of 1996–2006 was stable at the level of 50, but in the 2007 report it declined to 30, and in 2008–2009 reports it was at the level of 35. In Belarus, this indicator was 50 in 1995–1997 reports, but in the 1998 report, it declined to 30, was stable at this level until the 2005 report, and then since the 2006 report, it still is at 20. Some countries that lacked significant natural resources in other regions of the world demonstrated the same trend that was found for the above-listed post-Soviet countries. For example, for Morocco in reports of 1995–1997, the property rights score was 70, then in the publications of 1998–2001 it declined to 50, in 2002 it was lowered to 30, and only in 2008–2009 increased slightly to 35. Property rights in Nepal were valued at 50 in the 1997–2000 reports, but since 2001 this figure remained stable at the level of 30. And finally, in Zimbabwe, which has nothing to do with the export of oil and gas, the property rights score declined from 50 in 1995–1997 reports to 30 in 1999–2000 reports. From 2002 to 2008 it declined to 10, and in the 2009 report sunk as low as 5.[10] Furthermore, in Saudi Arabia, for example, the decline in its indicators of property rights took place during the period of the lowest oil prices in 1998–1999, and since 2000 it remained stable, with the exception of a certain decline in the 2008 report.

To summarize the evidence on the influence of revenues of the export of oil and gas on property rights, one could come to the following conclusions:

1. Evaluations of the protection and institutional guarantees of property rights differ considerably (compare the EFW and Index of Economic Freedom, tables 4.3 and 4.4). This fact poses major difficulties for conclusions of impact of various factors, including the flow of oil and gas export revenues.

2. The resource curse argument does not explain significant variations in the degree of observance of property rights within the group of oil- and gas-exporting countries. Traditionally, in Middle Eastern monarchies, these indicators are quite high, and often exceed those in a number of new member states of the European Union.

3. There are no plausible explanations as to why property rights in many countries that do not receive revenues from oil and gas export are no better protected than in many countries that are lacking them. If so, then there does not seem to be any grounds to support the argument that the resource curse is nothing more than an assumption, which has to be empirically tested alongside with other hypotheses.

OIL- AND GAS-EXPORTING COUNTRIES AND THE RULE OF LAW: INTERNATIONAL COMPARISONS

The World Bank Worldwide Governance Indicators (WGI) research project measures six dimensions of governance:

- Voice and Accountability
- Political Stability and Absence of Violence/Terrorism
- Government Effectiveness
- Regulatory Quality
- Rule of Law
- Control of Corruption

They cover 212 countries and territories for 1996, 1998, 2000, and annually for 2002–2008. The indicators are based on several hundred individual variables measuring perceptions of governance, drawn from thirty-five separate data sources constructed by thirty-three different organizations from around the world.[11] According to the authors of the project, the rule of law is defined as "capturing perceptions of the extent to which agents have confidence in and abide by the rules of society, and in particular the quality of contract enforcement, property rights, the police, and the courts, as well as the likelihood of crime and violence."[12]

The data of table 4.5 provoked the same questions posed earlier, when dynamics of the world oil prices and protection of property rights in oil- and gas-exporting countries were compared. In a number of cases, the changes of percentile ranks are indeed quite closely related with the dynamics of the world oil prices (Bolivia, Ecuador, Trinidad and Tobago, Turkmenistan, Venezuela), and in others this trend seems to be expressed not so clearly (Russia, Saudi Arabia, UAE, Uzbekistan). And, also besides the countries where a certain trend for the rule of law is hard to detect, there are some countries where the dynamics of indicators of the rule of law are totally opposite to the predictions of the argument of the resource curse (Algeria, Angola, Azerbaijan).

Table 4.5.   Rule of Law (Percentile Ranks)

	1996	1998	2000	2002	2003	2004	2005	2006	2007
Algeria	10	10	14	30	30	31	31	34	29
Angola	3	3	2	4	6	7	7	8	8
Azerbaijan	19	15	15	22	26	23	25	21	24
Bahrain	61	70	66	71	72	77	71	66	70
Bolivia	45	46	41	40	40	35	20	18	16
Ecuador	38	33	29	31	31	28	21	14	15
Kazakhstan	23	20	21	18	17	16	26	20	25
Kuwait	76	75	72	71	70	71	72	70	72
Mexico	37	37	42	45	44	42	40	42	36
Nigeria	5	8	12	5	4	5	7	12	10
Oman	78	74	71	70	70	74	68	69	70
Qatar	57	64	70	70	66	69	77	74	79
Russia	29	20	15	21	20	21	22	18	18
Saudi Arabia	65	62	57	57	60	59	57	56	58
Trinidad & Tobago	68	63	62	63	57	50	51	48	50
Turkmenistan	13	13	13	11	8	6	6	6	7
UAE	77	79	78	79	77	74	65	68	67
Uzbekistan	18	16	16	6	7	7	6	6	14
Venezuela	30	26	28	14	10	10	10	5	3

Source: *Governance Matters 2009. Worldwide Governance Indicators, 1996–2008,* http://info.worldbank.org/governance/wgi/index.asp (22 July 2009).

Finally, the argument of the resource curse cannot explain gaps in percentile ranks on the rule of law indicators for certain regions. For Middle Eastern monarchies, the average value for the years as shown in table 4.5 comes to 67.7: this, for example, exceeds the equivalent figure for Poland (65.0). At the same time, for African countries (including Algeria) the average value is 12.4 (without Algeria, it would be 6.5). For countries of the former Soviet Union, the equivalent average indicator is 16.3, and here, in their turn, two groups of countries are observed. For Azerbaijan, Kazakhstan, and Russia it is 20.7, while for Turkmenistan and Uzbekistan it is 10.0. Once again, these contrasts of indicators of the rule of law between various oil- and gas-exporting countries are difficult to explain using the resource curse argument alone.

In table 4.6, ten countries, where the rule of law indicators for 1998–2008 demonstrated a major decline, are compared. Among them are only four oil and gas exporters; the six others do not belong to this group. At the same time, there are some countries where the decline in the percentile rank of the rule of law would ideally fit the argument of the resource curse, if they exported oil and/or gas, for

Table 4.6.   Rule of Law (Negative Significant Changes)

	2008 (level)	1998 (level)	Change
Zimbabwe	−1.81	−0.53	−1.29
Eritrea	−1.24	−0.21	−1.03
Venezuela	−1.59	−0.71	−0.88
Bolivia	−1.12	−0.28	−0.84
Argentina	−0.61	0.08	−0.69
Cote D'Ivoire	−1.52	−0.90	−0.62
Trinidad & Tobago	−0.25	0.37	−0.62
Ecuador	−1.23	−0.63	−0.60
Kyrgyzstan	−1.26	−0.67	−0.59
Thailand	−0.03	−0.48	−0.51

Source: Kaufman, Kraay and Mastruzzi, "Governance Matters VIII," 35.

example, Poland (1996—70, 1998—71, 2000—70, 2002—68, 2003—65, 2004—63, 2005—60, 2006—59, 2007—59).[13]

In the recent study by Freedom House, *Nations in Transit 2009*, indicators of Judicial Framework and Independence may well demonstrate both the current state of the rule of law, and even, to a certain extent, the current state of property rights (lowest point is 7).[14] In table 4.7, assessments of Judicial Framework and Independence are presented for the according years for countries of the former Soviet Union (excluding Baltic countries).[15] The figures correspond to a larger degree with all the previous ratings examined above, and also cast doubts about the argument of the resource curse. For example, there is a decline of indicators in both oil-exporting countries, such as Russia and Azerbaijan, and non-oil states such as Georgia and Kyrgyzstan, while figures for Ukraine and Armenia are rather uneven. Belarus receives a stable low assessment in terms of Judicial Framework and Independence indicators.

If one further analyzes the indicators in table 4.7, then one may note that the average rating of non-oil countries of the post-Soviet region (Armenia, Belarus, Georgia, Kyrgyzstan, Moldova, Tajikistan, and Ukraine) came to 5.0 in 1999–2000, while for oil and gas exporters the average rating was 5.6. In the latest annual report of 2009 (covering the developments in 2008), the equivalent figures were 5.4 and 6.2, respectively. In other words, for the former group of countries the rating declined by 8 percent and by 11 percent for the latter group. The trend for a decline of Judicial Framework and Independence is clear in both groups of countries, but in oil and gas exporters it declined more quickly, and thus the gap between the indicators in these two groups increased.

Table 4.7. Judicial Framework and Independence

	1999–2000	2002	2003	2004	2005	2006	2007	2008	2009
Armenia	5.0	5.0	5.0	5.0	5.25	5.0	5.0	5.25	5.5
Azerbaijan	5.5	5.25	5.25	5.5	5.75	5.75	5.75	5.75	5.75
Belarus	6.5	6.75	6.75	6.75	6.75	6.75	6.75	6.75	6.75
Georgia	4.0	4.25	4.5	4.5	4.5	5.0	5.0	5.25	5.5
Kazakhstan	5.5	6.0	6.25	6.25	6.25	6.25	6.25	6.25	6.0
Kyrgyzstan	5.0	5.25	5.5	5.5	5.5	5.5	5.5	5.5	5.5
Moldova	4.0	4.0	4.5	4.5	4.75	4.5	4.5	4.5	4.5
Russia	4.25	4.75	4.5	4.75	5.25	5.25	5.25	5.25	5.25
Tajikistan	5.75	5.75	5.75	5.75	5.75	5.75	5.75	6.0	6.25
Turkmenistan	6.25	5.75	7.0	7.0	7.0	7.0	7.0	7.0	7.0
Ukraine	4.5	4.75	4.5	4.75	4.25	4.25	4.5	4.75	4.0
Uzbekistan	6.5	6.5	6.5	6.5	6.25	6.75	6.75	6.75	7.0

Source: Freedom House, *Nations in Transit 2009*.

To summarize the analysis of the developments of the rule of law, one may attribute these trends to the negative influence of the growth of revenues from oil and gas export. However, it is clear that this caused major changes only in several countries, which shifted from unstable democracy to various types of authoritarianism (such as Bolivia, Venezuela, or Russia). At the same time, in Middle Eastern monarchies, the inflow of oil revenues does not have any destructive influence on the rule of law. Thus, in looking for an explanation of the decline of the rule of law, just as, especially, property rights, it is necessary to analyze the historical developmental paths of various countries and their political and economic features, and not restrict just to references to the resource curse argument.

WHAT DO RUSSIAN ECONOMISTS THINK ABOUT THE POOR STATE OF PROPERTY RIGHTS AND THE RULE OF LAW?

In recent years, Russian economists have devoted a lot of attention to the problem of the influence of the revenues from export of resources on institutional changes. No doubt that their interest in these issues was connected with the developments in Russia, which at first glance could serve as a typical illustration of the resource curse argument. It's clear from figure 4.3 that, on the one hand, changes of the average annual export price of Russian oil, and on the other hand, the permanent decay of democratic institutions in the country, are indicated in changes in its democracy score. While the average annual price of Russian oil grew over seven years (2001–2008) from $21 to $91 per barrel, its democracy score degenerated below the 6.0 line, according to Freedom House Nations in Transit annual data. In other words, in the 2000s Russia joins the group of countries classified as consolidated authoritarian regimes.[16] At the same time, one should admit that authoritarian regimes of Middle Eastern monarchies do not break property rights and the rule of law. On the contrary, four Middle Eastern monarchies (UAE, Qatar, Bahrain, and Kuwait) are among the top 50 countries of 115 for IPRI value (see table 4.1) and five of them (Bahrain, Kuwait, Oman, Qatar, and UAE) are placed in the top third of percentile ranking for the rule of law (see table 4.5). Russia, however, is rated much lower than those Middle Eastern states in both these respects.

Konstantin Sonin proposed the economic theory of poor protection of property rights with an application to Russia. The major idea of his 2003 article is that the capacity to maintain private protection sys-

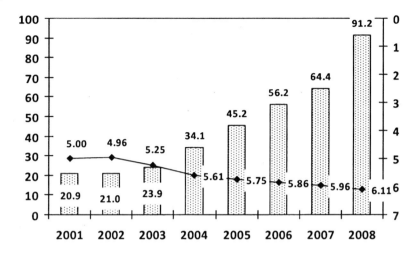

Figure 4.3. Average Export Price of Russia's Oil and Freedom House Democracy Score (Nations in Transit dataset)

tems makes the rich natural opponents of public property rights and precludes grassroots demand to drive the development of the market-friendly institution. The author argues that due to the oligarchs' political power, the Russian state has failed to establish and to enforce a system of clearly defined property rights.[17] Sonin published yet another article where he develops further the idea of the previous analysis.[18] Although these studies do not discuss the role of natural resources, it is clear that the so-called oligarchs primarily represented the oil and gas sector. In a later publication written with Sergei Guriev, Sonin proposed the assumption that the rise in the "oil bonus" increased rent-seeking, and weakened the demand for good and efficient institutions.[19] As an example of the influence of the resource curse on the quality of institutions, Sonin and his coauthors analyzed changes in media freedom (this may be seen as the case of its influence on the rule of law). They demonstrated that media freedom negatively depends on oil reserves, and this effect is evident in nondemocratic countries, but in developed democracies, this link is not observed.[20]

The analysis of property rights in connection with oil prices is analyzed by Guriev, Sonin, and Anton Kolotilin, with the focus on the problem of expropriation in the oil and gas sector.[21] The authors note that recent expropriations of foreign-owned oil assets in Venezuela, Bolivia, Russia, and Kazakhstan have generated renewed interest in the political economics of expropriations. The data allow them to test the conventional wisdom that expropriations are more likely to happen in the periods of higher oil prices and in countries with poorer institutions. They back this idea by considering a dynamic model with limited commitment on behalf of both government and the foreign oil company. In this model expropriations emerge in equilibrium when oil prices are high and political institutions are weak. This argument, at first glance, is plausible with the Russian experience of expropriations of major private oil companies such as Yukos (2003–2004) and Russneft (2007–2008). However, a closer look at the export price of Russian oil in 2003, when the Russian state launched the campaign against Yukos, shows that it did not greatly exceed the level of the two previous years (figure 4.3). Although in 2004 these prices jumped drastically, and it can be claimed that the final decision on the fate of Yukos was adopted under their influence. However, there is no clear evidence whether or not this was the case.

Also, the issue of the resource curse was analyzed by the well-known Russian economist Viktor Polterovich[22] together with Vladimir Popov and Aleksander Tonis.[23] They elaborate the argument of the so-called conditional resource curse. Its essence is in the authors' conclusion that "there is a threshold of the level of institutional development, below which resource wealth declines the quality of institutions, and above which it does not have significant influence."[24] In countries that lay below this threshold, resource abundance contributed to nonproductive investment into rent-seeking instead of technological developments and led to insufficient investment into human capital. A low level of human capital and the lack of interest of governments in progressive changes due to their high revenues from oil export play a decisive role in the further decay of institutions. In particular, among other institutions, the authors test the influence of resource abundance on the rule of law. Their calculations show that with the same level of GDP per capita in a country with a high share of natural resources in export, the indicators of the rule of law is lower, as a rule.[25] However, even the argument of "conditional resource curse" does not explain the paradox noted above, when property rights not only do not decline, but improve in several oil- and gas-exporting countries as oil prices increase, although it seems unlikely that these countries exceeded the threshold of institutional development above which resource abundance does not influence institutions negatively.

The effect of resource wealth on property rights was analyzed by Vitaly Tambovtsev and Lyliya Valitova.[26] Tambovtsev formulates the following initial statement: "A country's possession of natural resources influences a wide range of parameters of its social and political-economic development through the influence of the ruling elite on the fundamental economic institutions of *property rights.*"[27] Tambovtsev and Valitova tested the following hypothesis: "In new democracies, the very presence of a significant share of concentrated resources in the export will contribute to a low level of protection of property rights for the most of economic agents, which in its turn will lead to a strengthening of the authoritarian political regime."[28] Unfortunately, the economic calculations of the authors only confirmed a trend for strengthening of authoritarian regimes[29] as their dependent variable is presented by two components of the Freedom in the World index assessed by Freedom House: political rights (PR) and civil liberties (CL).[30] But the restrictions of political (merely electoral) rights of citizens are not always identical to restrictions of property rights (the oil-exporting Middle Eastern monarchies may serve as an example).

Finally, explanations of the poor protection of property rights in general, and in the oil and gas sector in particular, may also lie outside the theory of the resource curse. Some of them could be linked with mass values and attitudes: "In Russian society, there is almost a consensual hostility to privatization and the private ownership that forms on its base."[31] Numerous surveys confirm this argument (see, for example, table 4.8). Answers to the question about the legality of actions in this case show not so much the formal legality (adherence to legal norms), but rather their legitimacy in the eyes of Russians.[32] As one can see, even the privatization of small enterprises does not look justified, not to mention major businesses (privatized oil companies are in fact the largest enterprises in Russia). At the same time, Russian economists, discussing the problem of the legitimacy of property rights in the country, often refer to surveys conducted by the leading

Table 4.8.   Were Such Actions as . . . Lawful or Not? (% of survey respondents, early November 2003)

Type of actions	Yes	No	Difference of yes and no	Don't know
Privatization of the most part of state enterprises in the 1990s	17	71	−54	12
Privatization of major large enterprises in the 1990s	13	85	−72	12
Privatization of small enterprises of retail, services etc. in the 1990s	33	51	−18	12

Source: Lev Gudkov, "O legitimnosti sotsialnogo poryadka v Rossii," *Vestnik Obshchestvennogo Mneniya* 70, no. 2 (March–April 2004): 35.

research firm Levada Center, which demonstrated that from 78 percent to 83 percent of Russian respondents in 2000–2007 supported the idea of a complete or partial revision of privatization. Similar figures are confirmed from other surveys too.[33]

Some authors argue that in fact Russians have a better attitude to private property as such than to privatization. According to one of these studies, 44 percent of respondents in the nationwide survey felt positively about private property, 14 percent felt negatively, and 38 percent did not have any particular feelings about it. The equivalent figures for privatization were 22, 36, and 38 percent respectively.[34] However, the same study demonstrates that the attitudes of Russians to the idea of private ownership of factories and major industrial enterprises divided equally (40 percent of survey respondents approve it, 41 percent do not approve, 11 percent feel indifferent, and 8 percent said they did not know).[35]

At the same time, it is claimed that "the illegitimacy of privatization and major private ownership is a universal, cross-national phenomenon, typical for all transitional economies."[36] This conclusion is based on the study by Irina Denisova and her coauthors.[37] However, in fact, in Russia "the state (i.e., bureaucracy), relying on the above-mentioned and quite widespread moods, can quite easily launch actions directed towards the *erosion* of property rights."[38]

Yet, surveys of Russians also show the negative attitude toward the criminal prosecution of Yukos and its owners by the state. According to the survey conducted by Levada Center in July 2008, of 1,600 respondents, 17 percent saw the Yukos affair as evidence of illegality and arbitrary rule in the country, 21 percent considered its legal grounds dubious, and only 15 percent believed that it was the case for the rule of law, while 47 percent of respondents could not give an answer.[39] Nevertheless, this quite widespread recognition of illegality (or dubious legality) of the Yukos affair does not mean that Russians are prepared to agree with the outcomes of privatization of enterprises. According to an international survey, 36.7 percent of Russians (for post-Communist countries in total 29.0 percent) support the proposal to renationalize privatized companies and keep them in state hands, and only 18.5 percent (19.4 percent in all post-Communist countries) agree to leave them in the hands of current owners with no change.[40] In the new study of these issues, Denisova and her coauthors come to the following conclusion: "We find that under autocracy and bad governance, support for economic reform among individuals with market-relevant skills is not different than among individuals without market-relevant skills, but as quality of democracy and governance improves, the differences in support for economic reform between respondents with high and low market skills becomes large. Thus, market skills and good institutional environments are complements rather than substitutes. These results hold not only for public support for revising privatization, but also for a market economy more generally."[41]

Actually, the peculiarity of Russia in this respect is not in the negative attitudes of its citizens toward privatization (in fact, they are not much worse than in other post-Communist countries). The peculiarity of Russia is in the clearly insufficient demand for democratic institutions, separation of power, and societal control of the state.[42] In total, only 9 percent of Russians believe that Western-type democracy is necessary for Russia's development, while 35 percent believe that it is totally not suitable, or even destructive, for the country.[43] As a result, a vicious circle is formed: the improvement of the attitudes of workers with market-relevant skills to privatization, private property, and market reforms in general requires an improvement of the quality of democracy and governance, but there is no mass demand for these changes.

As a result, the Russian state may easily and arbitrarily take private assets under its control without major resistance or transfer these assets to Kremlin's cronies. Primarily, the Russian state is interested in expansion in the oil and gas sector. Since 2003, attacks to private business in this sector became tougher. According to the calculations of Vladimir Milov, the share of state-owned and state-affiliated companies in oil production has increased in Russia from 11.5 percent in 2004 to 39 percent in 2007, and in oil processing from 14.6 percent to 49.3 percent in the same period.[44] At the same time, the costs of these policies in the short-term period are less for the ruling elite in Russia than the advantages that they could take from gaining control over oil and gas rent and using it in their own interests beyond the public control.

NOTES

1. International Property Rights Index (IPRI). *2009 Report*. A Project of the Property Rights Alliance, www.InternationalPropertyRightsIndex.org (accessed 15 July 2009).

2. International Property Rights Index.

3. The *2009 Report* and *2008 Report* reflect the assessments of property rights with at least a one-year lag (2008 and 2007, respectively) so they demonstrate the data at the peak of world oil prices.

4. As of 1 September 2009, there were thirty countries in the OECD, but I exclude Mexico from this list, which is closer to emerging markets than to democratic countries with a stable market economy.

5. Central Bank of Bangladesh, www.bangladesh-bank.org.

6. Karla Hoff and Joseph E. Stiglitz, "After the Big Bang? Obstacles to the Emergence of the Rule of Law in Post-Communist Societies," *American Economic Review*, 94, no. 3 (June 2004), 753–63.

7. Ukraine shares 82–86th positions in IPRI with Mozambique, Madagascar, Kenya, and Peru. Armenia shares 98–99th positions with Ethiopia (IPRI, 2009 Report). The state of property rights in Belarus, Georgia, and Tajikistan is not reflected in the International Property Rights Index, but this can be judged by the *2009 Index of Economic Freedom* (Heritage Foundation), in which these countries received scores of 20, 35, and 30, respectively, in the property rights section (the highest possible score is 100). *2009 Index of Economic Freedom* (Washington, D.C.: The Heritage Foundation and Dow Jones and Company, Inc., 2009), heritage.org/Index (accessed 17 July 2009).

8. James Gwartney and Robert Lawson, *Economic Freedom of the World: 2009 Annual Report*, 18 July 2009, www.freetheworld.com/2009/reports/world/EFW2009_BOOK.pdf (accessed 17 November 2009).

9. *2009 Index of Economic Freedom.*

10. *2009 Index of Economic Freedom.*

11. Daniel Kaufman, Aart Kraay, and Massimo Mastruzzi, "Governance Matters VII: Aggregate and Individual Government Indicators 1996–2008," *World Bank Policy Research Working Paper*, no. 4978 (June 2009).

12. Kaufman, Kraay, and Mastruzzi, "Governance Matters," 6.

13. *Governance Matters 2009. Worldwide Governance Indicators, 1996–2008*, http://info.worldbank.org/governance/wgi/index.asp (accessed 11 February 2010).

14. Freedom House, *Nations in Transit 2009*, www.freedomhouse.hu/index.php?option=com_content&view=article&id=242:nations-in-transit-2009&catid=308&Itemid=92> (accessed 20 July 2009).

15. The lowest score is 7; 1 is the highest.

16. *Nations in Transit 2009.*

17. Konstantin Sonin, "Why the Rich May Favor Poor Protection of Property Rights," *Journal of Comparative Economics*, 31, no. 4 (December 2003), 715–31.

18. Konstantin Sonin, "Institutsionalnaya Teoriya Beskonechnogo Peredela," *Voprosy Ekonomiki*, no. 7 (July 2005), 4–18.

19. Sergei Guriev and Konstantin Sonin, "Ekonomika 'Resursnogo Proklyatiya,'" *Voprosy Ekonomiki*, no. 4 (April 2008), 61–74.

20. Georgy Egorov, Sergei Guriev, and Konstantin Sonin, "Media Freedom, Bureaucratic Incentives, and the Resource Curse," *CEPR Discussion Papers*, no. 5748 (2006).

21. Sergei Guriev, Anton Kolotilin, and Konstantin Sonin, "Determinants of Expropriation in the Oil Sector: A Theory and Evidence from Panel Data," *CEFIR and NES Working Paper series*, no. 115 (2008).

22. Polterovich is known primarily as one of the authors of the concept of "institutional traps": Viktor Polterovich, "Institutional Trap," in *The New Palgrave Dictionary of Economics Online* (Palgrave Macmillan, 2008), www .dictionaryofeconomics.com/article?id=pde2008_I000262, doi:10.1057/978023 0226203.0809 (accessed 10 August 2009); Viktor Polterovich, "Institutional Traps," in Lawrence R. Klein and Mark Pomer, eds., *The New Russia: Transition Gone Awry* (Stanford, Calif.: Stanford University Press, 2001), 93–116.

23. Viktor Polterovich, Vladimir Popov, and Aleksander Tonis, *Ekonomicheskaya Politika, Kachetstvo Institutov i Mekhanizmy "Resursnogo Proklyatiya"* (Moscow: State University—Higher School of Economics, 2007); Viktor Polterovich, Vladimir Popov, and Aleksander Tonis, "Mekhanizmy 'Resursnogo Proklyatiya' i Ekonomichaskaya Politika," *Voprosy Ekonomiki*, no. 6 (June 2007), 4–27.

24. Polterovich, Popov, and Tonis, *Ekonomicheskaya Politika*, 34.

25. Polterovich, Popov, and Tonis, *Ekonomicheskaya Politika*, 63.

26. Vitalyi Tambovtsev, "Mozhno li Ozhidat Uluchsheniya Zashchity Prav Sobstvennosti v Rossii?" in Andrei Zaostrovtsev, ed., *Problemy Ekonomicheskoi Teorii i Politiki* (St. Petersburg: MTsSEI "Leontievskyi Tsentr," 2006), 374–401; Vitalyi Tambovtsev and Lyliya Valitova, "Resursnaya Obespechennost Strany i Ee Politiko-Ekonomicheskie Posledstviya," *Ekonomicheskaya Politika*, no. 3 (September 2007), 18–31; Vitalyi Tambovtsev, ed., *Prava Sobstvennosti, Privatizatsiya i Natsionalizatsiya* (Moscow: Fond "Liberalnaya Missiya"; Novoe Literaturnoe Obozrenie, 2009), 385–407.

27. Tambovtsev, *Prava Sobstvennosti*, 391.

28. Tambovtsev, *Prava Sobstvennosti*, 395. By "concentrated resources," the author means the spatial profile of the location of natural resources (i.e., an oil and/or gas field may be regarded as a concentrated natural resource, unlike such a resource as fertile soil).

29. Tambovtsev, *Prava Sobstvennosti*, 398.

30. *Freedom in the World 2009*, www.freedomhouse.org/template.cfm?page =351&ana_page=354&year=2009 (accessed 10 August 2009).

31. Tambovtsev, *Prava Sobstvennosti*, 345.

32. Legitimacy in terms of this analysis means justification in the eyes of public opinion, corresponding to mass perceptions about justice in the society. Legitimacy may often be in conflict with formal legality.

33. Tambovtsev, *Prava Sobstvennosti*, 346.

34. Mariya Ordjonikidze, "Zapadnye Tsennosti v Vospriyatii Rossiyan," *Vestnik Obshchestvennogo Mneniya*, 88, no. 2 (March–April 2007), 29.

35. Ordjonikidze, "Zapadnye Tsennosti," 30.

36. Tambovtsev, *Prava Sobstvennosti*, 346.

37. Irina Denisova, Markus Eller, Timothy Frye, and Ekaterina Zhuravskaya, "Who Wants to Revise Privatization and Why? Evidence from 28 Post-Communist Countries," *CEFIR and NES Working Paper series*, no. 105 (November 2007).

38. Tambovtsev, *Prava Sobstvennosti*, 298.

39. *Obshchestvennoe mnenie 2008* (Moscow: Levada-Tsentr, 2008), 94.

40. Denisova, Eller, Frye, and Zhuravskaya, "Who Wants to Revise," 28.

41. Irina Denisova, Markus Eller, Timothy Frye, and Ekaterina Zhuravskaya, "Who Wants to Revise Privatization? The Complementary of Market Skills and Institutions," *CEFIR and NES Working Paper series*, no. 127 (April 2009).

42. In 2006, 43 percent of survey respondents approved the further strengthening of state power, and 42 percent favored the control of society over the state. Fifty-four percent suggested that legislatures should to a certain degree or even completely be controlled by executive authorities. Fifty-six percent suggested the same subordination to executives for judiciary (Ordjonikidze, "Zapadnye Tsennosti," 33).

43. *Obshchestvennoe mnenie 2008*, 147.

44. Vladimir Milov, "Russian Energy and Politics," 25 January 2008, www .milov.info/2008/01/russian-energy-and-politics (accessed 11 August 2009).

5

The Logic of Crony Capitalism

Big Oil, Big Politics, and Big Business in Russia

Vladimir Gel'man

Resource abundance in general, and "big oil" in particular, throughout the last decade have been seen as an important factor of many pathologies of political and economic development—starting from the decline of democracy and freedom of speech, and ending with corruption and civil wars.[1] Scholars, recognizing the key role of big oil in these processes, disagree in their evaluations of effects of its influence on big politics and big business. However, the most widespread opinion is that the negative influence of big oil is poisoning politics, economy, and society only in combination with a number of other factors, most of which are of structural or path-dependent nature.[2] As Terry Lynn Karl noted, "Petro-states are built on what already exists."[3] Russia and other countries of post-Soviet Eurasia are no exception in this respect,[4] as it is shown in other chapters of this book. The present chapter is devoted to the effects of big oil on relationships between big politics and big business in contemporary Russia. It will discuss dynamics of relations between the Russian state (i.e., the federal authorities), on the one hand, and major oil and gas companies, on the other. These relations, which have been analyzed in detail by numerous scholars,[5] demonstrated dramatic changes over the last few decades since the decline and collapse of state socialism, through the turbulent process of socioeconomic and political transformations in the 1990s, and then to the emergence of state capitalism, accompanied by large-scale redistribution of property rights in the 2000s. It is not surprising that the assessment of the current political-economic system in Russia as "crony capitalism" in recent years is becoming commonplace in assessments of numerous analysts and commentators.[6]

What caused the emergence of crony capitalism in Russia, and the logic of transformation of its major features in the 1990s and 2000s? Numerous studies devoted to an analysis of Russian politics and economy connect these developments with structural factors (including trends in the oil and gas sector and the dynamics of world oil prices)[7] or see crony capitalism as a side effect of special interests and opportunistic behavior by political and economic actors (including political leaders and oil companies).[8] However, in the framework of these analyses, political institutions are often becoming the missing link, serving as nothing more than a by-product of interactions between big politics and big business.[9] In this chapter of the book, the major attention is paid to political institutions, which along with big oil have given rise to the dynamic of crony capitalism in contemporary Russia. In the first part of the chapter, the framework of analysis is presented, based on comparative studies carried out by David Kang[10] and Pauline Jones Luong and Erika Weinthal,[11] and designed to explain the logic of the development of crony capitalism in Russia. Then in light of this approach, the interactions of big oil, big business, and big politics in the Soviet Union and in Russia in the 1990s and 2000s are examined against the background of processes of institution building and institutional decay. At the conclusion of the chapter, the mutual influence of political institutions and relationships between the state and major oil and gas companies in Russia, and the prospects for their subsequent transformation, are discussed.

CRONY CAPITALISM, BIG OIL, AND POLITICAL INSTITUTIONS: THE CASE OF RUSSIA

As a rule, the dynamics of interactions between the state and business in transitional societies are considered as an effect of structural features of economic actors, on the one hand, and the level of consolidation of the state on the other. This approach, which is presented in the study by David Kang, is oriented toward a comparative analysis of corruption within the framework of crony capitalism—from a laissez-faire model, which demonstrates a relatively low level of corruption, to the high level of corruption in the case of rent-seeking, when the state is captured by big business, and in the case of the predatory state, when the state apparatus essentially carries out "business capture." An intermediary model with a medium level of corruption is a structure-induced or ad hoc (i.e., situational) based equilibrium between political and economic actors, or a situation of "mutual hostages."[12]

Kang, who analyzed interactions of political and economic actors based on the cases of South Korea and the Philippines, pointed out two key factors that determine their nature. First, the national economic structure, which in the Philippines is deeply affected by a large number of rather dispersed business groups, and in South Korea by a small number of big multisectoral holding companies (chaebol) that were established under the state support. Second, the constellation of actors within the state apparatus, which in the authoritarian regimes in the 1970s and 1980s in both cases—both in South Korea and in the Philippines—were a relatively monolithic and consolidated group, while the democratization of these countries in the 1980s and 1990s led to the relative fragmentation of the power elites. Owing to these factors, the trajectory of interactions between the state and big business in both cases differed fundamentally (from "mutual hostages" to rent-seeking in South Korea, and from the predatory state to laissez-faire in the Philippines).[13]

The model of interactions of state and big business proposed by Kang is not specified in regard to various sectors of the economy and issues of property rights. These aspects, however, are examined in the analysis of Pauline Jones Luong and Erika Weinthal, which is focused on varieties of ownership structure and the mechanisms of control over natural resources in respective sectors of resource-based economies in connection with the incentives they provide for institution building. The authors pointed out several types of ownership structure—

Table 5.1. Typology of Interactions between the State and Big Business (level of corruption in parentheses)

		State actors	
		Coherent	Fractured
Business actors	Small-N (concentrated)	Mutual hostages (medium)	Rent-seeking (high)
	Large-N (dispersed)	Predatory state (high)	Laissez-faire (low)

Source: Adapted from David Kang, *Crony Capitalism: Corruption and Development in South Korea and the Philippines* (New York: Cambridge University Press, 2002), 15.

(1) state ownership with control, when the major natural resources (first and foremost, oil and gas) are controlled by the state, and the major economic actors in the oil and gas sector are state-owned oil and gas companies; (2) private domestic ownership, when the major actors are domestic private oil and gas companies; also (3) state ownership without control; and (4) private foreign ownership, when the major actors are foreign investors. Under conditions of state ownership with control, political elites and the bureaucracy establish blurred boundaries between business and the state, and thus enable the emergence of weak institutions. Examples of this kind are Venezuela and Mexico, where the oil business is concentrated in the major state-owned oil companies. On the contrary, private domestic ownership forces both the state and private oil and gas companies to clearer and more symmetrical relations, which provides foundations for the emergence of strong institutions in a long-term perspective (an example is the United States). Finally, the key role of foreign investors creates mixed incentives for institution building, and enables the emergence of "hybrid" institutions, which is shown by the rather contradictory experience of many countries of the Third World.[14]

Jones Luong and Weinthal convincingly argue that the appearance of certain ownership structures in the oil and gas sector of the economy is caused by the constellation of structural and political factors. On the one hand, a key role is played by the dependence of the economy of a certain country on the export of natural resources. If it is high, then in respective sectors of the economy of resource-rich states (and, in particular, oil states), domestic owners usually predominate (both state and private), while low dependence

Table 5.2.   Ownership Structure and Institutional Outcomes

Ownership Structure	Key Actors	State-Business Relationships	Incentives for Institution Building	Institutional Outcome
State ownership with control	Political elites + bureaucrats	Blurred + symmetrical	converge	weak
Private domestic ownership	Political elites + domestic owners	Clear + symmetrical	converge	strong
State ownership without control	Political elites + foreign investors	Clear + asymmetrical	diverge	hybrid
Private foreign ownership	Political elites + foreign investors	Clear + asymmetrical	diverge	hybrid

Source: Adapted from Pauline Jones Luong and Erika Weinthal, "Rethinking the Resource Curse: Ownership Structure, Institutional Capacity, and Domestic Control," *Annual Review of Political Science* 9 (2006), 247.

on export of natural resources opens the door for foreign investors. At the same time, the level of political competition (closely linked with features of political regimes) affects the role of private owners in resource sectors—in noncompetitive (i.e., authoritarian) regimes, the state ownership predominates, and competitive regimes open windows of opportunities for private economic actors (both domestic and foreign). Thus, political regime changes alongside the dynamic of dependence of states on export of natural resources explains changes in the ownership structure in resource-based economies in various countries.[15]

As we can see, these two approaches do not contradict each other, but are rather mutually cross-fertilizing. Political and economic determinants, which give rise to the features of interactions between big business and the state, and also the ownership structure and the quality of institutions are in many ways mutually connected and mutually dependent. However, their influence is indirect, especially in the wake of large-scale and simultaneous political and economic transformations. In this sense, post-Soviet cases (including Russia) are very interesting from the viewpoint of an analysis of the trajectories of their political and economic development. The uneven constellations of these factors—the dynamics of (1) political regimes and (2) state building against the background of (3) a growth of dependence on oil and gas export give rise to significant changes in ownership

Table 5.3. Determinants of the Ownership Structure

		Level of political contestation	
		Low	High
Dependence on export of natural resources	High	State ownership with control	Private domestic ownership
	Low	State ownership with control	Private domestic ownership

Source: Adapted from Pauline Jones Luong and Erika Weinthal, "Rethinking the Resource Curse: Ownership Structure, Institutional Capacity, and Domestic Control," *Annual Review of Political Science* 9 (2006), 257.

structure, processes of institution building, and changing interactions between the state and big business.

To put it bluntly, the trajectory of Russia on its map of interactions between the state and big business in recent decades looks as follows. In the Soviet period, the predominance of state ownership in the economy (an extreme case of state ownership with control) against the background of the Communist authoritarian regime would seem to be a classic example of a predatory state. However, starting from the 1970s, the Soviet economy experienced an increase in dependence from the export of oil and gas.[16] This factor contributed to the relative increase of the influence of state bureaucracy and top managers of the oil and gas sector, and caused a trend in state-business relationships toward the ad hoc type of "mutual hostages." In the late 1980s and early 1990s, the rise of principal-agent problems under conditions of major decline of the state capacity[17] and major changes from a noncompetitive Soviet rule to a more open and competitive political regime opened political opportunities for big business, which drastically increased its capacities for rent-seeking, especially in the oil and gas sector. In the mid-1990s, the nontransparent process of privatization of state assets (in particular, in the oil industry) enabled the emergence of private domestic ownership, which was accompanied by sudden and large-scale state capture. The overwhelming political influence of the "oligarchs" (tycoons) in this period was criticized by most observers.[18] In the early 2000s, the policy of "equal distance" of "oligarchs" proclaimed by the Russian authorities, and the search for compromises between the state and big business on property rights, tax policy, and centralization of the state would seem to have opened the door to the emergence of a structure-based equilibrium close to the model of mutual hostages.[19] However, just some years later, the rise of Russia's dependence on oil export, on the one hand, and the decline of political competition in the country, on the other, essentially caused a move to large-scale redistribution of property rights, partial restoration of state ownership with control, and the flourishing of a predatory state, for which the policy of business capture is a typical feature.[20] This model of interactions between the state and big business is persistent in contemporary Russia, but it is merely ad hoc rather than structure-induced, and in the medium-term perspective may be subject to major changes, because of both political and economic factors. Let's take a closer look at the dynamics of influence of these factors on big business and big politics in Russia.

BIG OIL AND THE PREDATORY STATE IN RUSSIA: SWINGS OF THE PENDULUM

Episode 1: Big Oil and the Rise of Big Business

The Soviet experience of relationships between the state and big business in the sector of natural resources is important for an understanding of the logic of crony capitalism in at least two important respects. First, it became the "point of departure" for the subsequent political and economic transformations in Russia and other post-Soviet oil states (such as Kazakhstan and Azerbaijan), and even today serves in many ways as a normative ideal for a number of leading Russian politicians and officials. Second, as Anna Bessonova correctly notes, despite the "cardinal changes of the developmental trends in the oil and gas sector of the Soviet times and of the recent period, the reactions of the ruling elites to foreign and domestic challenges to the oil sector and the economy in general are similar in many ways. The predominance of short-term solutions to problems of the sector, the inefficient management and the system as a whole have not created and are not creating incentives for development [of] . . . a system capable of responding to modern changes."[21]

Although scholars of the Soviet economy have discussed the thesis about its planned nature,[22] there is no doubt that it was not a market economy. The oil and gas industry, like the entire Soviet system, was a part of a vertically integrated hierarchy of governance, created by a centralized predatory state in the 1920s and 1930s. This hierarchy merely provided short-term incentives for all actors, and thus a favorable environment for special interest groups has emerged.[23] On the one hand, the Soviet state invested large-scale resources in the development of the oil and gas industry and managed its enterprises through industrial branch ministries and planning agencies. On the other hand, the top managers of the oil and gas sector themselves had considerable opportunities to lobby their interests, which were connected with the major development of the sector—an increase in centralized investments into production and processing of oil and gas, and a more extensive use of existing fields.[24] Branch ministries responsible for the oil and gas industry, as it developed, began to play the role of the major tools for lobbying the interests of the sector, while the geographic concentration of oil and gas enterprises across the vast territory of the country and the technological features of production and processing of oil enabled a strengthening of positions of territorial interest groups, which thus combined the phenomena of both "departmentalism" and "localism."[25] The Soviet system thus stimulated blurred boundaries between the government and big business in the oil and gas sector, and brought about the inefficiency of institutions for governing the industry, and the economy in general.

Starting from the period of the oil boom of the 1970s, the Soviet economy became increasingly dependent upon importing of food and consumer goods by exporting oil and gas, thus Soviet leaders were forced to make more concessions to the special interests of the oil and gas sector. In other words, both the leadership of the country and the top managers of the industry were interested in the short-term maximization of the amount of resource rent, at the expense of efficient development. Former Russian prime minister Yegor Gaidar, in analyzing the economic causes of the collapse of the Soviet system, referred to his predecessor, the chairman of the Council of Ministers of the Soviet Union, Alexei Kosygin, who was forced to call personally to top managers of the oil industry and ask them to increase oil production (and, accordingly, oil export) urgently, in order to buy the necessary amount of grain abroad with these export revenues.[26] It will be no exaggeration to state that the interactions of the state and the oil and gas sector in this period gradually moved more toward an ad hoc equilibrium of mutual hostages. An increase in the importance of the oil and gas industry was accompanied by a weakening in centralized control over its top managers from the Soviet political leadership, against the background of the rise of principal-agent problems in the country as a whole. The reverse side of this tendency was the investment crisis that hit the oil industry in the late 1970s and early 1980s as a result of its orientation almost exclusively on extensive development and short-term appropriation of resource rents. The decline of oil production in the 1980s led to an increase of centralized investments in the industry, but their amount proved insufficient to heal the pathologies, and the severe decline of world oil prices in 1985–1986 delivered an irrevocable blow, both to the oil and gas sector and to the entire Soviet economy.[27]

The comprehensive crisis of the Soviet system at the end of the 1980s, which eventually led to its complete collapse, undermined the patterns of sectoral governance of the economy that had formed over decades, including the oil and gas sector. The weakening of centralized control over enterprises, against the background of attempts to revive the production through institutional liberalization, led to the major turn of special interest groups from latent to open form. At the same time, after the first wave of market reforms and the Soviet collapse in the early 1990s there was a drastic change in the balance of forces between the state and economic actors, especially in the oil and gas sector. If the state after the Soviet collapse was subject to territorial fragmentation and a weakening of its coercive capacity, the economic actors went out of the centralized control and received almost unlimited capabilities for rent-seeking.[28] The consequence of this disequilibration was the collapse of the model of mutual hostages, and de facto the turn of many industrial enterprises under the control of their managers. The transformation of the gas industry clearly demonstrated these effects. For the first time, from the Ministry of Oil and Gas Industry of the Soviet Union, the Ministry of Gas Industry was established, and in 1989 Viktor Chernomyrdin, the minister at the time (and later the prime minister of Russia), proposed the special governmental decree on transforming the ministry into the largest state-owned company, Gazprom, which was headed by Chernomyrdin himself, and to which all the assets of the industry were transferred.[29]

Although in the early 1990s the major oil producing enterprises were transformed into joint stock companies, which were formally under state ownership, this did not change the trend in the industry, especially due to the weakening and fragmentation of the Russian state.[30] Several of oil producing enterprises, such as Tatneft and Bashneft went under the control of the republican elites of Tatarstan and Bashkortostan, which proclaimed their sovereignty and gained privileged conditions of taxation for the enterprises they owned.[31] In the majority of other enterprises of the oil and gas industry, the formal preservation of state ownership with control only served as a façade in the early 1990s, behind which the phenomenon of "red directors" was developed. The top managers of major state-owned enterprises were interested in the capture and subsequent looting of their assets, while the state was incapable not only of providing any efficient corporate governance of these industrial enterprises, but even of collecting taxes from them.[32] In particular, Gazprom remained a "state within a state" for a long time, only paying taxes due to informal personal bargaining with the Russian president.[33] As a result, the decline of production in the industry continued, and the complete exhaustion of the model of state ownership with control forced changes in relations between the state and big business.

Episode 2: The Rise and Fall of Oligarchs

The need for transformations of ownership structure in the oil and gas industry (as in other sectors of economy) in Russia in the 1990s was brought about not only by economic, but also by political factors.

First, the early period of post-Communist economic transformations in Eastern Europe was accompanied by an active drive of reformers to pursue a policy of privatization, not only for economic reasons, which were reflected in the concept of the "Washington consensus," but also because of the very ideology of liberal reforms.[34] Second, the collapse of the Communist party's monopoly on power and the emergence of a competitive political system meant that the denationalization of property rights became the center of the political agenda.[35] Third, the rise of new economic actors—domestic private businesses, and the opening of post-Soviet Russia for foreign capital—meant that the oil and gas sector became a potentially attractive object for them during privatization.

Essentially, the Russian government in the 1990s faced the choice between preservation of the existing status quo, that is, the continuity of rent-seeking in the oil and gas industry (and in other sectors) nearly by default, and selling major assets to foreign or Russian businesses.[36] As the preservation of the status quo clearly did not suit Russian economic reformers, privatization of the industry in 1994–1995 went on the agenda. However, the proposal of a large-scale transfer of industrial assets (especially in the oil and gas sector) under the control of foreign capital was greatly unpopular among the Russian society, and during competitive elections it could have been used by the left-wing opposition to accuse the government of "selling the Motherland to the West." In its turn, Russian business, which had just found its feet, was not interested in powerful foreign competitors coming into the country, and so lobbied for restrictions for participation of foreign capital in privatization of a number of attractive assets, including the oil and gas industry.[37] For their part, the political instability and weakness of the Russian state in the 1990s was not attractive for foreign investors, who did not strive for a mass invasion into the Russian market, limiting themselves to several projects for development of new fields, and lobbying their interests in Russian parliament through passing laws on agreements on production sharing laws and subsoil use laws. Also, the high dependence of the Russian economy on oil and gas export meant that the transfer of the major assets of the oil industry to the control of foreign businesses was rather unlikely.[38]

It is difficult to say what transformation paths the oil and gas industry in Russia could have taken, but under conditions of deep recession, high political uncertainty, and a harsh battle for power during a severe fiscal crisis, the Russian government used the mechanism of privatization in order to receive political and financial support from emerging Russian business. In 1995, the first deputy prime minister at the time, Anatoly Chubais, proposed the project of the "loan-for-shares deals," which was implemented in 1995–1996. The idea was that the government gave large stakes of some major enterprises in the oil, metallurgy, and other industries as a loan to several consciously selected Russian banks in exchange for their direct cash payments, which the government could use at its discretion. Formally, the government had the right to buy the shares back over the course of a year after the deal; otherwise, the shares would become the property of the bankers (this is what happened in the end). This practically meant that the Russian authorities gave control over a number of major assets (including oil) to arbitrarily selected Russian businessmen who were closely connected with them, and on their part, besides payment of money, also guaranteed the government their political support on the eve of the presidential elections scheduled for summer 1996. In particular, the Tyumen Oil company went under the control of Alfa Bank headed by Mikhail Fridman, the oil company Yukos was taken over by Menatep Bank headed by Mikhail Khodorkovsky, and Sibneft was acquired by the mutisectoral holding controlled by Boris Berezovsky.[39]

The "loan-for-shares deals" were harshly criticized from a number of positions. First, the amount of money that was paid to the Russian government was (according to a number of expert assessments) much lower than the market prices of the assets, if they had been sold on the open market in auctions. Second, the government arbitrarily used the money received from bankers in the loan-for-shares deals during the period before the presidential elections of 1996 to cover debts on pensions and salaries, and for targeted social payments. Some observers argue that these payments on debts played a considerable role in the successful reelection bid of then Russian president Boris Yeltsin over his Communist rival Gennadii Zyuganov.[40] Third, and finally, the government, by giving Russian big business major economic privileges in the wake of privatization, found itself in considerable political dependence on major businessmen (the "oligarchs"). This dependence increased during the presidential elections of 1996. Soon after the elections, a number of oligarchs and their protégés received high government positions as part of the "spoils," which opened up new opportunities for further rent-seeking.[41] Attempts by a number of economic reformers in the Russian government (including Chubais) to combat this process were not very successful: by the end of 1997 they suffered a defeat in the conflict with the oligarchs.[42] This trend gave many grounds for major concerns about "state capture" by big business in Russia, which began to have a key influence on the key political and economic decisions at the level of top leadership of the country.[43] Essentially, the state capture by big business was merely considered as an extreme manifestation of rent-seeking on the scale of Russia as a whole—unlike those of the "red directors," whose rent-seeking was rather decentralized and covered the scale of several enterprises and/or regions.[44]

Although the political consequences of the loan-for-shares deals were assessed very negatively from the viewpoint of interactions of the Russian state and big business, their consequences for the oil industry were not so straightforward. In particular, the coming of new private owners into the sector and their control over the major oil companies made it possible not only to overcome the phenomenon of red directors and significantly improve the quality of corporate governance, but also to attract investments to the industry, thus overcoming the protracted decline in production.[45] When they came to the oil business, the oligarchs were soon forced to put their efforts into a more efficient use of the assets they had received from the state. In terms proposed by Mancur Olson, one might say that after the loan-for-shares deals, the Russian oligarchs began to turn from the role of "roving bandits" that they played in the early 1990s to the role of "stationary bandits,"[46] like the American robber barons at the beginning of the twentieth century. In any case, if for the oligarchs, this process, which was of a centralized nationwide nature, took several years, if decentralized control over assets in the industry had stayed in the hands of the red directors and/or regional leaders, it could probably have taken decades.

The period of state capture by big business in Russia proved to be rather short-lived. After the financial crisis of 1998, the influence of big business on the government's decision-making was broken,[47] and the strengthening of the coercive capacity of the Russian state, at the time when power was transferred from Boris Yeltsin to his successor Vladimir Putin in late 1999 and early 2000, dealt a severe blow to the oligarchs. In summer 2000, at a private meeting with the oligarchs at his country residence, Putin made big business an informal "offer one can't refuse," which was unofficially dubbed the "barbeque agreement." The idea was that the state would not review property rights and would maintain "equal distance" toward the oligarchs, while big business would have to keep its loyalty toward the authorities and not interfere in the process of political decision-making.[48] The few oligarchs (including Boris Berezovsky) who did not agree with the conditions of this informal agreement soon lost their assets and were forced to leave Russia[49]; the remaining representatives of big business in Russia simply had no choice in this situation.

To a certain degree, the barbeque agreement marked a new stage in relationships of big politics and big business in Russia, which proved to be close to the model of mutual hostages. On the one hand, the Russian state took a step toward the oligarchs in promoting more favorable conditions for business. In particular, the Russian authorities strived to attract foreign investments in the oil industry (an example of which was the establishment of the joint company TNK with British Petroleum, TNK-BP), and improve tax legislation. During the tax reform of 2000–2001, the state found a compromise with the interests of big business, agreeing with representatives of oil companies on the rates and procedures for payment of corporate taxes, including a subsoil use tax.[50] On the other hand, big business, although it did not stop lobbying its interests in the Russian parliament and in regional legislatures, could not impose its proposals to the Russian state, as it did in the period of 1996–1998, and accepted the "rules of the game" developed by political leadership of the country. Furthermore, big business actively supported a number of steps by President Putin, including the policy of recentralization of the state, which destroyed local barriers on the development of business, and was directed toward the formation of a common national Russian market.[51] The president and the government of Russia recognized major associations of Russian entrepreneurs as their official junior partners in a framework of what appeared to be a corporatist model of interaction between the state and interest groups in Russia.[52] According to assessments of several commentators, this balance of forces between the state and big business had a favorable effect in the period 2000–2003, both on the policy of economic reforms and on the preservation of political pluralism in Russia.[53]

However, the equilibrium of mutual hostages in the period of 2000–2003 in Russia was only caused by ad hoc arrangements, not structure-induced, let alone on formal institutional guarantees.[54] As the barbeque agreement was only a tacit deal, its conditions could easily be revised unilaterally if the political and economic situation in Russia changed.[55] The Russian authorities had strong incentives for such revisions affected by both political and economic factors. In economic terms, the rapid growth of world oil prices and the increase of revenues from resource rent in the 2000s (especially compared with the period of the 1990s) against the background of the significant increase in the coercive capacity of the Russian state pushed the Russian authorities to a statist economic policy[56] and to a reexamination of the formal and informal rules of the game in relations with big business (including in the oil and gas sector). In terms of politics, this was the period when Russia faced the major trend toward authoritarian rule, which was accompanied by restrictions on political competition and an increase in the Kremlin's monopoly. All meaningful political actors—regional elites, media, and the parliament, where the progovernment party United Russia dominated—came under the Kremlin's control by 2003.[57] Under these conditions, the further extension of the political monopoly of the Kremlin on the economic arena became the logical next step of the Russian authorities, especially as the idea of revising the outcomes of privatization and restoring the predominance of state ownership also had significant support in Russian society.[58] A major revision of property rights in this sense looked like a very logical decision from the viewpoint of big politics, especially in the wake of the parliamentary elections campaign of 2003.

On 25 October 2003, the major owner and CEO of the major Russian oil company Yukos, Mikhail Khodorkovsky, was arrested on charges of tax evasion and later given a long sentence in jail. According to a number of observers, the basic reasons for his arrest were merely of a political nature. They were connected with Khodorkovsky's aspiration to lobby his interests in parliament, and his support of various parties at elections, in the lists of which his protégés were included; with his intentions to sell his business, Yukos, to American oil companies (possible buyers named were Chevron and Conoco Phillips); and his plans to actively participate in politics himself.[59] Khodorkovsky's arrest soon resulted in the collapse of Yukos—the key stakes of the company were sold to pay off its debts. At the same time, the Russian authorities, using nontransparent legal mechanisms and acting through dummy intermediaries, ensured the transfer of major assets of producing and processing enterprises belonging to Yukos to the control of the state oil company Rosneft, where the board of directors was headed by Putin's close ally Igor Sechin. At the same time, the assets of Yukos were acquired by Rosneft at a price that was much lower than market price.[60]

Anders Aslund and Vadim Volkov, analyzing the fate of the Russian oligarchs at the beginning of the twenty-first century in comparison with the American robber barons in the early twentieth century, noted the fundamental differences in the logic of crony capitalism in the Russian case. As a result of the Yukos affair, the outcome of the conflict between big business and the Russian state was not just the bankruptcy and subsequent decay of the oligarchs initiated by the authorities (as it was in the case of Standard Oil in the United States, for example), but a fundamental revision of property rights that was launched in subsequent years.[61] In fact, the Yukos affair was a turning point in relationships between the Russian state and big business, marking a major move from the temporary balance of mutual hostages to the policy of business capture by the Russian state, and a transfer (or return) of the oil industry to the model of state ownership with control, and the further establishment of the predatory state in Russia.

Episode 3: The Return of the Predatory State

The Yukos affair changed the configuration of economic actors in the Russian oil and gas industry, and in other sectors, in at least two ways. First, the Yukos affair opened the door for large-scale revision of property rights in the oil industry. In the atmosphere of the boom of oil prices in the period of 2004–2008, following the de facto nationalization of Yukos, the Russian state began to attack other assets owned by both Russian private capital and foreign businesses.[62] In 2006, the authorities increased pressure on the international Sakhalin-2 project on development of oil fields in the Sakhalin, which involved Shell and Japanese companies. Foreign companies were charged with violating Russian environmental legislation, and then they were forced to leave the project and sell their shares in this project to Gazprom subsidiaries. In 2005, Gazprom acquired major stakes in Sibneft oil company, which was previously under the control of Roman Abramovich, a businessman close to the Kremlin (the new subsidiary of Gazprom, Gazpromneft, became the third largest oil company in Russia). The price for these assets ($13.7 billion), according to many assessments, was much higher than their market value.[63] In 2006–2007, the authorities' attack on the private Russian company Russneft (its head Mikhail Gutseriev, like Khodorkovsky, was charged with tax evasion) finished only after Gutseriev's forced emigration to Great Britain. He sold stakes in the company to subsidiaries of Oleg Deripaska, a businessman close to the Kremlin.[64] Finally, in 2008 a corporate conflict was provoked inside the joint TNK-BP company, which led to personnel changes of top managers representing interests of British stakeholders, although the transfer of its assets under the control of Russian owners did not happen (at least as yet). On the whole, one might consider an increasing tendency since the Yukos affair to expropriate property in the oil industry, and transfer its assets to the control of state companies or private businesses connected with the Russian authorities, which serves as a clear indicator of business capture by the predatory state.

Second, at the same time of the growth of Russia's dependence on big oil (i.e., the export of oil and gas) and the increase in the amount of the resource rent in the 2000s (and especially after the Yukos affair), a further decline in quality of institutions continued in Russia. It was reflected in the systematic decline in indicators of Russia in international comparisons of governance and the rule of law,[65] and led to nontransparency of governance (both state and corporate governance), an increase of corruption, and the rise of inefficient expenditures, including and above all in the oil and gas sector.[66] In the mid-2000s, the previously unknown firm Gunvor, registered in Switzerland and led by a former KGB colleague of Putin, Gennady Timchenko, joined the list of major international oil traders. According to certain analysts, Gunvor delivered up to 40 percent of oil export from Russia to the world market, primarily by the state companies Rosneft and Gazpromneft; at the same time the information of the company itself and its ownership structure remains nontransparent.[67] During these years, there was a drastic decline in the economic indicators of the Russian gas monopoly, Gazprom. Against the background of a swift growth of operational expenses of the company (they increased by 3.9 times from 2000 to 2007), its debts increased, which in 2007 came to 66 percent of the annual turnover of Gazprom (for the period from 2000 to 2007, their amount grew by 4.6 times). According to the former deputy energy minister of Russia, Vladimir Milov, the cause of these developments was primarily the unjustified expenses of Gazprom in acquiring major assets in the oil industry and energy sector (both within the country and abroad) and other industries, and also the purchase of gas from producers from Central Asia and Kazakhstan.[68] At the same time, a number of assets were removed from Gazprom's control and transferred to persons and companies with close personal ties with Putin. As a result, the production of gas by Gazprom and its deliveries to the domestic market in the 2000s in fact just slightly increased, while investments into production were clearly insufficient.[69] Thus, the large-scale rise of the presence of the Russian state in the oil and gas industry under conditions of a predatory state led to a decline of the efficiency of big business, and its transformation into a "cash cow" for businessmen and officials connected with the authorities.[70]

Besides the domestic consequences, the rise of the Russian predatory state in the oil and gas industry also had foreign policy and international trade implications. The dominance of Russian gas and energy companies in a number of post-Soviet states was used as a mechanism of a carrot and stick in Russia's relations with neighbors such as Ukraine and Belarus, for a long time after the collapse of the Soviet Union; the economies of these countries were heavily subsidized by Russia due to reduced prices on gas. In their turn, the governments of these countries, thanks to their transit position for deliveries of Russian gas to Europe, could take resource rent, and Ukraine and Belarus merely acted as rentier states.[71] After the Ukrainian "orange revolution" of 2004, Gazprom and the Russian government that stood behind it unilaterally increased the cost of gas for Ukraine, attempting to put pressure on the regime, on the one hand, and receive control over the major transit gas pipelines in Ukraine, on the other. When these attempts failed, in early 2006 Gazprom turned off the gas supply to Ukrainian consumers, at the same time leaving European countries without gas, which had been delivered by gas pipelines passing through Ukrainian territory.[72] The conflict was resolved by establishment of a special intermediary company Rosukrenergo, under the control of Gazprom and Ukrainian businessmen connected with the Ukrainian authorities (this mechanism was severely criticized for lack of transparency).[73] When during the severe financial crisis of 2008–2009 the Ukrainian government once more proved unable to pay for gas supply, Gazprom once more resorted to turning off pipelines, provoking a new conflict with Ukraine. Although in the end the conditions for delivery and payment of gas were agreed upon, and intermediaries were removed from the deal, Gazprom was not able to resolve the problem of transit on its own conditions.[74] Similarly, Gazprom tried to put pressure on Belarus on several occasions, using the threat of raising the price of gas as a tool to gain control over gas pipelines on its territory, but these steps (at least, as yet) have not achieved their goal.[75] It is not surprising that Gazprom has noticeably complicated relations between Russia and a number of European countries, for which Russia's gas supply have key significance. The attempts made in recent years by the Russian authorities to review priorities of the export of natural resources and shift the major foreign oil and gas markets from Europe to China have also had a mixed reaction—both because of the conditions for export of oil to the Chinese market, which are rather disadvantageous for Russia, and because of the political risks involved with this turn in foreign policy and international trade.[76]

Despite to the swift expansion of the Russian state into the oil and gas sector in the 2000s, the problems of the industry itself have only deepened. The crucial exhaustion of many fields and/or increasing production costs in the sector caused a major decline in production of oil in early 2008, which in many ways resembled a similar crisis of the 1980s.[77] At Gazpromneft alone, the average daily production of oil in 2005–2008 declined by 11.5 percent.[78] As the economy requires the rise of production and deliveries of oil and gas, the prospects of a shortage of supply became increasingly real.[79] Besides the inefficiency of corporate governance, especially in state-owned companies, the strategic planning in the sector also contributed to these developments. Russian authorities and both state-owned and private oil and gas companies, in striving for short-term rents, did not invest enough resources in projects that aimed toward long-term returns. As in the Soviet period, the extensive use of old fields and major increase of the export of oil and gas were not backed up by technological innovations directed toward increasing the output of oil fields and oil processing, and purchases of expensive foreign equipment only partially solve the problems of the industry.[80] In its turn, this short-term planning was a forced choice for big business: in many ways it was caused by the low quality of institutions and the "uncertainty about the continuity of rules of the game" under conditions of the Russian predatory state.[81]

The international financial crisis of 2008–2009, which was accompanied by a severe decline in world oil prices and in production, dealt a considerable blow to the Russian oil and gas sector, and forced the Russian authorities and big business to think about changing their policies. In 2009, the Russian authorities announced a proposal to involve foreign investments in production and processing of oil and gas on conditions that were advantageous for investors, and also announced their intentions for the planned privatization of major oil companies.[82] However, there are grounds to doubt these statements: many observers believe that significant changes of the relationships between the Russian authorities and big business in general and the oil and gas industry in particular are unlikely at the moment. Indeed, despite the crisis (or even due to it), Russian oil and gas companies, above all state-owned companies, have remained nontransparent, not abandoning unjustifiably high salaries and bonuses for their top managers, or a series of ambitious investment projects. A typical example of this approach was the decision officially adopted in 2009, despite societal protests, to launch the construction project of the Okhta-Center in St. Petersburg—a new large-scale office complex of Gazprom, which according to the planners will be crowned by a tower over 400 meters high.[83]

To summarize, one might conclude that relationships between the Russian state and big business over the last decades have resembled pendulum-like swings. From the equilibrium of mutual hostages between the state and oil and gas enterprises of the Soviet period, in the late 1980s and early 1990s this pendulum began to move toward rent-seeking, reaching the extreme point of state capture in 1996–1998. In 2000, the pendulum began to swing back toward a strengthening position of the state, and passing the point of equilibrium of mutual hostages; from 2003 to 2004, after the Yukos affair, this pendulum moved toward a predatory state, where it remains to this day. The current state of relationships between the Russian state and big business in the oil and gas sector may be assessed as low-level equilibrium. But how stable is this equilibrium, and what are the possible factors for its changes?

POLITICAL INSTITUTIONS, BIG OIL, AND THE RUSSIAN STATE: A VICIOUS CIRCLE?

The pendulum-like swings in relationships between the Russian state and big business in many ways coincide with the dynamic of changes not only of the policies of the Russian authorities, but also the political institutions and the political regime in general.[84] In fact, the Soviet period was the heyday of a statist economic policy, stable political monopoly of the party-state, and the Communist authoritarian regime. In the 1990s, with the low world oil prices, the collapse of the former economic and political system gave rise to attempts of liberal economic reforms[85] and establishment of unstable transitional political institutions,[86] supporting "pluralism by default," and spontaneous emergence of competition of political and economic actors.[87] These changes, which in many ways accompanied the state capture of big business, were justly criticized as inconsistent and inefficient, but today they may rather be evaluated as the protracted severe growing pains of Russian political and economic reforms. However, the medicine against these growing pains in the 2000s caused severe chronic diseases in Russian political and economic developments, including pathologies in the oil and gas sector.[88] With the high world oil prices, a return to statist economic policy, political monopolism, and authoritarian rule in the short-term perspective looked self-enforcing. And so far, after the 2008–2009 world economic crisis, no major domestic and international challenges that undermined the existing status quo in this respect are observed.

Thus, the Russian experience allows us to propose that not only the resource curse (i.e., big oil) can have a negative influence on big business and big politics, but in its turn, big politics may affect this linkage, also undermining the performance of big business. Inefficient political regimes and their institutions such as the Soviet authoritarianism of the 1970s and 1980s, and Russian authoritarianism of the 2000s, contributed to an inefficient development of the country, and besides the resource curse, impose major barriers to economic and political reforms. Thus, big oil, big politics, and big business in the Russian case form a vicious circle, although testing this proposal in the comparative perspective lies outside the scope of this chapter.

Can this vicious circle of inefficient authoritarian institutions in Russia be broken, and if so, how will their possible changes influence the economic development of the country under conditions of the resource curse? Although in the short-term perspective, the chances for these changes are not very high, and Russia's dependence on the export of oil and gas are unlikely to decline in the foreseeable future, the country is not doomed to preserve the model of a predatory state forever. With the instability of world oil prices, and/or an exhaustion of technological and investment opportunities of increasing production in the oil and gas industry, Russia may, like the Soviet Union after 1985–1986, face a drastic reduction in resource rent.[89] In this case, it is more likely that the leaders of the country will be forced (as in the late Soviet period) not only to review economic policy in favor of greater liberalization, but also launch considerable institutional changes, including political liberalization. Also, the high level of socioeconomic inequality in Russia provokes the escalation of conflicts on the redistribution of the resource rent. A comparative cross-national study by Thad Dunning shows that these conflicts undermine the stability of political institutions, both democratic and authoritarian,[90] and in certain circumstances they may enable major economic policy shifts, and change the nature of relationships between the state and big business in various states and nations, including Russia.[91] Although there are no grounds to claim that a change of the current model of relationships between the Russian state and big business will inevitably enable greater efficiency of politics, policy, and governance, preserving the current status quo of the predatory state will probably lead Russia to a path of stagnation and subsequent decay. Once a predatory state has arisen, both in Russia and in other countries, it cannot be improved, it can only be destroyed, and often with considerable losses. The future will show whether Russia will be capable of diverging from the trajectory of the predatory state, avoiding losses that are not compatible with its future.

NOTES

1. Jeffrey Sachs and Andrew Warner, "Natural Resource Abundance and Economic Growth," *NBER Working Papers*, no. 5398 (1995); Terry Lynn Karl, *The Paradox of Plenty: Oil Booms and Petro-States* (Berkeley, Calif.:

University of California Press, 1997); Michael Ross, "The Political Economy of the Resource Curse," *World Politics*, 51, no. 2 (1999), 297–322; Michael Ross, "Does Oil Hinder Democracy?" *World Politics*, 53, no. 2 (2001), 325–61; Michael Ross, "How Does Natural Resource Wealth Influence Civil Wars," *International Organizations*, 58, no. 1 (2004), 35–67; Thad Dunning, *Crude Democracy: Natural Resource Wealth and Political Regimes* (New York: Cambridge University Press, 2008); Georgy Egorov, Sergei Guriev, and Konstantin Sonin, "Why Resource-Poor Dictators Allow Freer Media: A Theory and Evidence from Panel Data," *American Political Science Review*, 103, no. 4 (2009), 645–68.

2. Karl, *The Paradox of Plenty*; Dunning, *Crude Democracy*; see also chapter 4 in this volume.

3. Karl, *The Paradox of Plenty*, 74.

4. M. Steven Fish, *Democracy Derailed in Russia: The Failure of Open Politics* (New York: Cambridge University Press, 2005), 114–38; William Tompson, "The Political Implications of Russia's Resource-Based Economy," *Post-Soviet Affairs*, 21, no. 4 (2005), 335–59.

5. Joel Hellman, "Winners Take All: The Politics of Partial Reforms in Post-Communist Transitions," *World Politics*, 50, no. 2 (1998), 203–34; Sergei Peregudov, Natalia Lapina, and Irina Semenenko, *Gruppy Interesov i Rossiiskoe Gosudarstvo* (Moscow: Editorial URSS, 1999); Peter Rutland, ed., *Business and the State in Contemporary Russia* (Boulder, Colo.: Westview, 2001); Timothy Frye, "Capture or Exchange? Business Lobbying in Russia," *Europe-Asia Studies*, 54, no. 7 (2002), 1017–36; Andrei Yakovlev, "The Evolution of Business-State Interaction in Russia: From State Capture to Business Capture?" *Europe-Asia Studies*, 58, no. 7 (2006), 1033–56; Andrew Barnes, *Owning Russia: The Struggle over Factories, Farms, and Power* (Ithaca, N.Y.: Cornell University Press, 2006).

6. Thane Gustafson, *Capitalism, Russian Style* (New York: Cambridge University Press, 1999); Chrystia Freeland, *Sale of the Century: Russia's Wild Rule from Communism to Capitalism* (New York: Crown Publishers, 2000); David Hoffman, *Oligarchs: Wealth and Power in the New Russia* (New York: Public Affairs Books, 2002); Anders Aslund, *Russia's Capitalist Revolution: Why Market Reforms Succeeded and Democracy Failed* (Washington, D.C.: Peterson Institute for International Economics, 2007).

7. David Lane, ed., *The Political Economy of Russian Oil* (Lanham, Md.: Rowman and Littlefield, 1999); Younkyoo Kim, *Resource Curse in a Post-Communist Regime: Russia in Comparative Perspective* (Burlington, Vt.: Ashgate, 2003); Rudiger Ahrend, "Can Russia Break the 'Resource Curse'?" *Eurasian Geography and Economics*, 46, no. 8 (2005), 584–609; Clifford Gaddy and Barry Ickes, "Resource Rent and the Russian Economy," *Eurasian Geography and Economics*, 46, no. 8 (2005), 559–83; Peter Rutland, "Putin's Economic Record: Is the Oil Boom Sustainable?" *Europe-Asia Studies*, 60, no. 6 (2008), 1051–72.

8. Steven Fortescue, *Russia's Oil Barons and Metal Magnates; Oligarchs and the State in Transition* (New York: Palgrave Macmillan, 2007); Marshall

Goldman, *Petrostate: Putin, Power, and the New Russia* (New York: Oxford University Press, 2008); Richard Sakwa, *The Quality of Freedom: Khodorkovsky, Putin, and the Yukos Affair* (New York: Oxford University Press, 2009).

9. Pauline Jones Luong and Erika Weinthal, "Rethinking the Resource Curse: Ownership Structure, Institutional Capacity, and Domestic Constraints," *Annual Review of Political Science*, 9 (2006), 241–63; Pauline Jones Luong and Erika Weinthal, "Combating the Resource Curse: An Alternative Solution to Managing Mineral Wealth," *Perspectives on Politics*, 4, no. 1 (2006), 35–53.

10. David Kang, *Crony Capitalism: Corruption and Development in South Korea and the Philippines* (New York: Cambridge University Press, 2002).

11. Jones Luong and Weinthal, "Rethinking the Resource Curse."

12. Kang, *Crony Capitalism*, 12–18.

13. Kang, *Crony Capitalism*, 151–53.

14. Jones Luong and Weinthal, "Rethinking the Resource Curse," 246–50.

15. Jones Luong and Weinthal, "Rethinking the Resource Curse," 256–57.

16. Thane Gustafson, *Crisis Amid Plenty: The Politics of Soviet Energy under Brezhnev and Gorbachev* (Princeton, N.J.: Princeton University Press, 1989); Maria Slavkina, *Triumf i Tragediya: Razvitie Neftegazovogo Kompleksa SSSR v 1960–1980-e Gody* (Moscow: Nauka, 2002); Yegor Gaidar, *Gibel' Imperii: Uroki Dlya Sovremennoi Rossii* (Moscow: ROSSPEN, 2006), 179–96; see also Yegor Gaidar, *Collapse of an Empire: Lessons for Modern Russia* (Washington, D.C.: Brookings Institution Press, 2007).

17. Steven Solnick, *Stealing the State: Control and Collapse in Soviet Institutions* (Cambridge, Mass.: Harvard University Press, 1998); Andrei Shleifer and Daniel Treisman, *Without a Map: Political Tactics and Economic Reform in Russia* (Cambridge, Mass.: MIT Press, 2000).

18. Hellman, "Winners Take All"; Freeland, *Sale of the Century*; Hoffman, *Oligarchs*.

19. Andrei Zudin, "Neokorporativizm v Rossii (Gosudarstvo i Biznes Pri Vladimire Putine)," *Pro et Contra*, 6, no. 4 (2001), 171–98; Pauline Jones Luong and Erika Weinthal, "Contra Coercion: Russian Tax Reform, Exogenous Shocks, and Negotiated Institutional Changes," *American Political Science Review*, 98, no. 1 (2004), 139–52.

20. William Tompson, "Putting Yukos in Perspective," *Post-Soviet Affairs*, 21, no. 2 (2005), 159–81; Yakovlev, "The Evolution of Business-State Interaction in Russia"; Vadim Volkov, "Standard Oil and Yukos in the Context of Early Capitalism in the United States and Russia," *Demokratizatsiya: The Journal of Post-Soviet Democratization*, 16, no. 3 (2008), 240–64.

21. Anna Bessonova, *Neftedobycha v Rossii: Gosudarstvennaya Politika i Innovatsionnye Perspektivy* (Moscow: Carnegie Moscow Center, 2009), www.carnegie.ru/ru/pubs/workpapers/WP_anna_bessonova.pdf (accessed 10 October 2009), 6.

22. Peter Rutland, *The Myth of the Plan: Lessons from Soviet Planning Experience* (London: Hutchinson, 1985); Vitalii Naishul', "Vysshaya i Posled-

nyaya Stadiya Sotsializma," Tat'yana Notkina, ed., *Pogruzhenie v Tryasinu* (Moscow: Progress, 1991), 31–62.

23. Gordon Skilling and Franklyn Griffits, eds., *Interest Groups in Soviet Politics* (Princeton, N.J.: Princeton University Press, 1971); Peregudov, Lapina, and Semenenko, *Gruppy Interesov i Rossiiskoe Gosudarstvo*, 44–69.

24. Bessonova, *Neftedobycha v Rossii*, 6–9; Goldman, *Petrostate*, 39–43.

25. Peter Rutland, *The Politics of Economic Stagnation in the Soviet Union: The Role of Local Party Organs in Economic Management* (New York: Cambridge University Press, 1993), 91–108.

26. Gaidar, *Gibel' Imperii*, 181.

27. Gustafson, *Crisis Amid Plenty*, 53; Gaidar, *Gibel' Imperii*, 190–96.

28. Anders Aslund, *How Russia Became a Market Economy* (Washington, D.C.: Brookings Institution Press, 1995), chap. 2; Anders Aslund, "'Reform' vs. 'Rent-Seeking' in Russia's Economic Transformation," *Transition*, 2, no. 2 (1996), 12–16; Peregudov, Lapina, and Semenenko, *Gruppy Interesov i Rossiiskoe Gosudarstvo*, 69–75, 87–91.

29. Kim, *The Resource Curse*, 76–91; Yakov Pappe and Yana Galukhina, *Rossiiskii krupnyi biznes: pervye 15 let. Ekonomicheskaya khronika 1993–2008* (Moscow: State University—Higher School of Economics, 2009), 79–86.

30. Kim, *The Resource Curse*, 91–92.

31. Raj M. Desai and Yitzhak Goldberg, *The Vicious Circles of Control: Regional Governments and Insiders in Russia's Privatized Enterprises* (Washington, D.C.: World Bank, mimeo, 1999), siteresources.worldbank.org/INTWBIGOVANTCOR/Resources/wps2287.pdf (accessed 10 October 2009).

32. Aslund, "'Reform' vs. 'Rent-Seeking.'"

33. Boris Nemtsov and Vladimir Milov, *Putin i "Gazprom": Nezavisimyi Ekspetrnyi Doklad* (Moscow, 2008), 7, www.milov.info/cp/wp-content/uploads/2008/10/broshura_gazprom_1.pdf (accessed 10 October 2009).

34. Hillary Appel, *A New Capitalist Order: Ideology and Privatization in Russia and Eastern Europe* (Pittsburgh, Pa.: University of Pittsburgh Press, 2004).

35. Michael McFaul, "State Power, Institutional Change, and the Politics of Privatization in Russia," *World Politics*, 47, no. 2 (1995), 210–43.

36. Aslund, *How Russia Became a Market Economy*, chapter 7.

37. Freeland, *Sale of the Century*.

38. Vladimir Milov, Sovremennaya Situyatsiya v Rossii: Politika, Ekonomika, Budushchee: Stenogramma Seminara "Vechera v Evropeiskom" (St. Petersburg: European University at St. Petersburg, 28 November 2008), 15–16, 27, www.eu.spb.ru/images/pss_dep/vech_v_evro_281108.doc (accessed 10 October 2009).

39. Freeland, *Sale of the Century*; Hoffman, *Oligarchs*; Kim, *The Resource Curse*, 93–94.

40. Daniel Treisman, "Why Yeltsin Won: A Russian Tammany Hall," *Foreign Affairs*, 75, no. 5 (1996), 64–75; Michael McFaul, *Russia's 1996 Presidential Elections: The End of Polarized Politics?* (Stanford, Calif.: Hoover Institution Press, 1997).

41. Freeland, *Sale of the Century*; Paul Khlebnikov, *Godfather of the Kremlin: Boris Berezovsky and the Looting of Russia* (New York: Harvest Books, 2001); Hoffman, *Oligarchs*.

42. Russell Bova, "Democratization and the Crisis of the Russian State," in Gordon Smith, ed., *State-Building in Russia: The Yeltsin's Legacy and the Challenge of the Future* (Armonk, N.Y.: M. E. Sharpe, 1999), 17–40.

43. Hellman, "Winners Take All."

44. Desai and Goldberg, *The Vicious Circles*; Yakov Pappe, "Treugol'nik Sobstvennikov v Rossiiskoi Regional'noi Promyshlennosti," in Vladimir Klimanov and Natalia Zubarevich, eds., *Politika i Ekonomika v Regional'nom Izmerenii* (Moscow and St. Petersburg: Letnii Sad, 2000), 109–20.

45. Kim, *The Resource Curse*, 94–102; Valery Kryukov, "Adjustment to Change: The Case of the Oil and Gas Industry," Stefanie Harter and Gerald Easter, eds., *Shaping the Economic Space in Russia* (Burlington, Vt.: Ashgate, 2000), 113, 118–20.

46. Mancur Olson, "Dictatorship, Democracy, and Development," *American Political Science Review*, 87, no. 3 (1993), 567–76.

47. Hans-Henning Schroeder, "The 'Oligarchs': A Force to Reckon With?" in Stefanie Harter and Gerald Easter, eds., *Shaping the Economic Space in Russia* (Burlington, Vt.: Ashgate, 2000), 50–64; Pappe and Galukhina, *Rossiiski krupnyi biznes*, 90–92.

48. Lilia Shevtsova, *Putin's Russia* (Washington, D.C.: Carnegie Endowment for International Peace, 2003), chapter 4.

49. Khlebnikov, *Godfather of the Kremlin*; Hoffman, *Oligarchs*, chapter 6.

50. Jones Luong and Weinthal, "Contra Coercion"; Jones Luong and Weinthal, "Combating the Resource Curse."

51. Nataliya Zubarevich, "Prishel, Uvidel, Pobedil? Krupnyi Biznes i Regional'naya Vlast'," *Pro et Contra*, 7, no. 1 (2002), 107–20.

52. Zudin, "Neokorporativizm v Rossii."

53. Shevtsova, *Putin's Russia*; Jones Luong and Weinthal, "Contra Coercion"; William Tompson, "Putin and the 'Oligarchs': A Two-Sided Commitment Problem," in Alex Pravda, ed., *Leading Russia: Putin in Perspective* (New York: Oxford University Press, 2005), 179–203.

54. Philip Hanson and Elizabeth Teague, "Big Business and the State in Russia," *Europe-Asia Studies*, 57, no. 5 (2005), 657–80; Tompson, "Putin and the 'Oligarchs'"; Volkov, "Standard Oil and Yukos."

55. Philip Hanson, "Observations on the Costs of Yukos Affair to Russia," *Eurasian Geography and Economics*, 46, no. 7 (2005), 481–94.

56. Fish, *Democracy Derailed in Russia*, 139–92.

57. Shevtsova, *Putin's Russia*; Peter Baker and Susan Glasser, *Kremlin's Rising: Vladimir Putin's Russia and the End of Revolution* (New York: Scribner, 2005); Fish, *Democracy Derailed in Russia*; Vladimir Gel'man, ed. *Tretii elektoral'nyi tsikl v Rossii, 2003–2004* (St. Petersburg: European University at St. Petersburg Press, 2007).

58. See chapter 4 in this volume.

59. Tompson, "Putting Yukos in Perspective"; Aslund, *Russia's Capitalist Revolution*; Goldman, *Petrostate*; Volkov, "Standard Oil and Yukos"; Pappe and Galukhina, *Rossiiski krupnyi biznes*, 197–226.

60. Nina Pusenkova, "'Rosneft' kak zerkalo russkoi evolyutsii," *Pro et Contra*, 10, no. 2–3 (2006), 91–104.

61. Anders Aslund, "Comparative Oligarchy: Russia, Ukraine, and the United States," *CASE Network Studies and Analyses*, no. 296 (2005), papers.ssrn.com/sol3/papers.cfm?abstract_id=1441910; Volkov, "Standard Oil and Yukos."

62. Philip Hanson, "The Resistible Rise of State Control in the Russian Oil Industry," *Eurasian Geography and Economics*, 50, no. 1 (2009), 14–27.

63. Nemtsov and Milov, *Putin i "Gazprom,"* 22–23.

64. Hanson, "The Resistible Rise," 17–18.

65. *Governance Matters 2009. Worldwide Governance Indicators, 1996–2008*, info.worldbank.org/governance/wgi/index.asp (accessed 10 October 2009); see also chapter 4 in this volume.

66. Nemtsov and Milov, *Putin i "Gazprom."*

67. Catherine Belton and Neil Buckley, "On the Offensive: How Gunvor Rose to the Top of Russian Oil Trading," *Financial Times*, 14 May 2008.

68. Nemtsov and Milov, *Putin i "Gazprom,"* 51–52.

69. Jonathan Stern, *The Future of Russian Gas and Gazprom* (Oxford: Oxford University Press, 2005); Tat'yana Mitrova and Yakov Pappe, "'Gazprom': ot Bol'shoi Truby k Bol'shomu Biznesu," *Pro et Contra*, 10, no. 2–3 (2006), 73–85; Vladimir Volkov, "'Gazprom': Riskovannaya Strategiya," *Pro et Contra*, 10, no. 2–3 (2006), 86–90.

70. Hanson, "The Resistible Rise."

71. Rawi Abdelal, "Interpreting Interdependence: National Security and the Energy Trade of Russia, Ukraine, and Belarus," in Robert Legvold and Celeste Wallander, eds., *Swords and Sustenance: The Economics of Security in Belarus and Ukraine* (Cambridge, Mass.: MIT Press, 2004), 104–27.

72. Jonathan Stern, "Natural Gas Security Problems in Europe: The Russian-Ukrainian Crisis of 2006," *Asia-Pacific Review*, 13, no. 1 (2006), 32–59.

73. Nemtsov and Milov, *Putin i "Gazprom."*

74. Simon Pirani, Jonathan Stern, and Katja Yafimava, *The Russo-Ukrainian Gas Dispute of 2009: A Comprehensive Assessment* (Oxford: Oxford Institute for Energy Studies, 2009), www.oxfordenergy.org/pdfs/ng27.pdf (accessed 10 October 2009).

75. Chloe Bruce, *Fraternal Friction or Fraternal Fiction? The Gas Factor in Russian-Belarusian Relations* (Oxford: Oxford Institute for Energy Studies, 2005), www.oxfordenergy.org/pdfs/NG8.pdf (accessed 10 October 2009); David Marples, "Is the Russia–Belarus Union Obsolete?" *Problems of Post-Communism*, 55, no. 1 (2008), 25–35.

76. Dmitrii Travin, "Modernizatsiya Obshchestva i Vostochnaya Ugroza Rossii," *European University at St. Petersburg, M-Center Working Papers*, no. 3 (2009), www.eu.spb.ru/images/M_center/travin_modern_ob_ugroz.pdf (accessed 10 October 2009).

77. Bessonova, *Neftedobycha v Rossii*; Clifford Gaddy and Barry Ickes, "Russia's Declining Oil Production: Managing Price Risk and Rent Addiction," *Eurasian Geography and Economics*, 50, no. 1 (2009), 1–13.

78. Nemtsov and Milov, *Putin i "Gazprom,"* 22.

79. Stern, *The Future of Russian Gas and Gazprom*; Volkov, "'Gazprom': Riskovannaya Strategiya"; Nemtsov and Milov, *Putin i "Gazprom."*

80. Bessonova, *Neftedobycha v Rossii*.

81. Gaddy and Ickes, "Russia's Declining Oil Production"; Hanson, "The Resistible Rise."

82. Tat'yana Stanovaya, "'Rosneft' v Zhertvu," *Politcom.ru*, 23 September 2009, www.politcom.ru/8847.html (accessed 10 October 2009).

83. Tony Halpin, "Protests Ignored as Europe's Tallest Skyscraper Gets Green Light in St. Petersburg," *The Times*, 24 September 2009; Simon Shuster, "The Battle over a New Skyscraper in St. Petersburg," *Time*, 6 October 2009, www.time.com/time/world/article/0,8599,1927550,00.html (accessed 10 October 2009).

84. Vladimir Gel'man, "Party Politics in Russia: From Competition to Hierarchy," *Europe-Asia Studies*, 60, no. 6 (2008), 913–30; Vladimir Gel'man, "Leviathan's Return? Recentralization Policy in Contemporary Russia," in Cameron Ross and Adrian Campbell, *Federalism and Local Politics in Russia* (New York: Routledge, 2009), 1–24.

85. Shleifer and Treisman, *Without a Map*.

86. Lilia Shevtsova, *Yeltsin's Russia: Myths and Reality* (Washington, D.C.: Carnegie Endowment for International Peace, 1999); Michael McFaul, *Russia's Unfinished Revolution: Political Change from Gorbachev to Putin* (Ithaca, N.Y.: Cornell University Press, 2001).

87. Lucan Way, "Authoritarian State Building and Sources of Regime Competitiveness in the Forth Wave: The Cases of Belarus, Moldova, Russia, and Ukraine," *World Politics*, 57, no. 2 (2005), 231–61.

88. Nemtsov and Milov, *Putin i "Gazprom"*; Gaddy and Ickes, "Russia's Declining Oil Production"; Hanson, "The Resistible Rise"; Bessonova, *Neftedobycha v Rossii*.

89. Gaidar, *Gibel' Imperii*.

90. Dunning, *Crude Democracy*.

91. Dunning, *Crude Democracy*, 286–88.

6

Oil Boom and Government Finance in Russia

Stabilization Fund and Its Fate

Andrey Zaostrovtsev

RUSSIA: OIL DEPENDENCY AND CONSEQUENT MACROECONOMIC PROBLEMS

It is no secret for anyone in the world that the development, if not the very survival, of the Russian economy depends to a decisive degree on the trends of the international market of hydrocarbons. It is enough to point out the fact that in 2008 its share in the structure of Russian export came almost to two-thirds (crude oil—32.4 percent, oil products—16.7 percent, and natural gas—14.1 percent, which comes to 63.2 percent).[1] Russian statistics do not assess directly the share of the oil and gas sector in the national economy, and its contribution to GDP, so judgments may only be presented on the basis of expert assessments.[2] The most accurate calculations in this respect were made recently by three Russian economists: Evsei Gurvich, Elena Vakulenko, and Pavel Krivenko.[3] They included the entire calculated added value in the oil and gas sector as a whole (i.e., the production and processing of oil, production of gas, and their transportation by pipelines). The results of their analysis are presented in table 6.1.

On the basis of this data, at first glance there would seem to be no grounds to talk about the strong dependence of the Russian economy on the oil and gas sector. As one can see, its share in 1998–2007 never exceeded 25 percent, and in 2007 it even dropped below 19 percent. At the same time, econometric calculations by the same authors have shown that changes in Russian GDP are 83 percent determined by the price of oil.[4] Furthermore, revenues of this sector has a decisive importance for filling the federal budget, as is

Table 6.1.   Size of the Oil and Gas Sector in Russia (% of GDP)

Years	Oil	Gas	Total
1998	6.3	8.1	14.4
1999	12.1	7.6	19.7
2000	16.7	7.7	24.4
2001	13.2	7.0	20.2
2002	13.1	6.0	19.2
2003	14.1	6.4	20.5
2004	15.0	5.4	20.4
2005	17.6	5.7	23.3
2006	16.5	5.7	22.2
2007	14.0	4.7	18.8

Source: Gurvich, Vakulenko, and Krivenko, "Tsiklicheskie svoistva," 54.

clearly shown in figure 6.1. And at the same time, it is apparent that there is dependence of oil and gas revenues from fluctuations of the world markets, and accordingly the influence of these markets on all key parameters of the Russian economy with the effect of external shocks connected with them.

Oil and gas revenues account for a much lower share of subnational (both regional and local) budgets in Russia, because the federal center has drawn them to itself. If in 2002, these revenues of the federal budget came to 79.2 percent of all oil and gas revenues in the budget system of the Russian Federation as a whole, in 2006 this share came to 90.1 percent (however, in 2007 it dropped to

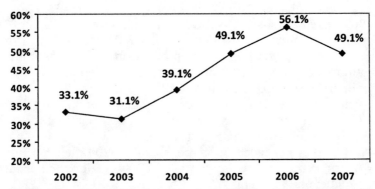

Figure 6.1.   Oil and Gas Revenues in the Russian Federal Budget (% of all revenues)

83.5 percent).[5] However, the importance of these revenues for subnational budgets of the Russian Federation is much greater, as one of the major items of expenditures of the federal budget (and the major source of revenues in subnational budgets) is interbudgetary transfers. In 2008, funds transferred from the federal budget to subnational budgets (i.e., regional and municipal governments) came to 2.67 percent of GDP. This is more than all expenditures on national defense (2.51 percent of GDP) or national security and law enforcement (2.63 percent of GDP).[6]

Economies that are so dependent on revenues from export of natural resources usually encounter three major problems caused by this dependency. The first is what economists called the "Dutch disease." The logic of development of the Dutch disease is presented in figure 6.2 (it is a somewhat simplified version of the scheme proposed by the Russian economist Vadim Gilmundinov).[7]

As clarification of this scheme, one should note that the appreciation of the real exchange rate of the national currency reduces competitive ability because of an increase of costs (expressed in foreign currency) for national production of tradable goods (i.e., those goods that are or may potentially be items of export or import). As a result, they not only lose foreign markets, but are forced out of the domestic market by imported goods that become increasingly cheaper. The decline in research and development and technological progress as a result of the Dutch disease is explained, first, by the fact that, as a rule, more venture enterprises, which require their products, are concentrated in the sector of nonresource sector tradable goods than in the sector of natural resources. Second, economists increasingly mention the so-called spillover effect, when technological innovations from one area spill over into others. It is believed that this effect is a most typical feature of the nonresource sector (for example, in the high-tech industry).

However, the very presence of the Dutch disease in the Russian economy is not an irrefutable fact: "We conclude that, while Russia does appear to have all of the symptoms, the diagnosis of Dutch Disease remains to be confirmed. Although we find evidence of real appreciation, a declining manufacturing sector, an expanding service sector, and rapid real wage growth, more research is needed to determine that these symptoms are not caused by other factors."[8] A number of Russian economists, indicating the impressive high growth rate of the industry and other sectors that did not lag behind the growth rate of the service sector in the period of highest oil prices in the international markets, claim that the Dutch disease is not present in Russia.[9] Still,

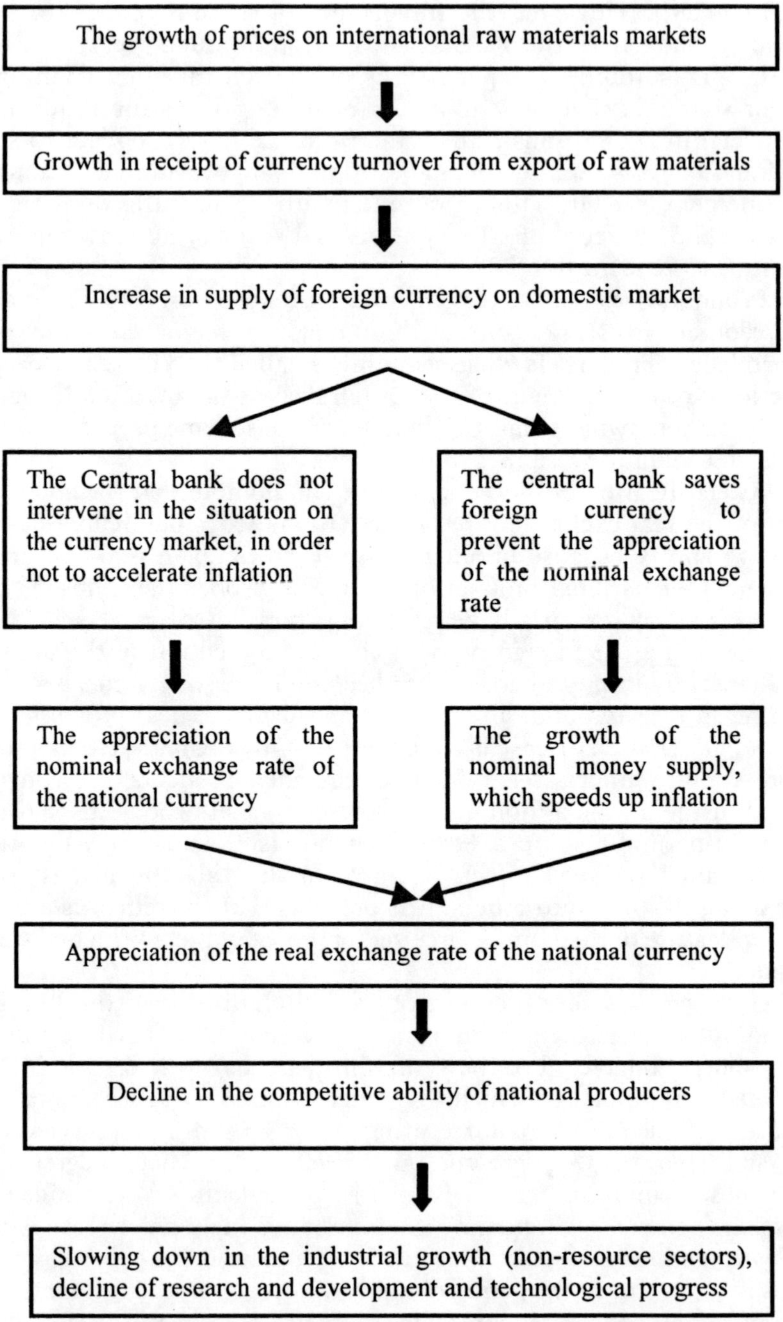

The growth of prices on international raw materials markets

↓

Growth in receipt of currency turnover from export of raw materials

↓

Increase in supply of foreign currency on domestic market

The Central bank does not intervene in the situation on the currency market, in order not to accelerate inflation	The central bank saves foreign currency to prevent the appreciation of the nominal exchange rate

↓   ↓

The appreciation of the nominal exchange rate of the national currency	The growth of the nominal money supply, which speeds up inflation

Appreciation of the real exchange rate of the national currency

↓

Decline in the competitive ability of national producers

↓

Slowing down in the industrial growth (non-resource sectors), decline of research and development and technological progress

Figure 6.2.   Evolution of the "Dutch Disease" and Its Consequences

some other scholars make confident claims for its existence and negative effects on the country.[10]

Second, the problem of resource-dependent economies is the unpredictability of budget revenues, because of unexpected fluctuations of international markets. In the period of large inflow of export revenues, the trend for macroeconomic populism increases considerably, primarily the increase of budget expenditures, many of which are connected with the new financial obligations of the state. In the period of a decline in prices of major export products, and therefore a decline of export revenues, there is an urgent need for a drastic cutting of budget expenditures, although it is not always possible because of the long-term nature of obligations taken on previously. As a result, a considerable budget deficit could appear, which leads to further macroeconomic instability. Furthermore, in a period of high export prices, governments often launch financing of various inefficient long-term investment projects using budget funds. For example, this was the case for the Soviet Union. Post-Communist Russia in the 2000s, however, conducted a policy of sterilization of excessive currency receipts and fiscal balance with the help of the Stabilization Fund, and later, its successor, the Reserve Fund, which was established on the eve of the international economic crisis of 2008–2009.

Third, besides the Dutch disease with all its consequences, unexpected declines in budget revenues, and partial expenditures, resource-exporting economies also face the challenge of redistribution of current export revenues over time. The present-day "happiness" because of the inflow of export revenues should be felt to a certain extent by future generations (or at least by the current generation, when a large section of it will be retired). In Russia this task was supposed to be solved by the Fund of National Prosperity that was established in 2008.

In principle, ideally energy-exporting countries should arrange things as if prices on energy resources did not increase in value and "purge" their economies from extra revenues as if they emerged on an ad hoc basis. In this case, all budget revenues should be divided into two parts: oil and gas, and non–oil and gas. Oil and gas revenues of the budget should consist of two parts: basic oil and gas revenues, and situational oil and gas revenues. The former included revenues to the budget at a fixed basic level of prices on exported oil (taking into account the actual or forecasted amount of oil and gas production), and the latter included extra revenues that come to the budget from an increase of actual oil prices above the basic level. With a correct calculation of this "threshold price" (or "cutoff price") in the long-term perspective, the average size of extra revenues should be equal to zero (because positive extra revenues in times of high oil prices will compensate the negative extra revenues in times of low oil prices). This picture is presented in figure 6.3, where P_B is a fixed and precisely calculated basic price, and the graph of actual prices (P_F) is a curve that emerged in prosperous intervals of time (t_G) segment, lying above the line of basic price (their areas are equal to positive extra revenues) and in bad times (t_B) segments lying below the line of the basic price (their areas are equal to negative extra revenues). Ideally, the task of the Ministry of Finance is to use some instruments to "cut" positive extra revenues in good times, save them, and then use these funds to cover the gaps in bad times that arise because of a decline in actual prices below the basis level (in other words, to compensate negative extra revenues). At the same time, the ideal finance minister should calculate non–oil and gas revenues of the budget (i.e., revenues if it is expected that the price on figure 6.3 is equal to zero) and compare them with the budget expenditures. The difference (usually negative) makes up the non–oil and gas balance of the budget. And then the finance minister should think about how much of oil and gas revenues to release to cover the deficit of the non–oil and gas budget. For example, this may be the calculated part of oil and gas revenues that is obtained with P_B. It becomes a so-called oil and gas transfer.

Of course, theoretically one could imagine absolutely ascetic finance ministers, governments, and parliaments of oil- and gas-exporting countries, which do not allow a deficit of the non–oil and gas budget, that is, it lives as if it did not export oil and/or gas at all. In this case, its non–oil and gas budget would be balanced, the non–oil and gas balance would be zero, and accordingly, so would be the oil

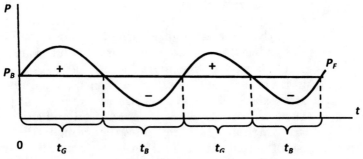

Figure 6.3. Smoothing of Budget Revenues Over Time

and gas transfer. In practice, this has never happened, and even Norway (the most efficient oil exporter in terms of balancing its budget) allows a non–oil and gas deficit, although its policy is based on saving all revenues from oil and gas (the principle of complete saving). In fact, various oil-exporting countries that faced the problems outlined above, caused by their dependence on the fluctuations of oil and gas revenues, propose different solutions.[11]

STABILIZATION FUND IN RUSSIA: FROM BIRTH TO DEATH

The period of the 1990s in Russia was marked by macroeconomic turbulence, which reached its peak during the financial crisis of 1998, which buried the modest hopes of financial stabilization that had arisen in the mid-1990s, when it seemed that the worst times of economic transition in Russia were already over. The fear of a repeat of those developments, and the desire to provide favorable conditions for economic growth, led to a major drive for further economic reforms. In the early 2000s, during the first years of Vladimir Putin's rule, a pragmatic approach, which is usually not typical among the Russian elites, dominated in solving macroeconomic policy issues in general.

In the early twenty-first century, the Russian government faced an unprecedented problem—not to combat a budget deficit, but on the contrary, to think about what to do with the revenues that unexpectedly came to the country, and had been unthinkable in the past, from the export of oil and gas. How to fight the threat of the Dutch disease? How to sterilize the money supply, and not allow inflation? And finally, how to avoid a populist fiscal policy because of wealth brought in from the outside because of the rally of oil prices on international markets?

The response was the establishment of a special financial reserve in the federal budget of the Russian Federation in 2002. This financial reserve played the role of predecessor of the Stabilization Fund (SF)—a more complex and efficient tool of macroeconomic policy. The creation of the SF as a special component of the federal budget was stipulated by amendments to the Budget Code of the Russian Federation, and it began to be filled from 1 January 2004. The fund was established under the conditions of an increase of the price of oil of "Urals" blend beyond a certain threshold (from 1 January 2004 it was equal to $20 per barrel, and from 1 January 2006 it increased to $27). The fund was filled by tax for the subsoil use levied from oil companies, in part received into the federal budget (95 percent of receipts under this tax), and export customs duties on oil.[12] Furthermore, the Russian government got the discretion to fill SF by extra revenues from the federal budget depending upon fiscal results of the previous year.

Nevertheless, one of the major shortcomings of the mechanism for filling the SF was the fact that it was far from covering all extra revenues from oil and gas export. This issue was also recognized by Russian finance minister Alexei Kudrin. He emphasized the fact that the tax for production of gas, export duties on oil products (i.e., not export duties on crude oil) and gas, and also the profit tax of the oil and gas sector were not included for calculations of the amount of money diverted to SF. These funds remained in the budget, and can be directed toward current budgetary expenditures. As a result, for example, in 2005 the SF received approximately half of all extra revenues of the Russian economy, or around 70 percent of extra revenues of the budget.[13] From the figures provided by the finance minister, it follows that extra revenues of the economy are higher than the extra revenues of the budget. It is also clear that the major reason for the incomplete capture of extra revenues of the economy into the SF is the privileged position of the gas industry (practically Gazprom). The rates for the subsoil use tax on gas (similar to the oil sector) are specific, but unlike the latter, they are not linked with world market prices. As Kudrin noted, "Due to the lack of a link of the subsoil use tax on gas to world prices, the taking of rent from the gas industry to the budget is not conducted in full."[14]

This issue was also considered as the major shortcoming of the mechanism for filling the SF by independent experts. Gurvich, indicating the incompleteness of sources for filling the SF, noted that from the economic standpoint, export duties on oil products and gas should be automatically transferred to it. In this case, the amount of funds in the SF would grow by one-quarter and come to 61 percent of the all extra revenues of the economy, 87 percent of the extra revenues coming to the budget of the expanded government, and 95 percent of the extra revenues of the federal budget.[15] "Incomplete transfer of extra revenues to the Stabilization Fund means that its mechanisms smooths over but does not completely eliminate fluctuations of budget parameters."[16] The privileged position of the gas sector in the Russian economy is clearly visible if one looks at the data calculated on the share of resource rent of the oil and gas sector that is allocated to the budget system of the Russian Federation (including the SF). As is shown in figure 6.4, a very important change occurred: from 2003, the gas sector allocates a lower share of received natural resource rent to the budget system in comparison with the oil sector. No wonder that

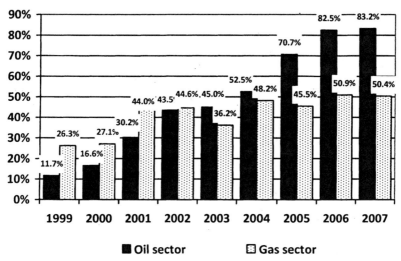

Figure 6.4.   Share of Natural Resource Rent in the Budget System of the Russian Federation (%)

the share of the SF in oil and gas revenues of the federal budget was far from satisfactory. In 2004 and 2006, it was almost equal to the oil and gas transfer (table 6.2). This once more confirms the fact that the SF, for all its importance, has not been able to fulfill completely the tasks that were laid upon it.

The SF was supposed to serve the goal not only of smoothing out fluctuations of budget revenues, but of smoothing out the external effects on the exchange rate. In other words, it should be an important tool to sterilize the superfluous money supply, which is usually conducted because of monetary policies by the central bank. In most countries, this happens because central banks sold government and treasury bonds to the private sector, that is, by taking money out of the economy. Furthermore, central banks may increase the inflow of money to their accounts from the banking system by increasing the refinancing rates and the reserve requirements. The first increases

Table 6.2.   Receipts to the SF and the Oil and Gas Transfer (% of GDP)

	2004	2005	2006	2007
Oil and gas revenues in the SF	4.1	7.0	6.1	6.0
Oil and gas transfer	3.9	4.5	6.4	3.2

Source: Gurvich, Vakulenko, and Krivenko, "Tsiklicheskie svoistva," 62.

the attractiveness of voluntary reserves in accounts of central banks (especially with high risks of crediting of private clients), and the second makes the increase of amounts of this reserve compulsory. If the amount of sterilized money is equal to the amount of extra revenues of resource rent, this means that the external shocks are completely compensated by monetary and fiscal policy measures, and do not influence macroeconomic indicators of the country. But insufficient centralization of funds leads to an appreciation of the national currency under the influence of a growth in export prices, and an increase of flow of foreign currencies caused by them, with all the consequences previously presented in the scheme of the development of the Dutch disease (see figure 6.2).

It is apparent that with this growth of world oil prices, which was observed from 1999 until mid-2008, no central bank could deal with this daunting task of sterilization on its own. The problem is that the central bank should take foreign currency from economic agents and exchange it for national currency (in Russia's case, rubles), when these agents need it to operate on the domestic market (when they are dealing with suppliers and consumers, paying taxes and salaries, etc.). It is practically impossible to get this money back by methods of monetary policy alone. As a result, quite a paradoxical picture is observed: on the one hand, the national currency of the oil- and gas-exporting country is appreciated because of the increase of demand for it, but on the other hand, the money supply increases, too, and as a result, the central bank faced difficulties in fighting inflation. Here the instrument of budgetary policy comes into play, which transfers money to the SF. National exporters exchange their dollars and euros for national currency to pay taxes and export duties, which are not spent by the finance ministry but are "frozen" at the SF, and thus disappear from the economy, as it would happen without the SF. In Russia, the government's role in sterilizing superfluous liquidity has grown over time. If in 2002–2003, the amount of sterilization from the federal budget came to 20–25 percent of the growth of Russia's international reserves, with the appearance of the SF in 2004, the growth of the amount of funds in the federal budget on accounts at the Central Bank of the Russian Federation reached 49 percent of the growth of reserves for the year, and in 2005 grew to 60 percent.[17] Furthermore, as is shown in table 6.3, in 2004 the government made the major contribution to the growth of sterilization of cash supply, and in 2005 it provided for it completely.

At the same time, as the economy improved, Russia was not able to avoid macroeconomic populism completely. The fact that the SF

Table 6.3. Dynamics of Amount of Removal of Superfluous Liquidity from
the Economy

	2004	2005
Growth of monetary base in previous year (%)	24.8	31.7
Sterilization of money supply, growth for the year (billion rubles)		
Federal government	612.7	1,291.4
Central Bank of the Russian Federation	185.4	−38.4
Reference: oil price ($/bl.)	34.4	50.6

Source: Kudrin, "Stabilizatsionnyi fond," 42.

did not take all of the extra revenues of the budget made especially high demands for conducting budgetary policy. Yet, in 2006, it was possible to reduce the total share of revenues of the federal budget in GDP (from 16.3 percent in 2005 to 15.9 percent in 2006), but 2007 was marked by a burst of budget expenditures, and their growth significantly exceeded the growth of GDP. As a result, the share of expenditures of the federal budget in 2007 reached 18.1 percent of GDP, and remained at the similarly high level in 2008 (18.2 percent of GDP).[18] This factor, among other things, contributed to the sharp rise of inflation in 2007 to 11.9 percent after eight years of permanent decline of its rate (from 84.4 percent annual inflation in the crisis year of 1998 to 9 percent in 2006).[19]

According to the legal regulations of the SF, its funds could have been used to cover a deficit in the federal budget if oil declined below the basic price. If the accumulated amount of funds of the SF exceeded 500 million rubles, then the excess money could have been used for other goals. The use of SF funds was determined according to the federal law on the federal budget for the appropriate financial year. For example, in 2005, the amount of SF exceeded a level of 500 billion rubles, and some of this money was directed to paying the foreign debt of the Russian Federation and to covering the deficit of its Pension Fund:

    93.5 billion rubles (equivalent to US$3.3 billion) was directed toward paying a debt to the International Monetary Fund.

    430.1 billion rubles (equivalent to US$15 billion) to paying a debt to member countries of the Paris club.

    123.8 billion rubles (equivalent to US$4.3 billion) to paying a debt to Vneshekonombank on loans provided to the Ministry of Finance in 1998–1999 to pay off and service the state foreign debt of the Russian Federation.

30 billion rubles (equivalent to US$1.04 billion) to covering the deficit of the Pension Fund of the Russian Federation.[20]

The government of the Russian Federation delegated to the Ministry of Finance authorities to use and distribute assets of the SF in terms of currencies and terms, and has approved the procedure for managing the SF funds. According to this procedure, the SF funds could be used by the following means (either separately or simultaneously):

- By acquiring securities and bonds of foreign states with SF funds.
- By acquiring foreign currency with SF funds and depositing it in foreign currency accounts at the Central Bank of the Russian Federation, which paid interest for using this money in the respective accounts.

Russian legislation on the SF has been often criticized. For example, Gurvich outlined a number of major shortcomings inherent to it. First, it was noted that there are no restrictions on opportunities for using its funds in case of very small inflow of export revenues: with a possible decline of oil prices by just $1 below the basic level, the government formally receives the right to spend all money from the SF. Second, the use of SF funds above the minimum level of 500 billion rubles in case of very large inflow of export revenues is not regulated at all. Third, this level set up in the federal law was not based upon serious calculations, and according to several economists, this rule was not needed at all, as extra revenues should only be spent if there is a major decline of their inflow.[21] At the same time, these shortcomings of legislation have had almost no effect on the real practice of the use of SF. Perhaps this resulted from the very fact that the SF was established and managed during the period of "oil prosperity" under the presidency of Vladimir Putin, when the growth of international oil prices far exceeded the most optimistic expectations of the Russian government. At any rate, the SF existed successfully until 30 January 2008. The dynamic of its growth is presented in figure 6.5.

From 1 January 2006, the funds from SF were used merely to pay off foreign debt of the Russian Federation. The only payment that was not used beyond this purpose was the deposit of the Russian Federation on 28 November 2007 in the prime capital of the state corporation Bank of Development and Foreign Economic Activity (Vneshekonombank), of the state corporation Russian Corporation of Nanotechnologies, and

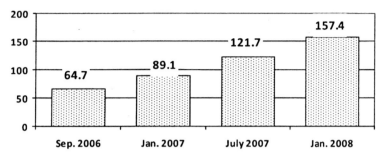

Figure 6.5.   Total Amount of Funds of the Stabilization Fund of the Russian Federation ($ billion)

the direction of funds to increase the amount of the Investment Fund of the Russian Federation (a total of 300 million rubles).[22] This was not an awfully large amount for a fund of 3.5 trillion rubles.[23] Nevertheless, a precedent was established: the previously sterilized liquidity was "injected" back into the national economy.

After 30 January 2008, the SF was divided into two different and independent funds—the already mentioned Reserve Fund and the Fund of National Prosperity. These developments will be discussed in the concluding section. Now it is worth discussing the great hostility that the SF met from a number of Russian economists, who objected to the very idea of taking extra revenues from the economy.

OPPOSITION TO THE STABILIZATION FUND

The idea to establish a Stabilization Fund for Russia had been proposed by the Institute of Economics in Transition, led by the former Russian prime minster and leading economic reformer Yegor Gaidar. The authors who developed the concept claimed that "the major goal to establish the Stabilization Fund of the Russian Federation was the accumulation of part of the revenues from the export sector of the economy in periods of high world prices on major Russian export goods and their use to pay off foreign debt and support the level of expenditures of the state budget in periods of an unfavorable situation, and also to slow down the growth of the real exchange rate of the ruble in periods of high export turnover."[24] At the same time, it is understandable that the very idea of rejecting the immediate use of the considerable available funds within the national economy draws severe opposition from various interest groups. Furthermore, from the very beginning it was clear that politicians would certainly use the very fact of investment of SF funds abroad for purely political purposes. It is no coincidence that the leading critics of the stabilization policy of Kudrin were those economists who were actively involved in political struggles. On the one hand, they attempted to show that the goals of the SF could not be achieved, and on the other hand, they offered their own suggestions for the use of extra revenues from export of oil and gas.

One of the major critics of Kudrin was the well-known politician and economist Sergei Glaziev. In many ways, he became a key figure in Russian economic policy due to his work in the reformist government of Yegor Gaidar as a deputy minister, and then as minister of foreign economic affairs. In September 1993, he left his position as a protest against the president, Boris Yeltsin, who had dissolved the Russian parliament. Subsequently, Glaziev increasingly distanced himself from supporting liberal market reforms, and in 1999 he joined the State Duma of the Russian Federation as a representative of the Communist Party of the Russian Federation. Later, he became one of the leaders of the newly formed nationalist coalition, Motherland (Rodina), and even ran in the presidential elections in 2004. As an economist, Glaziev was a major supporter of state interventionism and active industrial policy. This economic ideology directly affected his proposals for alternative use of extra revenues from the export of oil and gas. In particular, he suggested state guarantees to be provided to attract private investments in various projects of socioeconomic development in the country, for example, subsidizing interest rates and providing guarantees on mortgages and housing loans for Russian citizens; providing interest-free loans for major infrastructural projects, especially at the municipal level; subsidizing the import of promising high technologies; issuing interest-free loans to venture funds for stimulating innovations and implementing new technologies; establishing engineering centers and techno-parks in regions with high levels of unemployment and highly qualified personnel, and the like.[25]

Along with the promotion of the idea of the "budget of development," and expansion of budget financing of investment projects, Glaziev was also a proponent of macroeconomic populism with a social flavor: "If we compare the structure of expenditures of our budget with international standards, we will see that the state monstrously under-funded the social sphere. If the structure of the Russian budget was comparable with international standards, we would have to spend twice as much on education and public health than we do, and raise our expenditures on research by three times, and on culture by four times. Then there would not be any surplus, there would simply not be enough money."[26] It is difficult to imagine that the economist Glaziev does not see a problem in the strong volatility of oil and gas export revenues, when adoption of such extended budget obligations in favorable years may either result in their radical cutting, or an enormous budget deficit and therefore a need for loans (including foreign loans) at high interest rates in the period when export revenues decline. Furthermore, Glaziev, like many interventionist economists, takes the position of the state as a "benevolent despot."

Without entering into polemics with Glaziev, I should note that according to the analysis conducted in the project Worldwide Government Indicators (World Bank), Russia has a percentile rank equal to 45 (out of 100) in the section Government Effectiveness, 31 in the section Regulatory Quality, and 15 in the section Control of Corruption.[27] In a study of the peculiarities of the resource curse in Russia conducted by Younkyoo Kim, he states that "our analysis does not provide convincing evidence of developments towards a more benevolent petro-state in Russia."[28] Due to these conditions of Russia, following recommendations of an active industrial policy and expanding state investments may repeat the results of some petro-states such as Nigeria, where the government invested revenues from oil export into industrial development, but despite the 6 percent annual growth of investments over the period of two decades, industry stagnated.[29]

Another prominent critic of the SF in Russia is Oksana Dmitrieva. Like Glaziev, she is a professional economist and active politician, and currently she is a member of the committee of the Russian State Duma for budget and taxes on behalf of the left-wing pro-Kremlin party, Just Russia. One of the central points of her criticism is the argument that the "Stabilization Fund cannot fulfill one of its major tasks—the stabilization of the living standards over time, as this will mean stagnation of the social development in the country at an extremely low level."[30] Thus, Dmitrieva subsequently rejects the very possibility and relevance of using the SF as a tool for money and loan regulation on the basis that, according to her view, inflation in Russia is of a primarily nonmonetary nature. Furthermore, she concludes that a surplus of the budget that exceeds the growth rate of GDP actually means an economic decline, which is quantitatively equal to the difference between this surplus (expressed in share of GDP), and the growth rate.[31] As a result, inflation increases, as the cash supply is less than GDP. Therefore, Dmitrieva believes that diverting funds to the

SF and forcibly reducing the use of GDP within the country is not a recipe for fighting inflation, but of making it worse.[32]

On the basis of the model represented by the multiplier for a simple closed economy, Dmitrieva attempts to show that diverting revenues to the SF slows down economic growth, and spending this money would cause a significant increase in rates of economic growth, yet an insignificant rise in inflation.[33] These judgments, however, are based on ignoring the fact of the overheating of the Russian economy at the end of the oil boom.[34] Dmitrieva concludes her polemics with proponents of the establishment of the SF by pointing out that it contributed to the preservation of the inefficient structure of the economy that was oriented toward export of raw materials: "By taking money from the oil and gas sector, the state does not allow market agents to invest this money and diversify the assets, therefore it hinders the flow of capital."[35] Also, according to Dmitrieva, the SF also does not fulfill the role of a macroeconomic stabilizer, as "in the case of a major decline in oil prices and a decline of the inflow of funds into the country, the use of the Stabilization Fund is equivalent to printing money."[36]

Of the last two claims, the first is partially just, as perhaps the increasing removal of rent, especially from oil companies (see figure 6.4) in fact did restrict economic restructuring with private capital and, most important, the investment potential of these companies in the sector. However, the issue as to how much money to divert to the SF does not mean that all the extra revenues, or even the majority of these revenues, should be kept in the oil and gas sector. The indispensable role of the deductions of these revenues to the SF as a means of countercyclical policy is already examined above. As to the second claim in the conclusion, it will be discussed alongside with analysis of the latest changes in the fiscal policy of Russia, and also, naturally, of the effects of the world economic crisis of 2008–2009 on its financial reserves.

SPLITTING OF THE STABILIZATION FUND AND THE IMPACT OF THE CRISIS ON FINANCIAL RESERVES

The Reserve Fund has practically replaced the SF. It is a part of the funds of the federal budget, and is designed to ensure that the government could fulfill its expenditure obligations in the case of a major decrease in receipt of oil and gas revenues to the federal budget. Unlike the SF, besides the revenues of the federal budget from the production and export of oil, it also aimed to include the revenues of the federal budget from the production and export of gas. The maximum size of the Reserve Fund is set at the level of 10 percent of the annual forecasted GDP for the according financial year. Before the 2008 economic crisis, it was thought that this is a guarantee of the use of expenditures of the federal budget over the period of three years, in the case of a major decline of world oil prices.

From 2008, a certain part of oil and gas revenues[37] in the form of *oil and gas transfer* has been annually diverted to finance current expenditures of the federal budget. The size of this transfer is approved annually by the federal law on the federal budget for the respective financial year. Its amount is calculated as a share of the GDP forecasted for the respective year. In 2008 it was 6.1 percent of GDP. Initially it was planned that in 2009 this figure would be 5.5 percent, in 2010, 4.5 percent, and then from 2011 onward, 3.7 percent of GDP.[38]

According to the proposed model, after the financing of the oil and gas transfer, oil and gas revenues should go to the Reserve Fund. The normative amount of the Reserve Fund is approved annually by the federal law on the federal budget for the respective financial year, and in an absolute value its calculations are based on 10 percent of the GDP forecasted for the respective year. After the Reserve Fund is filled to the proposed amount, all remaining oil and gas revenues should go to the Fund of National Prosperity, described below in more detail. Another source of revenues for the Reserve Fund is revenues from investment of its money. The officially declared goals of the investment of funds of the Reserve Fund are to ensure the preservation of these funds, and the stable level of revenues from these investments in the long-term perspective. Of course, it is possible that these investments could bring some financial losses in the short-term perspective.[39]

According to the legal procedure, the funds of the Reserve Fund could be used by the following means: (1) by acquiring with its funds foreign currency and depositing it in foreign currency accounts at the Central Bank of the Russian Federation, which paid interest for using this money in the respective accounts; (2) by placing its funds in foreign currency and financial assets in foreign currency (deposits in foreign banks and funds, securities and foreign government bonds, state agencies and international financial organizations). In the second case, the government of the Russian Federation and the Ministry of Finance are both responsible for arranging special requirements for investment of funds of the Reserve Fund, according to the regulations of the Budget Code of Russia.

Funds of the Reserve Fund may be used for financial provision of the oil and gas transfer, and prescheduled payment of state foreign debts. The use of funds of the Reserve Fund to cover the oil and gas transfer is legally possible in the case of insufficient oil and gas revenues of the federal budget, received for the according financial year and designated for these purposes.[40] Initially, it was thought that the use of these funds in periods of unfavorable world markets would make it possible to conduct a balanced budgetary policy, ensure stable socioeconomic development of the country, and reduce its dependence on fluctuations in international oil markets. The Ministry of Finance received wide discretionary powers to conduct the new stabilization policy. During the implementation of the federal budget, it has the right to use funds of the Reserve Fund without making changes to the federal law on the federal budget for financial provision of the oil and gas transfer, in the case that oil and gas revenues actually received in the current financial year are insufficient for implementing this transfer. However, the maximum amount of funds for financial provision of the oil and gas transfer should be approved by the federal law on the federal budget.

The Fund of National Prosperity, like the Reserve Fund, is part of the funds of the federal budget. Money from the Fund of National Prosperity may be used only to provide state financing of voluntary pension savings of Russian citizens, and to provide balance (i.e., covering the current deficit) of the budget of the Pension Fund of the Russian Federation. The amount of funds from the Fund of National Prosperity used for these purposes is determined annually by the federal law on the federal budget for the current financial year.[41] In other words, it is filled on the base of oil and gas revenues after delivery of money for the purposes of the oil and gas transfer and filling of the Reserve Fund. Another source of funding of the National Prosperity Fund is from reinvestments of its revenues (which is organized similarly to the investment of money of the Reserve Fund, and is specified by a special decree of the Russian government).[42]

As a result, quite a strict and accurate scheme was proposed for the use of oil and gas revenues. It is presented in figure 6.6. First, on the basis of separately calculated oil and gas revenues, the oil and gas transfer is formed (the part of it that is supposed to fill the revenues of the federal budget, and may be spent during the current financial year) in a certain share of the GDP forecasted (see figure 6.6). Then the Reserve Fund is filled until its amount reaches 10 percent of GDP forecasted. Finally, the remaining oil and gas revenues (of course, if there are any) go to the National Prosperity Fund.

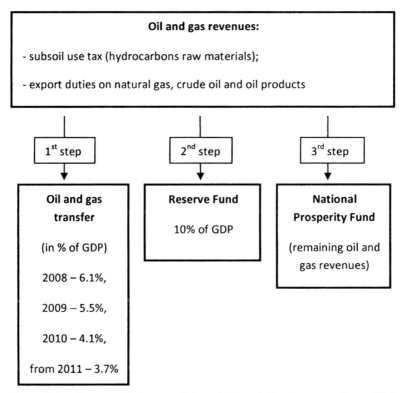

Figure 6.6.   Proposed Scheme of Use of Oil and Gas Revenues from 2008

However, starting from 2009, the world economic crisis turned the tables, so to speak. In general, the situation is as follows: oil and gas revenues have become insufficient, not only to fill the Reserve Fund, but also to provide for the oil and gas transfer. After the entire amount of money is submitted to the federal budget in the form of this transfer to the budget, a deficit of the federal budget still remains. To cover the remaining deficit, the funds that were previously accumulated in the Reserve Fund have been used for filling the financial gap. No wonder that the Reserve Fund is quickly dwindling (table 6.4), not to mention the very fact that nothing remains to fill the National Prosperity Fund. However, it demonstrated a small growth in 2009, which is explained by some revenues from investment of its funds (table 6.4). It is interesting that in September 2009, for the first time since these funds were established (February 2008),

Table 6.4. Total Amount of Funds of the Reserve Fund and the National Prosperity Fund

Date	Reserve Fund		National Prosperity Fund	
	In Billion $	In Billion Rubles	In Billion $	In Billion Rubles
November 2009	77.2	2,242.1	93.4	2,712.6
September 2009	85.7	2,706.8	90.6	2,863.1
April 2009	121.1	4,117.7	85.7	2,915.2
January 2009	137.1	4,027.6	88.0	2,584.5
September 2008	142.6	3,504.6	31.9	784.5
June 2008	129.3	3,069.9	32.6	773.9
February 2008	125.2	3,057.9	32.0	783.3

Sources: Ministerstvo Finansov Rossiskoi Federatsii: Sovokupnyi ob"em sredstv Rezervnogo Fonda, www1.minfin.ru/ru/reservefund/statistics/volume/index.php?id4=5796 (18 November 2009); Sovokupnyi ob"em sredstv Fonda Natsionalnogo Blagosostoyaniya, www1.minfin.ru/ru/nationalwealthfund/statistics/volume/index.php?id4=6412 (18 November 2009).

the amount of funds in the National Prosperity Fund exceeded those in the Reserve Fund.

According to the forecast, proposed by the Ministry of Finance of Russia, the use of the Reserve Fund to cover the current deficit of the federal budget will lead to its practically complete exhaustion by the end of 2010. Moreover, in 2011–2012 the fund will not be filled. All the funds that should have gone to it during these years will be directed toward financing the provision of current expenditures of the federal budget. After the funds of the Reserve Fund are exhausted in 2010, budgetary policy will be to a large degree focused on covering the deficit of the federal budget using state loans. The proposed use of funds of the National Prosperity Fund to finance part of the transfer from the federal budget to the Pension Fund, with the lack of the further filling of it, will also lead to a gradual decline in the amount of the fund. With the further use of the fund according to the same proposed scheme, it may be completely exhausted as early as 2014–2015, which will further aggravate the problem of providing for the pension system in Russia.[43]

At the end of August 2009, the government of Russia, after extensive discussions of the proposal for the federal budget for 2010, made a fundamental decision on delivery of revenues of the Reserve Fund and the National Prosperity Fund into the federal budget on common grounds, and made respective amendments to the Budget Code of Russia.[44] In other words, all oil and gas revenues will thus become the oil and gas transfer. This and other measures to bring tax receipts to the federal budget and fill its financial gaps will not completely cover this deficit, and the government will be forced to borrow money in the form of loans and credits.

To summarize, the consequences of the economic crisis in 2010 will finally eliminate all remnants of the solid financial reserves that were accumulated in Russia over five years (2004–2008). It is quite possible that the National Prosperity Fund will melt much earlier than the schedule proposed by the Ministry of Finance of Russia, because of Putin's prioritizing of the populist policy to significantly raise pensions.[45] The Ministry of Finance also announced its plans to establish the Russian Financial Agency—a government-sponsored organization that is supposed to manage state reserves and debts.[46] It is more than likely that by the time it is established it will only manage the latter.

In Russia, the financial prosperity caused by the oil boom of the early twenty-first century is coming to an end. The drastic rise of state expenditures over the five years between 2004 and 2008 led to the average production cost of a barrel of oil in the Russian Federation reaching $40, as opposed to $25 in countries of the Persian Gulf.[47] At the same time, the increasingly complicated conditions for the production of oil and gas in Siberia and the High North, along with expensive and ambitious investment projects (such as the construction of the Eastern Siberia–Pacific Ocean pipelines) forced the government of Russia increasingly to exempt oil and gas companies from paying the subsoil use tax and export duties for hydrocarbons produced in Eastern Siberia and in a number of other regions of the country. Thus, the very opportunities for filling the federal budget are decreased, while it is still built primarily on oil and gas revenues. In perspective, budget losses may be much higher larger than the losses that are actually forecasted by the Ministry of Finance, and thus amount of loans and credits for covering the budget deficit will increase. But even with a comparatively favorable development on the world oil markets, Russian government finances will face major problems. The period of financial abundance and prosperity in Russia is now a thing of the past.

NOTES

1. Federalnaya tamozhennaya sluzhba: Eksport-import Rossii vazhneishikh tovarov za 2008 god, www.customs.ru/ru/stats/ekspress/detail.php ?id286=5449 (accessed 13 August 2009).

2. World Bank, *Russian Economic Report*, no. 7 (February 2004), ns.world bank.org.ru/files/rer/RER_7_eng.pdf (accessed 14 August 2009); Masaaki Kuboniwa, Shinichiro Tabata, and Nataliya Ustinova, "How Large Is the Oil and Gas Sector in Russia? A Research Report," *Eurasian Geography and Economics*, 46, no. 1 (January-February 2005), 68–76.

3. Evsei Gurvich, Elena Vakulenko, and Pavel Krivenko, "Tsiklicheskie svoistva byudgetnoi politiki v neftedobyvayushchikh stranakh," *Voprosy Ekonomiki*, no. 2 (February 2009), 51–70.

4. Gurvich, Vakulenko, and Krivenko, "Tsiklicheskie svoistva," 68.

5. Gurvich, Vakulenko, and Krivenko, "Tsiklicheskie svoistva," 57.

6. *Rossiiskaya ekonomika v 2008 godu*, Vypusk 30. (Moscow: Institut ekonomiki perekhodnogo perioda, 2008), 68, 86.

7. Vadim Gilmundinov, "'Gollandskaya bolezn' v rossiiskoi ekonomike: Otraslevye aspekty proyavleniya," *Ekonomika i Organizatsiya Promyshlennogo Proizvodstva*, no. 12 (December 2008), 19.

8. Nienke Ooomes and Katerina Kalcheva, "Diagnosing Dutch Disease: Does Russia Have the Symptoms?" *IMF Working Papers*, no. 102 (April 2007).

9. Sergei Guriev and Konstantin Sonin, "Ekonomika 'resursnogo proklyatiya,'" *Voprosy Ekonomiki*, no. 4 (April 2008), 64; Sergei Zhuravlev, "Kholostoi vystrel," *Expert*, no. 30–31 (17–23 August 2009), 50–51.

10. Gleb Fetisov, "'Gollandskaya bolezn' v Rossii: makroekonomicheskie i strukturnye aspekty," *Voprosy Ekonomiki*, no. 12 (December 2006), 38–53; Anatolyi Chigrin, "Proizvodit nevygodno: posledstviya 'gollandskoi bolezni' v Rossii," *Ekonomika i Organizatsiya Promyshlennogo Proizvodstva*, no. 1 (January 2008), 3–18; Gleb Fetisov, "Dinamika tsen i antiinflyatsionnaya politika v usloviyakh 'gollandskoi bolezni,'" *Voprosy Ekonomiki*, no. 3 (March 2008), 20–36.

11. Ronaldo Ossowski, Mauricio Villafuerte, Paulo Medas, et al., "Managing the Oil Revenue Boom: The Role of Fiscal institutions," *IMF Occasional Papers*, no. 260 (April 30, 2008).

12. The subsoil use tax in Russia is a special tax designed for the oil and gas sector. Its rate is determined by the Tax Code of the Russian Federation in rubles per ton of oil produced (419 rubles in summer 2009), and is corrected for coefficients reflecting changes in world prices (monthly—since autumn 2008) and the level of development of the oil field. Export customs duties are determined by decrees of the Russian government in dollars per ton of crude oil exported, and also adjusted depending on changes in the world prices (since 1 February 2009 the rate was reduced from $119.10 to $100.90 per ton).

13. Aleksei Kudrin, "Mekhanizmy formirovaniya neneftegazovogo balansa byudgeta Rossii," *Voprosy Ekonomiki*, no. 8 (August 2006), 8.

14. Kudrin, "Mekhanizmy formirovaniya," 8.

15. Evsei Gurvich, "Formirovanie i ispolzovanie stabilizatsionnogo fonda," *Voprosy Ekonomiki*, no. 4 (April 2006), 40.

16. Gurvich, "Formirovanie i ispolzovanie," 34.

17. Aleksei Kudrin, "Stabilizatsionnyi fond: zarubezhnyi i Rossiiskii opyt," *Voprosy Ekonomiki*, no. 2 (February 2006), 41.

18. *Rossiiskaya ekonomika v 2008 godu*, 51.

19. Federalnaya sluzhba gosudarstvennoi statistiki: Indeks potrebitelskikh tsen na tovary i platnye uslugi naseleniyu po Rossiiskoi Federatsii v 1991–2008

gg., www.gks.ru/free_doc/new_site/prices/potr/2009/I-ipc91–08.htm (accessed 16 August 2009).

20. Ministerstvo Finansov Rossiiskoi Federatsii: O Stabilizatsionnom Fonde RF, www1.minfin.ru/ru/stabfund/about/ (accessed 16 August 2009).

21. Gurvich, "Formirovanie i ispolzovanie," 32.

22. Ministerstvo Finansov Rossiiskoi Federatsii: Ostatki na otdelnykh schetakh po uchety sredstv Stabilizatsionnogo Fonda, www1.minfin.ru/ru/stabfund/statistics/remains/index.php?id4=182 (accessed 16 August 2009).

23. Ministerstvo Finansov Rossiiskoi Federatsii: Sovokupnyi ob"em sredstv Stabilizatsionnogo Fonda RF, www1.minfin.ru/ru/stabfund/statistics/volume/ (accessed 16 August 2009).

24. Anna Zolotareva, Sergei Drobyshevskii, Sergei Sinel'nikov, et al., "Perspektivy Sozdaniya Stabilizatsionnogo Fonda v Rossiiskoi Federatsii," *Nauchnye Trudy*, no. 127 (Moscow: Institut ekonomiki perekhodnogo perioda, May 2001), 5–6.

25. Sergei Glaziev, "Stabfond obyazan rabotat' v obshchenatsionalnykh interesakh," *Nezavisimaya Gazeta*, 23 June 2006.

26. Sergei Glaziev, "Stabfond obyazan rabotat.'"

27. *Governance Matters 2009. Worldwide Governance Indicators, 1996–2008*, info.worldbank.org/governance/wgi/index.asp/ (accessed 28 August 2009).

28. Younkyoo Kim, *The Resource Curse in a Post-Communist Regime: Russia in Comparative Perspective* (Burlington, Vt.: Ashgate, 2003), 36.

29. Guriev and Sonin, "Ekonomika 'resursnogo proklyatiya,'" 66.

30. Oksana Dmitrieva, "Formirovanie stabilizatsionnykh fondov: predposylki i sledstviya," *Voprosy Ekonomiki*, no. 8 (August 2006), 22. However, this suggestion is rather contradictory. Maintaining and stabilizing the living standards (even at the low level, as the author believes) also means keeping them unchanged over time. This is why nobody set the task to raise the living standards with the help of the Stabilization Fund.

31. Dmitrieva provides the following example in order to confirm her theoretical argument. Based on the results of 2005, GDP growth came to 6.4 percent, and the surplus of the federal budget was around 8 percent of GDP. This means, according to her logic, that was a decline of a real GDP by 1.6 percent (Dmitrieva, "Formirovanie stabilizatsionnykh fondov," 26).

32. Dmitrieva, "Formirovanie stabilizatsionnykh fondov," 26. In this case, according to the famous quantity theory of money $MV = PY$, Y is not the total amount of GDP, but the much smaller spent part of GDP (the difference here in the Russian economy is significant because of the money accumulated in the Stabilization Fund that is taken out of spending). In Dmitrieva's calculations with the use of the above formula, Y therefore declines, and inflation increases as a result.

33. Dmitrieva, "Formirovanie stabilizatsionnykh fondov," 28–29.

34. Overheating of the economy was mentioned in the World Bank report presented in June 2008. The World Bank, *Russian Economic Report*, no.

16 (June 2008), siteresources.worldbank.org/INTRUSSIANFEDERATION/ Resources/rer16_ Eng.pdf (accessed 29 August 2009).

35. Dmitrieva, "Formirovanie stabilizatsionnykh fondov," 29–30.

36. Dmitrieva, "Formirovanie stabilizatsionnykh fondov," 30.

37. Since 2008, oil and gas revenues have been calculated separately from other revenues of the federal budget. They include (1) the subsoil use tax on production of all forms of hydrocarbon raw materials (oil, gas, natural fuel gas from all oil fields, and gas condensate from all oil fields); (2) export customs duties on crude oil; (3) export customs duties on natural gas; (4) export customs duties on all goods processed from oil.

38. Ministerstvo Finansov Rossiskoi Federatsi: Rezervnyi Fond, www1 .minfin.ru/ru/reservefund/accumulation (accessed 30 August 2009).

39. Byudgetnyi Kodeks Rossiiskoi Federatsii, chapter 13.2, article 96.11, paragraph 2, www.roskodeks.ru/codecs/201.html (accessed 30 August 2009).

40. Byudgetnyi Kodeks Rossiiskoi Federatsii, chapter 13.2, article 96.11, paragraphs 1, 3; Postanovlenie Pravitel'stva Rossiskoi Federatsii, no. 955, 29 December 2007, "O Poryadke upravleniya sredstvami Rezervnogo Fonda," www1.minfin.ru/ru/reservefund/legalframework/rf_pprf/index.php?id4=6600; Postanovlenie Pravitel'stva Rossiskoi Federatsii, no. 805, 6 November 2008, "O vnesenii izmenenii v trebovaniya k finansovym aktivam, v kotorye mogut razmeshchatsya sredstva Rezervnogo Fonda," www1.minfin.ru/ru/ reservefund/legalframework/rf_pprf/index.php?id4=6776; Prikaz Ministerstva Finansov RF, no. 3, 16 January 2008, www1.minfin.ru/ru/legislation/orders/ index.php?id4=5813; Prikaz Ministerstva Finansov RF, no. 4, 16 January 2008, www1.minfin.ru/ru/legislation/orders/index.php?id4=5811; Prikaz Minister-stva Finansov RF, no. 5, 16 January 2008, www1.minfin.ru/ru/legislation/ orders/index.php?id4=5812; Prikaz Ministerstva Finansov RF, no. 11, 17 Janu-ary 2008, www1.minfin.ru/ru/legislation/orders/index.php?id4=5814; Prikaz Ministerstva Finansov RF, no. 12, 17 January 2008, www1.minfin.ru/ru/ legislation/orders/index.php?id4=5815; Prikaz Ministerstva Finansov RF, no. 116, 24 January 2009, www1.minfin.ru/ru/reservefund/legalframework/ prikaz/index.php?id4=7148. Webpages accessed 30 August 2009.

41. Byudgetnyi Kodeks Rossiiskoi Federatsii, chapter 13.2, article 96.8, paragraph 4.

42. Byudgetnyi Kodeks Rossiiskoi Federatsii, chapter 13.2, article 96.10, paragraphs 1–2.

43. Postanovlenie Pravitelstva Rossiskoi Federatsii, no. 18, "O poryadke upravleniya sredstvami Fonda Natsionalnogo Blagosostoyaniya," 19 Janu-ary 2008, www1.minfin.ru/ru/nationalwealthfund/legalframework/fnb_pprf/ index.php?id4=6616 (accessed 30 August 2009).

44. Ministerstvo Finansov Rossiskoi Federatsii: Osnovnye napravleniya byudgetnoi politiki na 2010 god i planovyi period 2011 i 2012 godov, www1 .minfin.ru/common/img/uploaded/library/2009/08/Osnovnye_napravleniya _budzhetnoy_politiki.doc (accessed 30 August 2009); Ministerstvo Finansov Rossiskoi Federatsii: Vyskazyvaniya Nesterenko informatsionnym agentst-

vam po itogam zasedaniya pravitelstva RF, www.minfin.ru/ru/press/speech/ index.php?id4=8021 (accessed 31 August 2009).

45. From 2005 to 2007 the average size of the work pension grew by 1.76 times, in 2008–2009 it grew again by 78 percent, and in 2010 a further increase of the pension by 45 percent is scheduled (Sergei Aleksashenko, "Ekonomicheskaya politika: tsena reitinga," *Vedomosti*, 31 August 2009).

46. Dmitrii Dokuchaev and Pavel Chuvilayev, "'Tyani-Tolkai' na rynke," *The New Times*, no. 29 (24 August 2009), 32–33.

47. Aleksandr Koksharov, "Peredyshka posle buma," *Expert*, no. 32 (24–30 August 2009), 35.

7

Oil, Gas, Transit, and Boundaries

Problems of the Transport Curse

Nikolay Dobronravin

The majority of the nations that received or regained independence after the collapse of the Soviet Union belong to the group of Landlocked Developing Countries, also known as LLDCs. This group includes almost all the countries of the South Caucasus and all countries of Central Asia. In terms of resource-based economies, this means that raw materials produced in these countries often have to be delivered to customers with extensive efforts on transportation through the territory of one or several transit countries. Transit for LLDC countries is not just a technical problem. According to the World Bank's assessment:

> An inland location frequently results in high trade transaction costs, with logistics costs accounting for 30% of the GDP of LLDCs, double that of other emerging economies and three times that for developed countries. . . . Transit trade is highly vulnerable to rent-seeking activities, inefficient bureaucratic procedures, and the inadequate provision of private sector services. The deficiencies extend to the reliability of supply chains particularly in the context of the small, distant markets served by many LLDCs. The current political economy does not provide incentives for the emergence of efficient freight transit operations. In many regions, including Sub-Saharan Africa and Central Asia, this has led to systems which can favor informal rather than formal operators.[1]

For post-Soviet countries exporting oil and natural gas, the issue of transit is related not only to the problem of the almost complete lack of equipped sea ports,[2] but also to the lack of direct access on land to the most profitable markets. After the Soviet collapse in 1991, these countries, in fact, became victims of the "transport curse." The reasons for the emergence and further evolution of the post-Soviet "transport curse" were created in the Soviet period due to its socio-economic geography and the policy of spatial development. The major industrial regions of the Soviet Union were remote from oil and gas fields. To deliver oil and gas to customers, either major railroads or grandiose pipelines had to be used. The borders between then Soviet Union republics did not serve as any barriers back then, and were hardly taken into account in the process of centralized state planning on the scale of the country as a whole. Also, a part of the transport network was inherited by the Soviet Union from the Russian Empire, in which these internal borders were still unknown. The central government of the Soviet Union compensated the republics for oil and gas not so much with money but merely in kind (i.e., imported goods, benefits for workers of the oil and gas sector, privileges for local party and state officials). These informal settlements became especially noticeable after the Soviet Union began to export oil and gas to Germany and other hard-currency buyers in Western Europe in the 1970s and 1980s. At the same time, transit of oil and gas to the West provided additional opportunities to supply cheap gas to socialist countries of Eastern Europe and to several republics of the Soviet Union. So-called All-Union (i.e., nationwide) ministries, which were located in Moscow, arbitrarily divided almost free raw materials among customers. The classic problem of the Soviet economy was reciprocal deliveries. For example, Kazakhstan received oil from Russia for processing, and sent its own oil to Russia, and the like.

No wonder that in the late 1980s, even before the collapse of the Soviet Union, most of the republics of the Soviet Union desired to escape from Moscow's control in a political, economic, and cultural sense. They began to drift toward the new centers of attraction such as the United States, the European Union, Turkey (for Azerbaijan and for the majority of Central Asian countries, apart from Tajikistan), and, to a lesser degree, East Asia (above all China), as well as Pakistan, Iran, Saudi Arabia, and other countries of the Islamic world. At the same time, Russia also aspired to the West. As a result, the ties that bound the Soviet economic world together were broken.

After 1991, all post-Soviet countries producing oil and gas elbowed each other as they tried to deliver their oil and gas to anyone who would pay in U.S. dollars or any other convertible currency, flouting the interests of other producers. In their turn, transit states hoped to strengthen their own economic prosperity, demanding both real payments for oil and gas transit (instead of nearly free transit in Soviet times), but also the preservation of Soviet very low prices for the oil and gas they needed for themselves. Governments and companies of the United States and other developed countries had received open access to new and highly attractive oil and gas resources in post-Soviet states,[3] but this access proved to be restricted, in many ways because of the transport curse. Already in the early 1990s it became clear how difficult it was to overcome the Soviet legacy. New transit routes were planned and their construction began, above all in the western direction, that is, toward the European Union. "Pipeline diplomacy"[4] was developed in the 1990s and especially in the 2000s. Various international programs for development of transport networks were elaborated[5]; the political influence of international actors and the post-Soviet states themselves was used for lobbying various transport routes that did not always seem rational from an economic standpoint. In a number of cases, as stated above, the political logic of "escaping from Russia" typically predominated. From the viewpoint of foreign observers and active participants of the process, a new "great game" had been launched in the post-Soviet area, and the countries consuming oil and gas raised their voices loudly and decisively.

Often, the expectations of players were excessive. As Charles E. Ziegler wrote, "The costs of extraction and transportation of oil are considerably higher for Central Asia than for the Middle East. More importantly, Russia and the Caspian states combined account for less than 8 per cent of the world's reserves, compared with the Middle East's two-thirds. Russia and Central Asia do have a key advantage, natural gas, though, since their reserves, at 31 per cent of the global total, far exceed those of the Persian Gulf states."[6]

Despite the enormous number of international projects, agreements, and statements on radical changes in the post-Soviet area (for example, several announcements of Russia's monopoly breaches over the export of oil and gas from countries of the South Caucasus and Central Asia),[7] the transport curse forces countries that gained political independence almost twenty years ago to continue to use networks inherited from the Soviet Union, even in cases when the political elites strive to cut off economic ties with Russia, and the old transport infrastructure is underdeveloped and requires technological updating.[8]

The major transport problem of most Central Asian countries was and continues to be the need to deal with Russia and Kazakhstan as transit countries. As early as 1993, the president of Uzbekistan, Islam

Karimov, explained the link between transport problems, relation-ships with Russia, and independence as following:

> I always say: communications are Uzbekistan's weakest point. As for now we only have an outlet to the North. God forbid if anyone would block this road! Who will we share our concerns with then? . . .
>   We talked about the Northern gates of our republic. We should also open gates like this to the South. Through Afghanistan we should reach Pakistan, and further to the Indian Ocean. Through Iran we should establish routes to Turkey, to the Persian Gulf. Through China we must establish ties with the Far East. Only with communi-cations of this level will we be able to consider ourselves independent from the economic standpoint.
>   We need Russia like water and air. We need its possibilities and ties.[9]

From the market perspective the oil and gas of Central Asia and Azerbaijan are too far from the most profitable clients, that is, con-sumers in the West.[10] One should remember that the difficulties of transporting oil from the Caspian region were written about back in the nineteenth century by Russian geographer Pyotr Chikhachev, noting the "isolation of Baku from European markets." According to Chikhachev, "After the building of the Baku-Batum railway, the Cas-pian oil has two sea routes for distribution across Europe—through Constantinople, and also through St. Petersburg and the cities of the Baltic provinces."[11] One and a half centuries since this assessment was made, the political and economic developments in Europe and Asia have changed considerably, and even borders and names of cit-ies and countries have changed numerous times. But still, the major export routes noted by Chikhachev have remained quite stable. Oil and gas shipments from the Caspian region are still mostly Europe bound, and they are usually delivered either through Georgia (the western or southwestern direction, with Turkey participating as a transit country) or through Russia (the northern route, and also with the possible transit to Turkey). Transit of oil and gas by the northern route from Azerbaijan and the Caspian regions of Kazakhstan are rela-tively simple from the technical viewpoint. The direct transportation of hydrocarbons to Russia from Turkmenistan via the Caspian Sea is also possible. However, de facto gas from Turkmenistan is delivered to Russia solely by transit through Kazakhstan.

Since the 1990s, Central Asian countries have strived to develop export of oil and gas not only to Europe (either through Russia or by-passing it) but also to East Asia. The major proposed consumers of oil and gas are located in the eastern provinces of China, which are far from Central Asia. Michael Klare assesses this export route ("the most ambitious") as follows: "Aside from the various geographical impediments to this project—much of the terrain along this route is harsh and mountainous—the proposed pipeline would pass through several areas of instability, including China's remote Xinjiang province."[12] Over the last two decades, the Chinese infrastructure has swiftly developed. Despite ethnopolitical problems, new transport routes have been laid through Xinjiang, and continue to develop in the form of pipelines and railways connecting China with Central Asia, first and foremost with Kazakhstan. According to Chinese assessments, "In history, Xinjiang served as the key controlling section of the well-known Silk Road, while now it is an unavoidable part of the railway leading to the second Eurasia Continental Bridge."[13] However, even in choosing the East Asian direction, Uzbekistan and Turkmenistan depend on their transit neighbors, Kazakhstan, and to a much lesser degree, Kyrgyzstan.

Yet another transit route for oil and gas developed in the Soviet period. Gas pipelines were built from Iran and Afghanistan to neighboring regions of the Soviet Union. The redirection of this route in the opposite route, from Kazakhstan and Turkmenistan to Iran, began at the end of the 1990s. From a purely geographical point of view, the shortest route to the Indian Ocean from the Caucasus, Central Asia, and several regions of Russia lies in the southern direction, through Iran or Afghanistan. The southern route is swiftly supported by Iran, in particular through the Economic Cooperation Organization (ECO) in which all the countries of Central Asia, Azerbaijan, Iran, Turkey, and Pakistan are members.[14] However, even with the most favorable economic, political, and security developments in the region, Iran and Afghanistan primarily remain transit states on the way to Pakistan,[15] India,[16] and other consumer countries. Thus, in the southern direction the problem of the transport curse for Azerbaijan and Central Asian oil and gas producing countries remains nearly the same.

The issue of oil and gas transit as an additional heavy burden for exporter countries may be partially solved with the aid of economic and political integration.[17] The possible weakening of the transport curse also depends to a large degree on the direction and scale of regional economic integration. The major unresolved problem is that the final removal of the transport curse from exporter countries of oil and gas, for example, to provide free transit to sea ports in accordance with the New York convention of 1965 (Convention on Transit Trade of Landlocked States) is highly unprofitable for transit states, which received their revenues from the transportation of exported natural resources.[18] According to the World Bank, these "gateway countries" for Azerbaijan are Georgia, Turkey, Russia, and Iran; for Kazakhstan it is Russia; for Turkmenistan they are Russia, Kazakhstan, Uzbekistan, and Iran; and for Uzbekistan they are Russia and Kazakhstan.[19] Thus, the economic and political future of oil and gas producing countries in post-Soviet Eurasia depends on political and policy decisions taken by governments of transit states, and their influence is no less, if not more important, than the actions of consumer countries.

KAZAKHSTAN: THE CENTER OF POST-SOVIET EURASIA

Among the post-Soviet countries, Kazakhstan most resembles Russia in many ways. Both countries are geographically located in both Europe and Asia, and both Russia and Kazakhstan have seen the spread of the ideology of "Eurasianism." Like Russia, Kazakhstan is a major producer of oil and gas; it currently holds second position for oil production among post-Soviet countries (after Russia). In 1994, the president of Kazakhstan, Nursultan Nazarbaev, proposed to establish the "Eurasian Union" on the basis of the Commonwealth of Independent States (CIS), and later the Eurasian economic community arose with the active involvement of Kazakhstan. The Russian-Kazakhstan border is the longest in the world, and estimates of its length differ by over one thousand kilometers.[20]

In the Soviet period, industrial enterprises and the infrastructure of neighboring regions of Kazakhstan and Russia were closely connected. And until now, several major communication routes between the European part of Russia and Siberia—railways, automobile roads, and pipelines—cut through the northern regions of Kazakhstan. Owing to its geographical position, Kazakhstan may export oil and gas without intermediaries to Russia, China, and Iran (by the Caspian Sea). However, the most profitable western route requires cooperation and mutual understanding with transit states. Also, Kazakhstan itself is a transit country for Turkmenistan and Uzbekistan, and to a lesser degree for Russia. The production of oil in the Caspian area in modern western Kazakhstan has been carried out since the early twentieth century, when the first pipeline was built. In the late 1970s and early 1980s, the important pipeline Pavlodar-Chimkent (Shymkent) was built as a part of the Omsk-Pavlodar-Shymkent-Charzhou pipeline system, which aimed on delivery of Western Siberian oil to oil processing enterprises of Kazakhstan, Uzbekistan, and Turkmenistan.[21]

Kazakhstan was not a single unified economy until the Soviet collapse in 1991. Some regions and major enterprises were controlled by All-Union ministries, and the republic had absolutely no say in their development process, with both the consumers and suppliers outside Kazakhstan. The leading position in industry was occupied by ferrous and nonferrous metallurgy, and considerable centralized investments from the Soviet Union budget were accounted for by oil, coal, and the mining and chemical industry. [22] In the political sense, Kazakhstan, like other republics of the Soviet Union that were established in the Soviet period, gradually underwent the process of state formation with its own ruling elite. Since 1989 the republic was headed by Nursultan Nazarbaev. On 16 December 1991, Kazakhstan declared its independence, after Russia, Ukraine, and Belarus announced the dissolution of the Soviet Union. Fifteen years later, the ambassador of Kazakhstan to Russia, Krymbek Kusherbaev, said, "It is not our fault that the Soviet Union collapsed. We were the last in the post-Soviet region to declare independence—on the 16th of December. Kazakhstan was also the last to leave the ruble zone."[23]

Despite numerous predictions, serious separatist movements did not emerge in Kazakhstan. Also, Kazakhstan did not turn into a mono-ethnic ethnocratic state. Political reforms in Kazakhstan generally followed the same model as in the neighboring Russian Federation, but occurred less turbulently. Two major propresidential parties, Asar and Otan, initially emerged, and in 2006 the united "party of power," Nur Otan, had been established.[24] In 1997, the capital of the country was transferred from Almaty (southern part of Kazakhstan) to Akmola (from 1998 renamed Astana) in the north of Kazakhstan. The move of the capital symbolized the break of Kazakhstan with the Soviet past. Also, tasks for more efficient governance of the country were solved more successfully.

In terms of economic reforms, a significant role during the first years of independence was played by young reformers (mainly ethnic Kazakhs), who proposed radical economic changes, as in Russia, but faced less visible resistance from political and economic actors. In 1997, in place of the ministry of oil and gas industry, the national companies Kazakhoil and Kazakhgaz were established. Also, the national company KazTransOil was established to manage all the major oil pipelines, oil product pipelines, and water pipelines. The gas transport system was managed in concession by the Belgian company Tractebel, and its affiliated firm Intergas Central Asia. The international consortium began to develop the major Kashagan oil field. In 2000, transportation of gas moved back into the hands of the state, and went under the control of KazTransGaz company. In 2001, the National Fund of the Republic of Kazakhstan was established for sterilization of revenues from oil and gas export; its assets were invested abroad, and their use was only allowed if world oil prices fell below $19 per barrel.[25] According to some assessments, during the period of 1996–2001 economic reforms in Kazakhstan reached their peak.[26] The developmental goal set up for Kazakhstan was its entry into the list of fifty most competitive countries in the world.

The pipeline transportation system of independent Kazakhstan is still closely linked with Russian oil pipelines. Oil was delivered from fields in western Kazakhstan by pipeline for further processing in Russia (in Orsk). Also, Western Siberian oil was transported for processing in Kazakhstan, and in exchange oil was delivered to Russia by the Atyrau-Samara pipeline. Only some of the Kazakhstan oil was exported, bypassing Russia, through the Caspian port of Aktau.[27] Gas to the southern regions of Kazakhstan was delivered from Uzbekistan, and from western Kazakhstan it was supplied to Russia. However, economic relationships of Kazakhstan with Russia and with Russian oil companies were rather complicated. On the one hand, according to some assessments, "oil barons of Kazakhstan were able to bribe Russia, which even to the detriment of national companies increased the quota by almost three times for the flow of oil export from Kazakhstan through its pipelines."[28] In the meantime, a conflict over revenues from sale of Kazakhstan gas became visible. In 1997, Nursultan Nazarbaev was said to lash out: "Gas processing in Orenburg, due to the efforts of Mr. Vyakhirev [then the CEO of Gazprom] and condensate processing at the factory in the Bashkir town of Salavat Yulaev is conducted in such conditions that from 1 dollar Kazakhstan gets only 13–17 cents. Why the hell do we need this gas?! I gave an order to close all these fields! We will move the pipeline inside the country, to Western China."[29] In practice, deliveries of gas to Russia continued, but under conditions that were much more beneficial for Kazakhstan. Also, in Russia after the major private oil company Yukos went bankrupt in the 2000s the Kazakhstan state corporation KazMunaiGaz became the major stakeholder in the oil processing enterprise in Lithuania, which formerly belonged to Yukos. However, the Russian company Transneft soon after that began a major repair of the pipeline for delivery of oil to Lithuania. The European Union demanded an urgent renewal of deliveries, but its efforts were unsuccessful.

In the 1990s, a conflict between Kazakhstan and Russia arose over fields located on the Caspian Sea shelf. The line of limitation of powers of the oil and gas ministries of Azerbaijan, Kazakhstan,

Turkmenistan, and the Russian Federation, which was established in the Soviet period, played the role of a conventional sea boundary. At last, in 1998, Kazakhstan and Russia agreed on a delimitation of the bottom of the Caspian Sea, and on a joint development of previously disputed fields.[30]

In 2005, the transportation of oil via Atasu-Alashankou pipeline, which connected Kazakhstan fields with Xinjiang in China, had been launched. The opening of this pipeline meant also that Kazakhstan could now serve as a transit country for deliveries of Western Siberian oil from Russia to China. As Russian diplomat Dina Gil'mutdinova notes, "For Kazakhstan, the development of the pipeline route to China is a geo-strategic task and is connected with its plans for independent export of raw materials without participation of transit countries."[31] Besides that, Kazakhstan joined the participants of the pipeline system Baku-Tbilisi-Ceyhan. Kazakhstan actively supported the proposed project to build the Trans-Caspian Gas Pipeline and its extension through Turkey to Central Europe (the Nabucco project). However, the Kazakhstan leadership did not intend to abandon completely the Russian route for transporting oil and gas to Europe. In 2001, Kazakhstan oil began to flow through Russia via the Caspian Pipeline Consortium (CPC) pipeline. In 2002, an agreement was signed on oil transit from Kazakhstan to the Russian port of Primorsk. A Russian route was also proposed for transit of natural gas from the Karachaganak gas condensate field, which is located near the Russian border. In 2007, an agreement was signed on construction of the Caspian gas pipeline, and on the reconstruction of the oil Soviet gas pipeline from Central Asia to Russia through the territory of Kazakhstan.

From 1997, according to the swap scheme, Kazakhstan oil was delivered to the processing plants in Iran, and in exchange, for the sake of Kazakhstan, Iranian oil was exported from the Persian Gulf. After a period of interruption connected with a scandal in the United States (the so-called Kazakhgate, involving supposed involvement of American oil businesses in this deal), deliveries were renewed.

As the general director of KazTransOil Askar Smankulov wrote in 2003, "The success of the further economic development of Kazakhstan will depend not only on the presence of oil and gas reserves, but primarily on the provision of transport independence of the republic in the export of hydrocarbon raw materials."[32] Already announced projects for transportation of gas and oil are so extensive that there are doubts whether Kazakhstan has enough of its own resources to fill new pipelines.[33]

During the period of growth of world prices on oil and gas, the oil and gas industry, which brought considerable revenues to Kazakhstan, served as the major driving sector of the economy. The growth of export receipts not only stimulated the major rise of expenditures among those people "sitting on the pipes," but also caused severe disappointment for those who were not allowed access to or were distanced from the "oil tap." Kazakhstan oil workers were dissatisfied with the low salaries, in particular when compared with the salaries of workers from Turkey. In the 2000s, this discontent was expressed in several spontaneous protests and interethnic tensions. Nevertheless, nationwide political stability has been preserved as yet.

In explaining why a color revolution did not happen in Kazakhstan, political analysts often refer to the need of maintaining stable deliveries of oil and gas.[34] This is an important issue indeed for Europe, China, and transit countries (including Russia), as they wish to avoid any domestic political crisis in Kazakhstan, which could lead to the "drying up" of pipes, challenging the stability of delivery of oil and gas. In its turn, the Kazakhstan ruling elite has incentives for the use of democratic rhetoric, which has helped in maintenance and development of economic and political ties with Europe and the United States.

With further economic growth, Kazakhstan's aspiration to political dominance in post-Soviet Central Asia becomes increasingly noticeable. However, Uzbekistan, which during the Soviet era claimed its leadership in Central Asia, along with other neighbors in the region, except Kyrgyzstan, did not support the Kazakhstan initiatives for regional integration. For Kazakhstan as an oil and gas producing country, the proposal of new Central Asian unity looks undoubtedly attractive. However, the possible loss of oil and gas transit revenues reduces the interest of Kazakhstan companies and ministries in a new unification of Central Asia.

TURKMENISTAN: A GAS POWER IN A
RING OF TRANSIT COUNTRIES

It was probably Turkmenistan that found itself in the worst position among post-Soviet oil and gas producing countries that gained independence in 1991. Transit of oil and gas from Turkmenistan to Europe is possible either by the Caspian Sea and then through two or three countries (Azerbaijan-Georgia, or Turkey), by sea through Russia, or by land through two or three countries (Kazakhstan-Russia or Uzbekistan-Kazakhstan-Russia). Transportation of its natural resources to China is impossible without transit through neighboring countries of Central Asia. And neither Iran nor Afghanistan today seems a reliable transit partner, either because of foreign pressure, or a continuing military conflict.

By the end of the Soviet period, the major sectors of the Turkmenistan economy were cotton and the oil and gas complex. From the 1960s, natural gas was produced in the country, primarily for consumption in Russia. A major railway and the gas pipeline system Central Asia–Center were laid through the territory of Uzbekistan and Kazakhstan to Russia.

In 1985, Saparmurat Niyazov became the Communist Party leader of the republic. In 1990 he was elected the first president of Turkmenistan, and in October 1991, Turkmenistan declared its independence.

In Turkmenistan, for the first time in post-Soviet Eurasia, an original national ideology was elaborated in the 1990s. According to Andrey Zaostrovtsev, it was the world's first "relatively successful project of non-religious and non-Marxist-Leninist ideological foundation of an autocracy."[35] The major book for all the people of Turkmenistan was *Rukhnama* by Saparmurat Niyazov. In 1993, he, as the founding father of the new Turkmenistan, was awarded the official title of the head of the Turkmens, or Turkmenbashi.[36] There was public recognition of the importance for Turkmens to belong to one of the five officially recognized tribes.[37] Unlike in Kazakhstan or Azerbaijan, a ruling family based on kinship ties was not established, though.

In the Turkmenistan economy, import substitution was encouraged, including oil processing. The oil and gas sector became the dominant industry of the economy of independent Turkmenistan. In the west of Turkmenistan, the Soviet oil and gas legacy went to the state company Turkmenneft and in the east to the company Turkmengaz. Foreign companies were allowed to participate in production and processing of oil and natural gas. Russia remained the major consumer and reseller of Turkmenistan gas. In 1997, a "gas conflict" arose, and deliveries through Russia were suspended because of the Ukrainian debt for Turkmenistan gas. The issue was resolved, and in 2003 Turkmenistan and Russia agreed on deliveries of Turkmen gas until 2028.

Revenues from the export of oil and especially gas have turned the sparsely populated Turkmenistan into a kind of post-Soviet Kuwait. The population of Turkmenistan received the right to free consumption of water, salt, gas, and electricity (within norms of consumption set up by the authorities). The low-income population groups were given free flour. Cheap petrol, and low costs on accommodation, telephone, and public transport have added to the picture of nearly universal "prosperity."[38] However, the genuine nature of the development of the Turkmenistan economy under Saparmurat Niyazov's rule is difficult to assess, as national statistics were classified information or unreliable. In 2003, a program for development of the country until 2020 was officially adopted. According to the program, by this time "Turkmenistan will join the group of most developed countries of the world. . . . The works on setting up a transportation infrastructure and implementation of the international oil and gas pipelines projects will be continued to provide targeted output of hydrocarbon resources and their delivery to international markets."[39]

After 1991, the construction of several new transit routes began, bypassing neighboring Uzbekistan. In 2006, the railway Ashgabat-Dashoguz (Tashauz) was opened; the north of Turkmenistan, which is historically and economically closely connected with Uzbekistan, received a direct link with southern regions and the capital of the country.[40] However, despite the regular exacerbation of relationships with the neighboring country, the major export route of Turkmen gas to Russia and Europe remained unchanged, passing through the territory of Uzbekistan. In 1996, the Tedhzen-Serakhs railway was opened, which links Turkmenistan with Iran. From the Turkmenistan point of view, this road "made it possible to connect the railways of Europe and Asia, and restore the Great Silk Road in a steel version."[41] In 2007, the presidents of Russia, Turkmenistan, and Kazakhstan agreed on the proposal of construction of a railway passing along the Caspian Sea as part of the corridor North-South (to the Persian Gulf).

Turkmenistan was faced with two major problems of its gas transit—the dilapidated system of its pipelines, and the not always friendly transit countries. Turkmenistan proposed to establish an international system of guarantees of reliable and stable transit of energy resources under the auspices of the United Nations.[42] Also, possibilities of diversification of export routes of Turkmen gas were the subject of permanent discussions. In particular, it was proposed to build the gas pipeline Turkmenistan-Iran-Turkey-Western Europe, the Trans-Caspian Gas Pipeline from Turkmenistan to Azerbaijan, the Trans-Afghan pipeline (Turkmenistan-Afghanistan-Pakistan with an extension to India), and also gas pipelines to South Asia (through Iran) and to China (through Uzbekistan and Kazakhstan, with an extension to Japan). In 1997, the first alternative route for the export of natural gas, a pipeline from Turkmenistan to northern Iran began to function.[43] Michael Klare noted about the Iranian direction of gas transit:

"By far the shortest and most expedient routes for carrying Caspian energy to world markets would extend southward from Azerbaijan and Turkmenistan through Iran to existing oil terminals on the Persian Gulf coast. But this route, of course, would clash with the official U.S. policy of isolating the Iranian economy."[44] In 1999, Turkmenistan, Azerbaijan, Georgia, and Turkey agreed on the proposed construction of the Trans-Caspian Gas Pipeline.[45] However, Turkmenbashi later refused to participate in this project because of complications in relationships with Azerbaijan. The construction of the other export gas pipelines did not begin under Saparmurat Niyazov's rule because of the complex situation surrounding Iran, war in Afghanistan, and difficult relationships with Uzbekistan, so most of these projects remain on paper as yet.

Maneuvering between several foreign partners, Turkmenbashi tried to avoid excessively strong dependence on any of them. In 1995, Turkmenistan declared its neutrality, remaining on the sidelines of international regional organizations in Central Asia. In 2005, Saparmurat Niyazov announced that his country was leaving the CIS. Turkmenistan was the only country in Central Asia to establish good neighborly relations with the Taliban regime in Afghanistan, but after 2001 it in fact assisted the antiterrorist coalition.

In December 2006, after the death of Turkmenbashi, the former deputy prime minister and minister of public health Gurbanguly Berdimuhamedov came to power. The major features of the socioeconomic development of the country, including free social benefits (free petrol was added in 2008) remained unchanged. To this day, the incomparably high oil and gas revenues received by Turkmenistan have not resulted in the rising demand for the large-scale modernization of this Central Asian country. According to an official Turkmenistan assessment, by 2030 "Turkmenistan will occupy one of the leading places in the world due to the considerable expansion of the delivery of hydrocarbons to the world market."[46] As the most profitable market for gas is still Europe, Turkmenistan, like Kazakhstan, will strive to improve relations with the West, at the same time developing ties with other customers, and if possible, preventing any radical changes within the country.

In May 2007, in the city of Turkmenbashi (formerly Krasnovodsk), the leaders of Turkmenistan, Russia, and Kazakhstan agreed on construction of the Caspian gas pipeline and reconstruction of the Central Asia–Center gas pipelines. At the same time, Turkmenistan did not reject the trans-Caspian route of gas export to Europe. In July

2009, at the cabinet meeting of ministers, President Berdimuhamedov announced:

> The independent audit of our gas fields carried out last year, and geologists' recent discoveries unveiled huge reserves of natural gas in the territory of our country for global community. Our duty is to back these discoveries with diligent effective work.
>
> I would like to note that today Turkmenistan has surplus tank gas. We are able to sell a required volume of gas on the border of our state. This opens up the opportunities to implement a number of the projects, including the NABUCCO Project. [47]

Relationships with Russia were also affected by the conflict over the temporary suspension of transit through the gas pipeline in April 2009. The accident was seen as an openly unfriendly act, according to the Foreign Ministry of Turkmenistan, "careless and irresponsible actions posing real threat to the life and health of people and fraught with unpredictable environmental consequences."[48] Also, in 2006, an agreement was signed on construction of the Turkmenistan-China gas pipeline (through Uzbekistan,[49] Kyrgyzstan, and Kazakhstan). This pipeline, inaugurated in December 2009, is supposed to be completed by 2011. In 2008, the preparation process for the construction of the Trans-Afghan gas pipeline (TAPI) to Pakistan and India has resumed, but at the moment the construction is planned for 2010–2015.[50]

Turkmenistan, a major producer of natural gas in Central Asia, may also become an important transit country, if transport corridors will develop from Kazakhstan and Russia to the south (through Iran and Afghanistan). However, today Turkmenistan is still in a ring of transit countries and the impact of the transport curse remains very significant.

AZERBAIJAN: THE ENERGY HUB OF THE CASPIAN

At first glance, Azerbaijan is the most prosperous among the countries analyzed in this chapter. The country is located closer to European customers than Kazakhstan or Turkmenistan. Also, the Azerbaijan transportation system today has outlets to the north, to the Russian Federation, to the south (to Iran), and to the west (to Georgia and Turkey). But still, since the end of the 1980s (i.e., from the late-Soviet period), Azerbaijan also encountered the problem of the transport curse. It was exacerbated by the geographical and geopolitical peculiarities of Azerbaijan, which was divided into two parts by the territory of neighboring Armenia, and also by the Armenian-Azerbaijan conflict and the security crisis in the North Caucasus.

Unlike Kazakhstan and Turkmenistan, Azerbaijan had previously existed as an independent state after the collapse of the Russian Empire (in 1918–1920). At the time, the western border of the Azerbaijan Democratic Republic remained undetermined because of the conflict with Armenia. After the Sovietization of all of Transcaucasia, Nagorno Karabakh, with a considerable Armenian population, became a part of Azerbaijan, receiving the status of an autonomous oblast. Nakhchivan, where Azeri people predominated, was also recognized as a part of Azerbaijan, but turned into an exclave, geographically isolated from the rest of the republic.[51] During World War II, the Soviet Red Army occupied southern (Iranian) Azerbaijan, and the Azerbaijan Democratic Republic was established there.[52] Then Soviet troops left Iran, and, as Robert Canfeld wrote, "following World War II the definitiveness of the boundary between north and south [in Azerbaijan and the Turkic-Iranian world in general] was further emphasized by the American decision to build up the Shah's Iran as a defensive barricade against any Soviet ventures into the oil-rich Middle East."[53]

Soviet Azerbaijan gradually turned into a quasi-independent nation-state. From 1969, the real power in the republic was concentrated in the hands of Heydar Aliyev, a native of Nakhchivan. By the late-Soviet period, Azerbaijan was no longer the major center of oil production in the Soviet Union, but ethnic Azeris played an important role in the development of the oil and gas sector in other republics and regions of the country. The transport network of Azerbaijan was primarily oriented toward the north (to Russia through the North Caucasus) and the west (to the Georgian ports of the Black Sea). Also, in 1971, a gas pipeline was built for supply of gas from Iran to Azerbaijan. Proposals for the further transit of Iranian gas to Europe through the Soviet Union were not implemented because of the Islamic revolution in Iran.

During the perestroika period, Moscow unsuccessfully attempted to rule Azerbaijan without Aliyev, while the Armenian-Azerbaijan conflict turned into a full-fledged war. On 30 August 1991, the independence of the Azerbaijan Republic was restored, and on 2 September the Nagorno Karabakh Republic declared its independence from Azerbaijan. Nakhchivan, which was ruled by Heydar Aliyev, was now de facto cut off from the rest of the territory of Azerbaijan. In 1992, Nakhchivan native Abülfaz Elçibay was elected as president of Azerbaijan. He was oriented toward close collaboration with Turkey under the slogan "two countries, one nation." Economic ties with Armenia were completely broken off, and transport routes to the north were regularly broken because of the military conflict in Chechnya.[54] Last but not least, the permanent instability in neighboring Georgia also damaged the Azerbaijan economy.

In 1993, Elçibay was overthrown by a military insurrection led by Colonel Surat Huseynov. Soon afterward Heydar Aliyev returned to power in Baku. In 1994, the leaders of Azerbaijan, Armenia, and Nagorno Karabakh agreed on a ceasefire. However, the Armenian-Azerbaijan border and the frontline in Karabakh have remained closed for Azerbaijan transit to Europe. During the years of Heydar Aliyev's second rule (1993–2003), political stability was restored in the country.[55] The president led the "party of power," Yeni Azerbaijan (New Azerbaijan). A new national ideology was elaborated by the leadership of the country. In 2000, Heydar Aliyev said in an address to the Azerbaijan people:

> Azerbaijan was destined to be a land dividing the East and the West and as such, was exposed to mighty influences of both the western and oriental civilisations. . . .
>
> The launch of the TRACECA programme, aimed at the restoration of the Silk Road, has facilitated further development in Azerbaijan's relations with European countries. As a country located in the centre of this major transportation corridor, Azerbaijan has become an important link between the East and the West. . . .
>
> The vast intellectual potential, natural wealth and a unique geographic location between Europe and Asia mean that Azerbaijan can assume a worthy place in the world community. The forthcoming restoration of the Great Silk Road under the TRACECA project represents an opportunity for the intensive development of communications and the global information system.[56]

Azerbaijan joined the GUAM bloc (Georgia, Ukraine, Azerbaijan, Moldova), which was created as a political counterbalance to Russia in the post-Soviet region. After the death of Heydar Aliyev, his son Ilham became the new leader of Azerbaijan, who continued the same policies. Under conditions of political stability, land reform and privatization were implemented, and the economy began to recover, primarily due to the major growth of the oil and gas sector.[57] In 1994, the "deal of the century" was signed for joint development of the offshore Caspian oil fields Azeri, Chirag, and Gunashli by an international consortium, the Azerbaijan International Operating Company (AIOC). Yet another international consortium launched the development of the deep sea gas condensate field Shah Deniz. Initially, Azerbaijan requested for the Caspian Sea to be divided into sectors, but the borders of the

Azerbaijan sector were determined without agreement with neighboring countries, which caused tension in relationships with Iran and Turkmenistan on several occasions. In the 2000s, the rise of prices in international oil markets led to a major inflow of petrodollars to Azerbaijan. The State Oil Fund was established for the concentration of extra revenues from export of natural resources.

The European aspirations of Azerbaijan were symbolically expressed in the appearance of the national currency, *manat* (after its denomination of 2006), because the design of its banknotes looks very similar to those of the euro. In 2006, the national committee Forward to Europe was established.[58] In 2009, Azerbaijan, like other countries of the South Caucasus, and also Belarus, Ukraine, and Moldova, joined the European Union program Eastern Partnership. For the export of oil to Europe, initially the northern route was used through the Russian port of Novorossiisk. But then, oil transit had been diverted, and in 1999 the Baku-Supsa pipeline through Georgia was opened. In 2005, the construction on the Baku-Tbilisi-Ceyhan pipeline was completed, and Azerbaijan oil reached the world market bypassing Russia and Black Sea ports.[59] In 2007, the gas pipeline Baku-Tbilisi-Erzurum was built, and Azerbaijan gained another point of entry to the Western markets. Also, Azerbaijan joined the European Nabucco pipeline project. It is planned to fill the Azerbaijan pipelines with oil and gas from Kazakhstan and Turkmenistan. At the same time, supply of Azerbaijan gas has also been promised to Gazprom, for export to the north.

The deficit of gas for domestic consumption was supplemented by import from Russia and Kazakhstan (through Russia). At the end of 2004, a conflict arose over gas prices, and from 1 January 2005 deliveries from Russia were stopped, so the need for an alternative route of gas transit became apparent.[60] In early 2006, Gazprom once again raised gas prices, and Azerbaijan reoriented itself to deliveries from Iran, by a gas pipeline that was built in the Soviet period.[61] Even before the crisis of relationships of Azerbaijan with Gazprom, the gas to Nakhchivan Autonomous Republic was delivered from Iran, and Baku covered these expenditures from the national budget.[62] From early 2007, Azerbaijan stopped importing gas from Russia.

Major differences in calculations and forecasts make it difficult to assess the potential of Azerbaijan as an oil and gas producing country. The position of Azerbaijan as a transit country for export of hydrocarbons from Central Asian countries is much more promising. According to the most optimistic calculations, "if, as expected, cargo transit through Azerbaijan increases by 8–10 times in the near future, this will bring annual revenues of over $1 billion."[63] One should note that Azerbaijan's major competitor as a transit country is Russia, though. In the future, the development of export of Central Asian hydrocarbons to South Asia and China may also reduce Azerbaijan's likelihood to turn into an energy hub of Eurasia and completely abandon the "transport curse."

NOTES

1. Trade Logistics Group, World Bank, *Trade and Transit Facilitation in Landlocked Countries*, siteresources.worldbank.org/INTTLF/Resources/Transit_Project_Brochure.pdf (accessed 30 July 2009).

2. Despite its long shoreline, this also applies to Russia to a significant degree. Only in the post-Soviet period did export of oil begin from Primorsk (Leningrad Oblast, at the Baltic Sea) and Arctic ports, and also of natural gas from Sakhalin.

3. In geopolitical literature, the Caspian region belongs to the so-called strategic triangle, or, together with Russian Western Siberia, to the strategic ellipse. See Michael T. Klare, *Resource Wars: The New Landscape of Global Conflict* (New York: Owl Books, repr. ed. 2002), 49; Robert L. Canfield, "Continuing Issues in the New Central Asia: Addenda in Appreciation to Géopolitique de la nouvelle Asie centrale," in Mohammad-Reza Djalili, Alessandro Monsutti, and Anna Neubauer, eds., *Le monde turco-iranien en question* (Paris: KARTHALA Editions, 2008), 22–23.

4. See Mohammad-Reza Djalili and Thierry Kellner, *Géopolitique de la nouvelle Asie centrale de la fin de l'URSS à l'après-11 septembre* (Paris: Presses universitaires de France, 2006), 203–73, especially the notion on "*bataille des pipelines*" (i.e., "pipeline battle").

5. Interstate Oil and Gas Transmission to Europe (INOGATE), Transport Corridor Europe Caucasus Asia (TRACECA), and other international programs and projects with the participation of economically developed countries of Europe and Asia.

6. Charles E. Ziegler, "China, Russia and Energy in the CCA Region and East Asia," in Richard Auty and Indra de Soysa, eds., *Energy, Wealth & Governance in the Caucasus & Central Asia: Lessons Not Learned* (New York: Routledge, 2006), 232.

7. See, for example, Klare, *Resource Wars*, 81–108.

8. In an undoubtedly apologetic book on modern Kazakhstan, Roi Medvedev wrote, "The republic does not have enough railways, and especially highways. It is considered that up to 50% of pipelines in Kazakhstan require replacement." See Roi A. Medvedev, *Kazakhstanskii proryv* (Moscow: Institute for Economic Strategies, 2007), 81.

9. Islam Karimov, "Perekhod na novuyu valyutu ravnoznachen revolyutsii," Speech at the XII session of the Supreme Soviet of Uzbekistan, 7 May 1993,

Press Service of the President of the Republic of Uzbekistan, 2004, press-service .uz/rus/knigi/9tom/1tom_9.htm (accessed 5 July 2009).

10. On the peripheral nature of Central Asia after the fifteenth century, see Djalili and Kellner, *Géopolitique*, 31–32.

11. Pyotr A. Chikhachev, *Stranitsa o Vostoke* (Moscow: Nauka, 1982), 205–6.

12. Klare, *Resource Wars*, 104.

13. *Atlas of China* (Beijing: SinoMaps Press, 2008), 120.

14. See, for example, a discussion of the eleven routes of export of oil and gas from the Caspian region with arguments in favor of the Iranian route: J. Hashemi, "The Caspian Sea: Calm Past and Turbulent Future," *Envoy* (April 1997), 26–29. See also Directorate of Transport and Communications, Economic Cooperation Organization, "Economic Cooperation Organization: A Presentation on the ECO Activities: Transport Facilitation for Landlocked Countries," April 2009, unece.org/trans/doc/2009/wp5/GE2-wkshp1-ECO3 .pdf (accessed 3 August 2009).

15. Pakistan supports construction of pipelines both as a consumer and as a potential transit state. See Dr. Raja Muhammad Khan, "Pakistan as Future Energy Corridor," *South Asia Research and Analysis Studies*, 10 May 2009, saras.org.pk/viewarticle.php?topicid=1042 (accessed 5 August 2009).

16. Nirmala Joshi notes, "In the changed context of 1991, India began to look upon the five states of Central Asia as part of its 'extended neighborhood.'" See Nirmala Joshi, "India-Russia Relations and the Strategic Environment in Eurasia," *Acta Slavica Iaponica*, no. 16 (2007), 196–97, src-h.slav.hokudai.ac.jp/coe21/publish/no16_1_ses/10_joshi.pdf (accessed 1 August 2009).

17. On the poor development of intraregional trade, see Thierry Kellner, "L' 'axe turco-iranien': Vers un nouveau concept géopolitique," in Mohammad-Reza Djalili, Alessandro Monsutti, and Anna Neubauer, eds., *Le monde turco-iranien en question* (Paris: KARTHALA Editions, 2008), 37–55.

18. See Kishor Uprety, *The Transit Regime for Landlocked States: International Law and Development Perspectives* (Washington, D.C.: World Bank, 2006). In 2007, Kazakhstan joined the convention.

19. World Bank, *Trade and Transit Facilitation in Landlocked Countries*.

20. See Sergei V. Golunov, *Rossisko-kazakhstanskaya granitsa: problemy bezopasnosti i mezhdunarodnogo sotrudnichestva* (Volgograd: Volgograd State University Press, 2005).

21. Askar Smankulov, "Sistema treuboprovodnogo transporta nefti respubliki Kazakhstan: Realii i perspektivy," *Sayasat*, no. 1 (2003), 8–10, www.sayasat -policy.freenet.kz/num1/smankulov.htm (accessed 5 August 2009).

22. See Z. Saktaganova, "K voprosu o meste i roli Kazakhstana v obshchesoyuznoi ekonomicheskoi integratsii v poslevoennyi period," in Sergei V. Golunov, ed., *Rossiya i Vostok: problemy vzaimodeistviya* (Volgograd: Volgograd State University Press, 2003), 66–78.

23. Krymbek Kusherbaev, "Kazakhstan dob'etsya udvoeniya VVP k 2008 godu, a utroeniya-k 2015-mu," *Rossiiskaya Federatsiya segodnya*, no. 11

(2005), 11, www.russia-today.ru/2005/no_11/11_neighbours.htm (accessed 20 July 2009).

24. For a brief overview of the economic developments of Kazakhstan after 1991, see Andrey Zaostrovtsev, "Kazakhstan: Avtokraticheskaya model' ekonomicheskogo vzleta," in Otar Marganiya, ed., *SSSR posle raspada* (St. Petersburg: Economicus, 2006), 197–229.

25. See Zaostrovtsev, "Kazakhstan: Avtokraticheskaya model'," 210–13, 225–28.

26. Zaostrovtsev, "Kazakhstan: Avtokraticheskaya model'," 218. Some of the other authors considered either 1997 or 1998 as the "point of departure."

27. Smankulov, "Sistema truboprovodnogo transporta."

28. Sagyndyk Mendybaev and Viktor Shelgunov, *Kleptokratiya. Kazakhgate. Novoe rassledovanie* (Moscow: Company Sputnik +, 2001), 44.

29. Mendybaev and Shelgunov, *Kleptokratiya*, 135.

30. Golunov, *Rossiisko-kazakhstanskaya granitsa*, 64–66.

31. Dina A. Gil'mutdinova, *Politika SShA v Kaspiiskom regione: Na primere Azerbaijana, Kazakhstana i Turkmenistana* (Moscow: Nauchnaya kniga, 2007), 93.

32. Smankulov, "Sistema truboprovodnogo transporta."

33. Petr Svoik, "Rasskazy o nefti," *Sovmestnyi proekt gazety "Epokha" i Interner-gazety "Navi-II,"* 2005, www.zonakz.net/ (accessed 20 July 2009).

34. See Andrey Scherbak, "Neftyanoe proklyatie i postsovetskie rezhimy: Politiko-ekonomicheskii analiz," *Obshchestvennye nauki i sovremennost'*, no. 1 (2007), 47–56. See also chapter 3 in this volume.

35. Andrey Zaostrovtsev, "Idealy konstitutsionnoi ekonomiki i rossiiskaya real'nost'," in Leonid Limonov, ed., *Aktual'nye politicheskie problemy Rossii* (St. Petersburg: Leontief Center, 2005), 155. Political opposition in Turkmenistan used the term *bashism* for labeling of this political system.

36. For an overview of the political developments of Turkmenistan in 1991–2006, see Nikolay Dobronravin, "Turkmenistan: Velikoe odinochestvo," in *SSSR posle raspada*, 455–76.

37. On the tribal, kinship, and clan-based groups of the Turkmenistan elite, see Shokhrat Kadyrov, "Central Asia, The Ethnology of Political Management: Yesterday, Today & Tomorrow" (a special report for the seminar on Turkmenistan, Oslo, 6 June 2005), www.igpi.ru/bibl/other_articl/1119947605.html (accessed 30 July 2009).

38. Saparmurat Niyazov, "Ukaz Prezidenta Turkmenistana: O bezvozmezdnom predostavlenii naseleniyu Turkmenistana prirodnogo gaza, elektrichestva, vody i povarennoi soil do 2030 goda," *Turkmenistan: The Golden Age*, 25 October 2006, www.turkmenistan.gov.tm/_ru/laws/?laws=01cn (accessed 1 August 2009).

39. "Turkmenistan: Gosudarstvennye programmy," trm.gov.tm/countri/gos&prog.html (accessed 3 July 2009); "National Program 'The Strategy of Economic, Political and Cultural Development of Turkmenistan until 2020.' Main Goals and Tasks for the Period until 2020," www.turkmenistan

.ru/?page_id=5&lang_id=en&elem_id=5598&type=event&sort=date_desc (accessed 5 July 2009).

40. See Sergei A. Tarkhov, "Novye zheleznye dorogi v postsovetskom prostranstve," *Pervoe sentyabrya: Geografiya*, no. 3 (January 2000), 2–3, geo.1september.ru/articlef.php?ID=200000301 (accessed 31 July 2009).

41. "Stal'nye magistrali v budushchee," *Turkmenistan: The Golden Age*, 14 May 2007, www.turkmenistan.gov.tm/ekonom/ek&trans.htm (accessed 5 August 2007).

42. United Nations General Assembly Resolutions, Resolution 63/210, "Reliable and Stable Transit of Energy and Its Role in Ensuring Sustainable Development and International Cooperation," 2008, daccessdds.un.org/doc/ UNDOC/GEN/N08/483/39/PDF/N0848339.pdf?OpenElementt (accessed 4 August 2009).

43. S. Gozhiy, "Yugo-zapadnyi neftegazovyi kompleks: Den' segodnyashnii i perspektivy," 7 March 2007, www.turkmenistan.gov.tm/ekonom/ek&oil.htm (accessed 5 July 2009).

44. Klare, *Resource Wars*, 100.

45. Jim Nichol, "Turkmenistan: Recent Developments and U.S. Interests," *Congressional Research Service, Library of Congress*, 13 May 2004, www.fas .org/sgp/crs/row/97-1055.pdf (accessed 5 July 2009).

46. Ministry of Economy and Development of Turkmenistan, *Investigation Guide*, www.economy.gov.tm/arhiw/GID/GID_eng.doc (accessed 1 August 2009).

47. "President of Turkmenistan Gurbanguly Berdimuhamedov addressed the enlarged sitting of the Cabinet of Ministers of Turkmenistan (July 10, 2009)," *Turkmenistan: The Golden Age*, 11 July 2009, www.turkmenistan .gov.tm/_en/?idr=4&id=090711a (accessed 25 July 2009).

48. "CAC-4 Gas Pipeline under Reconstruction," *Turkmenistan: The Golden Age*, 10 April 2009, www.turkmenistan.gov.tm/_en/?idr=5&id=090410a (accessed 10 July 2009).

49. See "Tranzit-delo vygodnoe," *Газета.uz*, 9 July 2009, www.gazeta .uz/2009/07/09/gas/ (accessed 20 July 2009).

50. "Govt to Reactivate TAPI Gas Pipeline Project," *Daily Times*, 14 May 2009, www.dailytimes.com.pk/default.asp?page=2009%5C05%5C14%5Cstory _14-5-2009_pg7_16 (accessed 20 July 2009); Aftab Maken, "TAPI Gas Pipeline Finalised. Work on Four-Nation Project to Start from 2010," *News International*, 25 April 2008, thenews.jang.com.pk/top_story_detail.asp?Id=14300 (accessed 20 July 2009).

51. See Rakhman Mustafa-zade, *Dve respubliki: Azerbaijano-rossiiskie otnosheniya v 1918–1922 gg.* (Moscow: MIK, 2006), 234–35.

52. This pro-Soviet republic had little in common with the Azerbaijan Democratic Republic of 1918–1920.

53. Canfield, "Continuing Issues in the New Central Asia," 22–23.

54. On the oil aspect of the wars in Chechnya, see Yahia Said, "Greed and Grievance in Chechnya," in Mary Kaldor, Terry Lynn Karl, and Yahia Said, eds., *Oil Wars* (London: Pluto Press, 2007), 130–56.

55. On the political developments of this period, see, for example, Nikolay Dobronravin, "Azerbaijan: 'poslednii rubezh' Evropy na granitse s Iranom?" in *SSSR posle raspada*, 338–42.

56. Haydar Aliyev, "Address of Haydar Aliyev, President of Azerbaijan, to the Azerbaijani People at the Beginning of the New Year of 2001, the New Century and the New Millennium December 29, 2000," *"Heydar Aliyev's Heritage" International Online Library*, library.aliyev-heritage.org/en/2541517 .html (accessed 4 August 2009).

57. "Noveishaya istoriya azerbaijanskoi nefti," *Caspian Energy*, www.casp energy.com/19/history_r.html (accessed 5 July 2009).

58. B. Safarov, "'Vpered k Evrope.' Sozdan natsional'nyi komitet," *Echo*, 11 February 2006, www.echo-az.com/archive/2006_02/1264/politica09.shtml (accessed 30 June 2009).

59. On the role of Nagorno Karabakh in oil transit, see Mary Kaldor, "Oil and Conflict: The Case of Nagorno Karabakh," in *Oil Wars*, 157–82.

60. Volodimir Saprykin, "Iz zhizni gazoprovodov: Yuzhnyi Kavkaz idet ot Rossii k Iranu?" *Zerkalo nedeli*, 22–28 January 2005, 1, www.zn.kiev.ua/ 2000/2229/48978/ (accessed 10 July 2009).

61. Mina Muradova and Rufat Abbasov, "Azerbaijan Eyes Iran as Baku Seeks to Diversify Energy Imports," *EurasiaNet*, 6 January 2006, www.eurasianet .org/departments/business/articles/eav010506.shtml (accessed 20 July 2009).

62. See the interview with the chairman of the Supreme Majlis of the Nakhchivan Autonomous Republic (Naxçıvan Muxtar Respublikası): Oleg Tsyganov, "Vasif Talybov: 'Esli by ne kommunikatsionnaya izolirovannost', Nakhchivan razvivalsya by gorazdo intensivnee," *Izvestiya*, 25 November 2004, www.izvestia.ru/azerbaijan/article752034 (accessed 5 July 2009).

63. "Azerbaijan Development Gateway: Biznes i ekonomika," www.gate way.az/rus/country/business.shtml (accessed 5 July 2009).

8

Oil, Gas, and Modernization of Global South

African Lessons for Post-Soviet States

Nikolay Dobronravin

During the period between World War II and the end of the 1980s, the Soviet Union, the People's Republic of China, North Korea, Cuba, and other countries belonging to the so-called socialist camp had a huge influence on many oil and gas producing countries in Asia, Africa, and Latin America. Today it may seem surprising that the economic influence of the socialist countries was typically rather modest, or even completely incomparable with the ideological charm of socialism. The influence of the "Red East" was manifested in the aspiration to spurt into further economic and social developments, following the path that had already been taken by the Soviet Union and other "socialist brothers." But foreign economic relations of countries of the global South, despite the charm of Soviet or Chinese socialism, were still oriented toward the "capitalist West."

In the African countries that were building state socialism ("countries of socialist orientation," as they were known to their Soviet and Eastern European allies), the oil and gas sector of the economy passed through the stage of nationalization and the battle with major transnational companies from Europe and North America. The results of these policies were ambiguous everywhere. On the one hand, the export revenues of these countries and the prosperity of their leaders quickly increased. On the other hand, the dependence of these countries on oil money proved destructive for the national economy. The effects of "imitator's hangover"—disappointment in the imitated ideology of state socialism—led these countries to deep political crises. In sum, the project of "noncapitalist" modernization of the 1950s and 1980s brought African oil and gas producing countries to both economic and political dead ends. However, as will be shown in this chapter, an "oil hangover"[1] also affected those African resource-rich countries that did not attempt to build a socialist society. Yet, as Leo Tolstoy wrote in his famous novel *Anna Karenina*, "Happy families are all alike; every unhappy family is unhappy in its own way." All the oil-dependent countries suffered in different ways. However, despite the romantic ideas of both left-wing and right-wing ideologists, different versions of the oil hangover in countries of the global South proved to be surprisingly similar.

Oil-rich African states, regardless of the ideological preferences of their national governments, are presented, probably, as the most vivid example of the incredible monotony of the effects of the resource curse than any other regions of the world. The extensive growth of production and export of oil and gas was accompanied by degradation of non-oil sectors of their economies. In various countries, the scope of scale of their crises against the background of the oil boom was considerably different. For example, according to Jean-Philippe Koutassila, the "oil curse" in fact did not affect Cameroon.[2] On the contrary, Nigeria is typically considered to be a classic case of all negative effects of the resource curse. Case studies and comparative analyses of national versions of the oil boom and the subsequent hangover are well presented in numerous publications by economists and political scientists.[3] In recent years, a critical analysis of the consequences of the developments of oil and gas producing countries of Africa (such as poverty, corruption, environmental crisis, and several bloody wars) turned into more skeptical yet more realistic assessments of their chances and possibilities. For example, Ghazvinian wrote:

> Even if a *rentier* state is led by inspired and visionary politicians determined to behave with integrity and the best interests of the population at heart—always a big if—there may be a real limit to how much they can achieve. To begin with, an extreme dependency on oil exports for national revenue leaves a country vulnerable to the frequent, unpredictable fluctuations in the price of oil. In a country like the Republic of Congo, for example, where petroleum accounts for a staggering 90 percent of export revenue, it is difficult to plan budgets from one year to the next or to put long-term macroeconomic strategies in place when you know that, within a couple of years, oil can dive from $80 a barrel to $20 a barrel. But even if a politician takes the brave decision to invest an oil windfall in developing traditional agriculture and industry, it is not always clear how he can go about doing so. If you are one of the world's poorest nations and your traditional economic mainstay is primitive cassava farming, such a small cottage industry does not have the capacity to absorb a sudden

investment of billions of dollars. Therefore, even the best-intentioned leaders in a *rentier* state find that at least a portion of the country's windfall is better invested in overseas brokerage accounts, where a reasonable return on investment seems guaranteed over the long term. And so there the money sits, collecting interest and gathering dust, dipped into occasionally by unscrupulous politicians or spent on military hardware to put down rebellions, but rarely used to develop cassava farming.[4]

African exporters of oil and gas, and especially countries of the Gulf of Guinea, became victims of rapid urbanization and the sharp rise of the state sector. All of these countries experienced the inflow of large amounts of legal and illegal immigrants. The arrival of foreigners caused xenophobia at the level of the state, something totally unknown before because of the peculiarities of the colonial history of Africa.[5] A typical manifestation of this was the launching of discussion about the origins of leaders of African states. For example, the second president of Gabon, Omar Bongo, was accused by the opposition of being Congolese; in the neighboring Republic of Congo (Congo-Brazzaville), President Denis Sassou Nguesso was also accused by the opposition of being of West African origin, and the like. The president of Angola, José Eduardo dos Santos, according to his official biography, was born into a family of migrants from the then Portuguese-held island of São Tomé (part of today's Democratic Republic of São Tomé and Príncipe) in the Angolan capital of Luanda, but the opposition claims that he was in fact born on São Tomé. Also, the competition between political actors transferred into an institutionalized form of conflicts between the "ruling" and "opposition" ethnic groups, for example, between the Bateke and Fang in Gabon. Under the first president of Gabon, Léon M'ba, the Fang, who are the largest ethnic group in the country, dominated in politics and occupied key governmental posts. After the death of President M'ba, the Bateke became the "ruling" ethnic group, while opposition politicians from the Fang accused the second president of Gabon, Omar Bongo, of "*fangophobie.*"

The political developments of petro-states of the Gulf of Guinea vastly differed. In 1960, Gabon, Congo-Brazzaville, and Nigeria became independent, followed by Angola in 1975. Gabon and Nigeria oriented themselves toward the West, while Angola and Congo-Brazzaville were for a long time pro-Soviet "people's republics." Despite the differences in official ideology, the countries continued to keep close relations. The best example of these ties, undoubtedly, was the establishment of the "family bloc" of Congo-Brazzaville and Gabon, when Edith Lucie Sassou Nguesso, the daughter of the Marxist-Leninist

Congolese president, became the wife of Omar Bongo, the pro-Western president of Gabon. Besides Nigeria, all of these countries were almost permanently ruled by personalist powers of their postcolonial leaders. The typical examples are the president of Gabon, Omar Bongo, who ruled the country from 1967 to his death in 2009, and the president of Angola since 1979 José Eduardo dos Santos. Essentially, the president of the Republic of Congo (Congo-Brazzaville), Denis Sassou Nguesso, who ruled the country from 1979 to 1991 and again since 1997, also belongs to this respected and feared postcolonial elite (known as "African dinosaurs" to their critics).

Although the governments of most of the petro-states of the Gulf of Guinea joined the Extractive Industries Transparency Initiative (EITI), in fact the stimulation of transparency rarely went beyond vague declarations. Revenues from export of hydrocarbons ensured a swift growth of prosperity of elites of these countries, and a rise in nationwide corruption and unfulfilled expectations among the rest of the population. Depending on the ratio of oil and other sectors, experts tend to distinguish between oil-dependent economies (Gabon, and also Equatorial Guinea) and oil-dependent states (Congo-Brazzaville, Angola, and Nigeria).[6] Among these states, the share of oil revenues in GDP is highest in Angola. It is followed by Nigeria, Congo-Brazzaville, Equatorial Guinea, Gabon, and Cameroon. But the share of oil in export is highest in Nigeria, followed by Congo-Brazzaville, Angola, and Gabon, and then Equatorial Guinea and Cameroon.[7]

The development of oil and gas fields began onshore and then continued deep into the Gulf of Guinea continental shelf. Oil and gas production offshore would be impossible without at least a few onshore facilities and a delimitation of maritime boundaries. As a result, the water area was divided between states in the region.[8] São Tomé and Príncipe, together with Nigeria; and Congo-Brazzaville and Angola agreed to establish joint development zones (JDZ). The relatively peaceful nature of the division of the continental shelf between nations of the Gulf of Guinea is probably explained by the very fact that the offshore blocks awarded by African governments for oil and gas exploration and production are de facto not controlled by national governments, but rather by major foreign oil and gas corporations. In spite of growing criticism from nongovernmental environmental organizations and the local population, positive evaluations of the role of Western oil companies in the Gulf of Guinea are still widespread. These assessments are typical not only for the advertising of the companies themselves, but for independent political analysts, who stressed the importance of oil and gas for the development of Africa, and the strategic role of African hydrocarbons for international security.[9] On the contrary, the role of non-Western companies and/or states such as China, India, and Russia is usually seen as destructive, although all the recent political conflicts and widely discussed environmental problems in the region of the Gulf of Guinea are primarily connected with the involvement of Shell, Elf, BP, and other European and North American companies into political and economic developments of this region.

GABON AND THE REPUBLIC OF CONGO: "CAPITALIST CORE" AND "SOCIALIST SHELL"

Both the Gabon republic and the Republic of Congo (Congo-Brazzaville) may be traced back to the nineteenth-century administrative units of the French colonial empire. Between 1910 and 1958 both were parts of a single *gouvernement général*, French Equatorial Africa, with porous internal borders. The axis of development of the French Congo was the Congo River, while Gabon developed upstream along the Ogowe River. As a result, two different territorial units were formed, which resembled a core (Gabon) and its shell (Congo). Finally, in 1960 these two divisions turned into independent states, retaining much of their original intertwining. Gabon and the Congo share a common currency—the CFA franc, and both countries are part of the Economic and Monetary Community of Central Africa (CEMAC). After decolonization and the development of major oil fields, Gabon served as a kind of window of the West in Central Africa, and the People's Republic of the Congo (as the country was called from 1969 to 1990) was oriented toward the Soviet Union, China, and other socialist countries. But despite different slogans the political systems of these two countries were fundamentally similar. Since the late 1980s, after the beginning of Soviet perestroika, both Gabon and the Congo entered a period of democratization. Gabon suffered from these political reforms less than the Republic of the Congo, and continues to play the role of a relatively stable "core" in the region.

Although the territory of Gabon is about half of the size of France, its population is about 1.5 million residents. Foreigners (West Africans, Lebanese, French, etc.) make up 35 percent of the population and dominate in business. Immigrants from other African countries in Gabon are often accused of banditry and other crimes, and the opposition is more hostile toward them than the government.[10] Natives of the Republic of the Congo held a special position among immigrants in Gabon: the majority of immigrants from Congo-Brazzaville came to Gabon to flee the civil war. There were refugees from both sides of the conflict.[11]

The first political regime of independent Gabon was established after competitive multiparty elections were held in the colonial period, and then turned into a one-party regime of the Gabonese Democratic Bloc (BDG). In 1967, the first president of Gabon, Léon M'ba, died; his post was taken over by vice present El Hadj Omar Bongo Ondima (initially under the name of Albert-Bernard Bongo). Under the second president of Gabon, only the Gabonese Democratic Party (PDG) has been legally recognized for a long time. In 1973, the president of Gabon converted to Islam, although the absolute majority of the population is Christian. Simultaneously, a policy of partial nationalization (*gabonisation*) of the oil industry has been launched, and state revenues from export of oil increased significantly. In 1975, Gabon became a member of OPEC, and in 1979 the national oil company Petrogab (*Société Nationale des Pètroles Gabonais*) was established. The oil boom ended with a "hangover" during the period of major decline of prices in the late 1980s. In 1987, the notoriously inefficient Petrogab was at last dissolved. Democratization began in 1989, and in 1990, the multiparty National conference was held, and a major wave of protests hit the country under the slogan "Bongo must go" (*"Bongo doit partir,"* BDP) in Libreville, the capital of the country, and in Port-Gentil, the "oil capital" of Gabon. In 1991, the new constitution of the Gabon Republic was adopted. In 1993, Omar Bongo won the presidential elections. In 1998, after yet another election victory, Omar Bongo called Gabon citizens to a so-called *démocratie conviviale*. The ruling group of the regime, which the opposition called *"Bongocrature,"* nevertheless was able to cope with major economic crises in 1994 (due to the devaluation of the CFA franc) and also in 1998 (after a severe decline in oil prices).[12]

In 2003, the constitution of Gabon changed, and presidential elections were held according to plurality rather than a majority formula, while presidential term limits were abolished (previously, presidents could serve only two terms for seven years each). The president's son, Ali Bongo, defense minister and one of the deputy chairmen of the ruling party, since that time was widely regarded as the future president of Gabon. The PDG, according to Omar Bongo, "is the only multi-ethnic party in the country, and this is where its power and influence lies."[13] The opposition to the ruling regime was intense but it was organized on regional and ethnic grounds (on the Fang people), and thus its chances were rather limited. Omar Bongo gradually became the patriarch of African politics. He took part in the management of numerous conflicts in neighboring countries. Maintaining close ties with France (French military troops were located in the country from 1960), the president severely criticized the neocolonialism of the former colonial power.[14]

During 2005 presidential elections, El Hadj Omar Bongo Ondimba received 79 percent of the vote. In October 2006 he announced, "There is no heir apparent. Who says that the succession is up for grabs? I will be a candidate in 2012 if God gives me strength."[15] Omar Bongo remained in power for forty-two years. In March 2009, his wife died, and in June the president himself passed away; in August his son Ali Bongo Ondimba won the early election, with a relatively low 41.73 percent of the vote. Immediately after the election, there were mass protests in Port-Gentil, with some violent attacks on the French consulate and the headquarters of Total Gabon.

French companies (Elf, and then Total) played a leading role in the history of Gabon as a petro-state. Onshore oil fields were discovered in 1956. Later on the major area of oil production was moved to offshore fields. According to experts, "Gabon has been a major oil producer for many decades. Historically, oil revenues accounted for approximately 60 percent of the government's budget, more than 40 percent of GDP, and 75 percent of export earnings. Despite holding Sub-Saharan Africa's third largest oil reserves, oil preeminence in Gabon's economy is expected to decline due to maturing oil fields."[16] The peak of oil production was reached in 1998, and then a decline of the entire oil sector began. In 1996, the country left OPEC. More than half of oil export is now accounted for by the United States. Oil export to East Asia grew rapidly after 2004, when an agreement was signed on deliveries of Gabon crude oil to China. Foreign companies dominated production and export of oil in Gabon; they operate according to contracts on development and production sharing agreements, stated in the law of 1983. The leading positions are held by Shell Gabon and Total Gabon, two joint ventures of subsidiaries of major international companies with the participation of the Gabon government. Only a small number of Gabon residents are employed in the oil industry. The oil workers' trade union (*Organisation nationale des employés du pétrole*, ONEP) only has around four thousand members. In 2007, according to the assessment of Omayra Bermúdez-Lugo, "crude petroleum accounted for 49.4 percent of the country's GDP compared with 52 percent in 2006. Gabon's current proven petroleum reserve base was estimated to be 2 billion barrels. Crude petroleum output, however, has been on a declining trend since 1997 primarily because of the exhausting of old oil fields."[17]

The preliminary results of the oil-driven period in the history of Gabon may be regarded as rather ambiguous, as well as in all the other African oil states. For a long time, the oil money meant that political stability was maintained, and public sector jobs were provided. The Transgabon Railway (*Transgabonais*) was built with revenues from the oil export, and was privatized in 1999.[18] At the same time, oil money to a large degree was used for the prosperity of the small ruling group. In the "good old days" of president Omar Bongo's rule, Gabon was (in)famous as the major international importer of French champagne. According to Ghazvinian, "In Gabon, the curse of oil has nothing to do with guns and speedboats and ultimatums, and everything to do with the price of Brie."[19] Public health conditions remain at a rather low level even by African standards and the literacy of the population is just around 60 percent. The infrastructure of Gabon is still deeply underdeveloped, and only 10 percent of all roads in the country are hard covered.[20] As long as the offshore maritime production of oil maintains the economic growth of Gabon, the threat of an even more severe oil hangover than at the end of the 1980s remains the major risk for the country's economy.

The territory of Gabon's neighbor, the Republic of the Congo (Congo-Brazzaville, the former French Congo) is about two-thirds the size of France. Brazzaville, the capital of the country, was the capital of French Equatorial Africa during the colonial period, and during World War II it was the temporary capital of *France Libre* under the leadership of General de Gaulle. It was in Brazzaville that the decisive battles of the civil war in the Congo took place.

After multiparty elections at the end of the colonial period, politicians who represented the more economically developed southern region and the capital of the country came to power in the Congo. The first president, Fulbert Youlou, represented one of the branches of the ethnic group Bakongo (Kongo). In 1963, left-wing parties and politicians (also mainly southerners under the leadership of Alphonse Massamba-Debat) took power, due to the support of trade unions. In 1968, more radical revolutionaries headed by the leader from the north, Marien Ngouabi (killed in 1977), asserted power in the Congo. The new government of the Congo declared its adherence to the ideals of Marxist-Leninism, a "people's republic" was proclaimed, and the single-party regime of the Congolese Labour Party (PCT) was introduced. The south found itself at the periphery of the country's political life, and this caused continuous major conflicts. After Ngouabi was killed, Joachim Yhombi-Opango came to power, and in 1979 he was replaced by Denis Sassou Nguesso. The fierce political struggle within the PCT was accompanied by Marxist slogans borrowed from the history of Soviet and Chinese communist parties.

Until the mid-1970s, the leading industry in the Congolese economy was forestry. It accounted for over 50 percent of national export. Agricultural products were also exported (coffee, cacao). Furthermore, foreign trade was developed through the ports of the Congo with other countries of Central Africa. The beginning and development of the production of oil caused a major restructuring of the Congo economy. By 1985, oil had virtually become the only source of export revenues. Oil production was concentrated offshore in the region around the city of Pointe-Noire. In other sectors of economy, the major decline of export became sensitive not only in relative, but also in absolute terms, especially in the forest industry. Also, due to the process of the spontaneous urbanization in Brazzaville and Pointe-Noire, more than half the country's population began to be concentrated there.

The transformation of the People's Republic of the Congo into a rentier state took place more quickly and severely than in Gabon. The state became the major employer in the country. While the high-level conspicuous consumption of the ruling group of Marxist-Leninists was oriented toward top Western brands, the Congo also demonstrated a drastic increase in the import of food.[21] The major decline of oil export revenues in 1986 hit the Congo harder than neighboring Gabon. At the end of the 1980s, democratization began in the country, and in 1991 the National conference that constituted a new political regime was held. After multiparty elections, Pascal Lissouba came to power. However, the competition between major parties soon turned into an open conflict along the "north-south" line, and then caused a civil war. Almost a third of the population of the Congo became refugees. In 1997, with the support of Angolan military troops, the leader of the north, Denis Sassou Nguesso, returned to power. A period of relative calm began only in the early 2000s, when oil prices began to increase again; peace agreements were signed in 2003. Due to these developments, the president strengthened his power, winning the elections of 2002 and 2009.

The major oil producing region of Pointe-Noire did not suffer from military conflict. Moreover, in the 1990s the amount of oil production in the Republic of the Congo reached the level of neighboring Gabon. Oil production was primarily developed on the basis of production sharing agreements with major international companies. As in Gabon, a French business (Total Exploration & Production Congo) played the leading role in oil production. By 2007, according to Philip M. Mobbs,

"The economy of the Republic of the Congo, also known as Congo (Brazzaville), was based largely on the production of hydrocarbons (crude petroleum and natural gas). The petroleum sector output was estimated to account for about 92 percent of the country's exports, about 82 percent of Government revenues, and about 62 percent of the country's gross domestic product. Petroleum products also accounted for about 32 percent of total imports."[22] At the same time living conditions for the majority of the population of the Congo had declined since the end of the 1980s, while not only state revenues but also the personal wealth of many officials increased.

These trends caused severe dissatisfaction with the regime among the deprived part of the country. In 2002, Catholic bishops openly expressed a negative assessment of the development of the situation in the country.[23] In 2008, in a declaration by an association of residents from the region of Kouilou (*Collectif des Originaires du Kouilou*), three major conflicts (or rather, *fractures*) in the region were outlined as the major contentious issues: the intergenerational conflict, political conflict, which led to violations during the conduct of elections, and socioeconomic conflict ("in a country where the mafia dominates in allocating jobs," law-abiding residents of Kouilou were said to face unemployment).[24] Crime remains at a high level, and the government is forced to spend a large amount of revenues from oil export on financing and maintaining law enforcement agencies.

However, the government often proposed more extravagant ways of spending state revenues, including moving the remains of the French colonial figure Pierre Savorgnan de Brazza from Algeria, and building his mausoleum. The history of colonization is now interpreted in the Congo as the peaceful establishment of contract relations between the French and traditional elites, primarily between de Brazza and the head (*makoko*) of his Bateke allies. Emphasizing the role of the Bateke people in the history of the Congo once more turns the country into a kind of "family-like political center" in its relationships to the Gabon periphery. In fact, the continuity of political stability in the Republic of the Congo now heavily depends on patronage from Angola and France.

The oil sector still dominates the country's economy, and the future of the Republic of the Congo depends to a significant degree on its prosperity. The influence of Marxist-Leninism was probably reflected in the scope of the major interethnic conflicts during the period of decline in oil prices in the 1990s. Also, disappointment in the socialist model of development led to a severe "imitator's hangover," and the consequences of this hangover have yet to be overcome.

ANGOLA AND NIGERIA: "BLOODY OIL"
AND REGIONAL LEADERSHIP

In an international and comparative perspective, both Angola and Nigeria serve as typical examples of major oil-induced conflicts,[25] and lessons of their developmental trajectories are rather important for oil- and gas-exporting countries of post-Soviet Eurasia.

Nigeria, the most populous country in Africa, has emerged as a unified administrative division since 1914. As a part of the British colonial empire, Nigeria successfully developed its agriculture (palm oil, cacao, peanuts, cotton) and mining industries (tin, zinc, coal), and by the mid-1950s, Nigeria surpassed countries of Southeast Asia in terms of its economic development and growth rate. In 1956, oil was discovered in the east of Nigeria, and in 1958 oil export was launched.[26]

By the time of the declaration of independence in 1960, Nigeria became a federation that included the north (more than half of the entire territory of the country, but without direct access to the sea), the west (in fact the southwest), and the east (from the geographical viewpoint, the southeast). In the north, ethnic groups known by the common name of Hausa-Fulani (mainly Muslims) dominated, in the east the Igbo (mainly Christians), and in the west the Yoruba held dominant positions, respectively. From 1960 to 1966, the postcolonial system of informal agreements between regional elites was elaborated in a relatively peaceful way, with leadership from the north, which in the south of Nigeria was considered to be a backward "feudal" part of the state. In 1966, the military (primarily the Igbo) attempted to transform Nigeria into a unitary state. Then the independent republic of Biafra was declared in the east, while all the oil fields of Nigeria were located on its territory. No wonder that the secessionist attempt of Biafra caused the major conflict in Nigerian history that turned into a bloody civil war.

During the period of civil war, 1967–1970, "progressive" or even "socialist" separatist Biafra was supported by both France and the People's Republic of China, while the Soviet Union provided military assistance to the federal government, which was led by General Yakubu Gowon (a Christian from the north; his surname was used in the media as an acronym for the phrase "go on with one Nigeria").[27] Simultaneously, in order to diminish the threat of separatism, the Nigerian federal authorities began to divide the territory and establish new states (their number has by now increased from four up to thirty-six), including those in the coastal Niger delta region, now officially termed

"South-South" zone. After the civil war, the states were ruled by military governors, usually natives of other regions. Under Gowon's presidency, Nigeria did not attempt to follow the Communist ideology of the Soviet Union. Still, partial nationalization (*Nigerisation*), including in the oil sector (on the basis of the Petroleum Act of 1969), began in the country. In 1971, the Nigerian National Oil Corporation was established (in 1977 it was transformed into the Nigerian National Petroleum Company, NNPC); and in the same year Nigeria joined OPEC. The major players in the oil sector were joint enterprises with foreign capital such as the Shell Petroleum Development Company of Nigeria Ltd. (SPDC).

In 1975, Gowon's government was overthrown, and less than a year later the subsequent president from the north, Murtala Muhammed, was killed. Soon after this, General Olusegun Obasanjo, who represented the Nigerian west, came to power. The oil sector grew, and the agrarian sector deteriorated, as well as the railways, which were used to transport agricultural products to the coast. Everything in Nigeria became dependent almost entirely upon oil. In 1979, General Obasanjo handed power over to the civilian government. Shehu Shagari, a poet famous in the north, was elected president. With money from the oil export revenues, the new capital of the country Abuja was built, along with roads and pipelines, the gigantic steel plant in Ajaokuta (with the participation of the Soviet Union), and Peugeot and Volkswagen assembly factories were opened.

In 1984, as a result of a new military coup, General Muhammadu Buhari, also a representative of the north, came to power. Buhari started a new campaign of purges, the so-called War Against Indiscipline (WAI), but he was unsuccessful. After the next coup in 1985, the next northerner became the head of state, General Ibrahim Babangida. The Structural Adjustment Plan (SAP), developed with the assistance of the IMF, did not save the economy from the hangover after the major decline in oil prices. In 1993, after an unsuccessful attempt to establish a civilian regime, the military staged yet another coup. Yet another representative of the north came to power, General Sani Abacha. Under his rule, financial machinations, drug trafficking, corruption, and international sanctions destroyed the national economy, but did not affect the oil sector to a large degree. After Abacha's death (in 1998), presidential elections were held, and Obasanjo came to power once again (but this time as a civilian). Assessing the increasingly apparent degradation of the Nigerian economy, governance, and society, Obasanjo stated:

It has not always been like this in Nigeria. Some of us old enough can remember service delivery when you could post a letter on an Express Train, and it would get to its destination, and you would get a reply. A large number of people can still remember the days when public servants would greet one with: "Can I help you Sir?" and they meant it, because one would be treated accordingly.

So how did our service delivery degrade into the present circumstances, when public servants, if they serve you at all, do so as a favor, or at a price? How and when did the so called "Nigerian way of doing things" become the norm?

Many Nigerians would claim to know the answer. It is that the public servants have to "chop," and "chopping" is given higher priority than the duty to deliver service. With this attitude, the public servants cannot allow the system to become efficient, where the criteria for efficiency are based on satisfaction of the citizens.

Hence, the vicious circle: in order to get through the inefficient system, one has to bribe one's way, yet the public officials, who operate this system, make sure it stays inefficient so that they can continue to collect toll.

We accept that any comprehensive reform of the service delivery needs to involve institutions in other tiers of government.[28]

In the period from 1966 to 1999 in Nigeria a system of proportional representation of the major regions was established, so all states had their quotas in the national government and public agencies, while social benefits were distributed among citizens of Nigeria on the basis of their territorial origins. The oil producing region of Niger delta was for a long time on the periphery of the political system. By the end of Sani Abacha's rule, all the states were grouped into six territorial zones including the so-called South-South (this zone includes oil producing states of the Niger delta). The Service Compact with All Nigerians (SERVICOM) was the basis of reforms during the second term of President Obasanjo (in 2008). Also, under Obasanjo in Nigeria the democratization of the political system occurred but this caused numerous intensive conflicts, and power struggles at the level of Nigerian states began. State governors often used local youth criminal gangs as instruments of violence against their opponents.

Under Abacha, the dissatisfaction of residents of the Niger delta was already evident, as they gained little from the production of oil and gas "on their territory" (not to mention the impact of economic and political crises). The first organized protest movement was the Movement for the Survival of the Ogoni People (MOSOP); its leaders were executed in 1995. Under Obasanjo in 2001, the special Niger

Delta Development Commission was established, and the federal government began to allocate to Niger delta states 13 percent of export revenues from oil extracted in the territory of each respective state. However, the process of political transformation of the South-South region had already gone too far. According to the assessment of Ibeanu and Luckham, "it spawned active grassroot movements, which arose in the Niger Delta to protest against environmental degradation and the mal-distribution of oil revenues. But in the train of the protest movements, there emerged a new political economy of privatized violence, fuelled by oil."[29] By 2003, in some states of the Niger delta, control to a significant degree moved to armed youth criminal gangs, which operated under the slogans for just distribution of oil revenues.

The population of Nigeria is now around 140 million. After the rise in oil prices at the beginning of the twenty-first century, the growth rates of the economy began to catch up with the growth in population. Nigeria became one of the world leaders in foreign investments. In 2004, a plan of development for fifteen years was developed (National Economic Empowerment and Development Strategy, NEEDS), in which the goal of liberalization of the economy and a move away from oil dependence was set up. Due to economic and political liberalization, national businesses and financial and industrial groups received access to development of the energy resources of Nigeria. However, the level of transparency in the oil sector under Obasanjo remained rather low and insignificant. In 2005, it was found that there were "over US$800m of unresolved differences between what companies said that they paid in taxes, royalties and signature bonuses, and what the governments said it received."[30]

In April 2007, Umaru Musa Yar'Adua, the former governor of the northern Katsina state won the presidential elections in Nigeria. The new president once again announced the launching of war against corruption. The Ministry of the Niger Delta was created, and the Ministry of Energy was divided into the Ministry of Power and the Ministry of Petroleum Resources. Goodluck Jonathan, representative of the South-South region, became the vice president of Nigeria. The illness of Umaru Yar'Adua and his absence from the country for medical treatment since November 2009 led to Goodluck Jonathan assuming the post of acting president in anticipation of the 2011 elections. Yar'Adua died in May 2010, and Jonathan was sworn in as president.

The authorities of the South-South states coordinate efforts, trying to ensure security and integration of the economies of the region.[31] Nevertheless, the crisis in the South-South zone continues, fuelled by very little local employment and severely disgruntled youth. Different political movements have been involved in the battle for oil and gas revenues with national government, including the separatist Movement for the Emancipation of the Niger Delta (MEND). Under such circumstances, foreign companies try to produce most of the oil and gas offshore. There is still potential for local conflicts in other regions of Nigeria. At the same time, Nigeria has good chances of continuing the diversification of its economy, including by expanding the production and export of gas. According to Philip M. Mobbs, in 2007 "despite the increase in the prices received for crude oil, Government revenue from hydrocarbons declined to $35.5 billion (which was about 79 percent of total revenue) compared with $41 billion (about 88 percent) in 2006."[32] During the world crisis of 2008–2009, this trend has changed, and especially the automobile industry has suffered considerably. At the moment, oil remains the major source of export revenues of Nigeria (up to 95 percent, according to the assessment by Ibeanu and Luckham),[33] and the problem of the Nigerian "kleptocracy" is still far from being solved.[34]

Angola, which borrowed Soviet ideology in the 1970s and 1980s, is in fact little different from "bourgeois-feudal" Nigeria. Even the difference that the Angolan political leaders are permanently in office is in practice not all that important for developmental trends and the impact of the resource curse on the country. Ghazvinian notes: "Boasting one of the continent's biggest and (sadly) most experienced armies, but also blessed with prodigious reserves of oil, diamonds, gold, timber and copper, Angola has long given its people reason to believe it has the potential to be one of Africa's real power-houses, on the level of Nigeria, South Africa and Egypt."[35] At the same time, the postcolonial development of Angola (besides the oil sector) cannot be called an example for imitation. In digesting an analysis of the situation in the country, Philippe Le Billon wrote, "I argue that the 'developmental' record of the oil sector in Angola has so far been abysmal, and suggest that it will remain so as long as the ruling élite fails to make a decisive transition to a more democratic and accountable governance."[36]

Like Nigeria, Angola formed as a single administrative unit in the colonial era, albeit with a much longer history of direct European domination. Different ethnic groups such as Ambundu (Umbundu, Mbundu), including the inhabitants of Luanda, the major city of the country; Bakongo (Kongo); Ovimbundu; and other peoples were under the rule of Portugal. Many Portuguese lived in colonial Angola (after proclaiming its independence in 1975 more than three hundred thousand Europeans fled the country). Three major organized forces fought against Portuguese rule in Angola, the MPLA (Popular Movement for the Liberation of Angola), FNLA, and UNITA. Each of these movements had different ethnic-regional coloring:

> The MPLA was a socialist movement which emerged from the mixed-race, urban population, and the Umbundu ethnic group of Central Angola, under the leadership of the poet Agostinho Neto and since 1979 by Eduardo dos Santos. . . . Despite rejecting any ethnic or "tribalist" character it remained strongly affiliated—most notably through its "popular defense" scheme—with Mbundu populations in and around the capital city of Luanda who represented about 15 per cent of the population. The National Liberation Front of Angola (FNLA), headed by Roberto Holden, represented about 15 per cent of the national population and had a strong ethnic base among the Bakongo, located in the North-West. While the leadership of the FNLA initially attempted to recreate the former Kongo kingdom through secession, it later moved to a national independence agenda and received the assistance of Western powers and Zaire. Finally, the National Union for the Total Independence of Angola (UNITA) emerged, headed by Jonas Savimbi, and comprising provincial assimilados, with a dominant ethnic base of Ovimbundu from the central highlands (planalto) who represented the largest ethnic group, with the 35 per cent of the population. While these ethnic differences contributed, at least in the early stages, to defining the lines of Angola's conflict, they almost never served as a motivation for it. With time, however, Jonas Savimbi did increasingly portray UNITA as the party of the black Africans, struggling to free Angola from the domination of the white and mixed-race MPLA.[37]

Angola is a resource-rich country with large mineral deposits. In the colonial period in Angola, there was an export-oriented mining industry (above all diamonds and iron ore) and agriculture (primarily coffee). In 1958, the Cabinda Gulf Oil Company began industrial production of oil. From the end of the 1960s, the center of the oil industry became the province of Cabinda, an enclave (or, more precisely, a geographical exclave) separated from the main territory of Angola by the Congo River and the territory of the former Belgian Congo—Zaire (now the Democratic Republic of the Congo). Since 1973, oil production has been the leading sector of the Angolan economy.

From 1975 to 2002 (with interruptions) there was a civil war in Angola, with the participation of soldiers from South Africa, Cuba, and the Soviet Union. The number of refugees reached two million, and there was spontaneous urbanization. Parallel to the changes in the Soviet Union, reforms and liberalization began in Angola in 1985, and since 1990 the authorities abandoned the people's republic and Marxist-Leninism. The existence of opposition parties was allowed, but the

MPLA remained the ruling party. At the 1992 elections, the MPLA received 53.74 percent of the vote, and 81.64 percent in 2008. President dos Santos has been in power since the 1992 presidential elections, and since that time presidential elections have not been held.

Under the people's republic, the country's mineral resources were declared to be state property. In the oil sector, the state-owned company *Sociedade Nacional de Combustíveis de Angola* (Sonangol) was formed. Sonangol received major stakes in joint enterprises, but the operators of the oil fields remained foreign companies. Despite the war, the production of oil and diamonds continued, because all sides of the military conflict heavily depended on the oil export revenues: "Oil funding the MPLA and diamonds funding UNITA is a simplistic yet relatively accurate reading of the Angolan war economy."[38] In 1992, the state monopoly in the resource sectors was abolished. Oil in Angola proved more important than ideology: "For years in Cabinda, a revolutionary Marxist government depended on money from an American oil corporation whose operations were defended by Cuban soldiers against attacks by an American-backed rebel army."[39]

Almost all the sectors of the Angolan economy, including the diamond industry, suffered considerably from the war. Angola joined the Kimberley process, which stipulates the growth of transparency in the diamond industry. However, according to some assessments, the international struggle for transparency was used for "killing competition using methods that have nothing to do with the market economy."[40] The oil sector developed relatively successfully, but in almost complete isolation from the rest of the country:

> In total, Angola's oil industry employs only about 10,000 Angolans. It is in every way—physically, socially and economically—an extreme example of an enclave sector. Physically, most of the oil is produced offshore, loaded straight from the rigs onto tankers, and shipped off to international markets without ever coming into contact with Angolan terra firma. . . . While agriculture and manufacturing collapsed as a result of both Portuguese mass departure at the time of independence and the wars, oil has continued to grow. Even in a time of low oil prices, such as 1998, the oil sector accounted for 61 per cent of GDP, and 74 per cent of government revenues. Thus an industry which employs less than 0.2 per cent of the active population, and which is barely present physically in the country, accounts for the lion's share of the country's income.[41]

One may judge the scope of participation of Angolans in the oil industry by the data from Chevron (from its subsidiary, the Cabinda Gulf Oil Company), the largest employer in this sector: "Today, Angolan employees compose 88 percent of our workforce of about 3,000. By 2010, Angolans will account for 90 percent of our professional, technical and managerial employees."[42] For a country with a population of fifteen million, this figure is tiny. Around ten thousand people are also employed in the diamond industry (although illegal diamond mining is more extensive).

During the war, the oil sector of the Angolan economy was far from transparent. ("Besides the government's 'general misuse' of oil revenues, it has also allegedly paid for arms purchases through funds generated from signature bonus payments for oil exploration, of which BP-Amoco, Exxon and Elf Aquitaine were the main contributors. According to the Angolan foreign minister, these funds were earmarked for the 'war effort.'"[43]) After the war, the Republic of Angola refrained from active participation in the Extractive Industries Transparency Initiative. As Job Graça, vice minister of finance of Angola, explained, "The Angolan government decision to hold an observer status—which I would like to reiterate—is consistent with the commonly agreed principle of the sanctity of contracts, on the one hand, and is determined by the fact that the government still faces institutional capacity and legal constraints, on the other hand."[44]

In the beginning of the twenty-first century, Angola became the fastest-growing economy in the world. According to the assessment of Chevron, "never in the history of Chevron's six decades in Angola have opportunities for growth and progress been so great."[45] In 2007, the country joined OPEC. The ruling regime keeps control over the developments in the country, and long-term contracts have been signed with international oil producing companies. But still, the basis of prosperity in Angola remains extremely narrow, and is subject to major risks. The Cabinda enclave remains an especially problematic region. In this province, it was only in 2006 that partial reconciliation was reached with separatists from the previously active Front for the Liberation of the Enclave of Cabinda (FLEC). As in the Niger delta, Cabinda residents have gained little from oil production, especially as Angola is a unitary state, with appointed governors of provinces.[46]

A comparison of the trajectories of development of African petrostates shows that both countries that borrowed Marxist-Leninist slogans and experimented with socialism and pro-Western exporters of oil and gas were unable to avoid major negative effects of the resource curse. But the choice of the model of a people's republic (such as Angola or the Republic of Congo) had more devastating consequences, comparable to the crisis in post-Soviet states and nations in the first years after the collapse of the Soviet Union. In such countries as Nigeria and Gabon, the political influence of the oil factor was less cata-strophic, although it was also evident and destructive. Still, post-Soviet oil- and gas-exporting countries in many ways resembled developmental trends of postcolonial African states and nations. For last several decades, African petrostates experienced long-term nondemocratic patrimonial rule by inefficient and heavily corrupt elites, who often were able to impose dynastic leadership succession, predatory use of mineral resources, the sharp rise of inequality, and arbitrary revisions of property rights, including nationalization of oil companies. Even though oil producing post-Soviet countries, at least as yet, were less vulnerable than African petrostates in terms of separatism, domestic political conflicts, and environmental crises, their institutions are rather weak and inefficient, thus risks of potential troubles and possible failures are increasing: in fact, Nigeria could become the future of Russia. Also, the oil and gas sector, as the African experience has shown, is capable to exist de facto autonomously and independently of political and economic changes in respective states and nations, turning into "states within the states" and swallowing up resources that are necessary for modernization. This autonomy of oil and gas sector is especially high in the development of oil production offshore, and this is also an important lesson for the future for post-Soviet nations.

NOTES

1. The concept of "hangover" is used, for example, by John Ghazvinian: "Gabon's recent history is best understood as that of a small, struggling country that won the lottery, went on a binge, and is just now waking up to an almighty hangover." John Ghazvinian, *Untapped: The Scramble for Africa's Oil* (New York: Harcourt Books, 2007), 107.

2. Jean-Philippe Koutassila, "Le syndrome hollandais: Théorie et vérification empirique au Congo et au Cameroun," Pessac: Groupe d'Economie du Développement de l'Université Montesquieu Bordeaux IV, 1998. Documents de travail 24, ced.u-bordeaux4.fr/ceddt24.pdf (accessed 4 August 2009).

3. Nicholas Shaxson, "Oil, Corruption and the Resource Curse," *International Affairs*, 83, no. 6 (November 2007), 1123–40; Ludvig Söderling, "Escaping the Curse of Oil? The Case of Gabon," *International Monetary Fund Working Papers*, no. 02/93, 2002, www.imf.org/external/pubs/ft/wp/2002/wp0293.pdf (accessed 5 September 2009); Karin Alexander and Stefan Gilbert, "Oil and Governance Report: A Case Study of Chad, Angola, Gabon, and Sao Tome é Principe," Institute for Democracy in South Africa (IDASA), 2008, www.idasa.org.za/gbOutputFiles.asp?WriteContent=Y&RID=2154 (accessed 4 September 2009).

4. Ghazvinian, *Untapped: The Scramble for Africa's Oil*, 104–5. Attempts to use oil revenues for modernization in the producing and processing of cassava, such as the Presidential Cassava Initiative under President Obasanjo, evidently did not bring the proposed results.

5. Athanase Bopda, "De l'usage de fonds mythiques dans les remaniements territoriaux en Afrique et au Cameroun," *Cahiers de Géographie du Québec*, 45, no. 126 (December 2001), 451–78.

6. Boungou Bazika and Jean Christophe, "Le pétrole: Ressource géostrate-gique et incidence sur les pays de la CEMAC," paper presented at CODESRIA Anniversary Conference, Central Africa Sub-region, Douala, Cameroun, 4–5 October 2003, www.codesria.org/Links/conferences/central/christophe.pdf (accessed 4 August 2009).

7. Albert Yama Nkounga, "Pétrole et développement en Afrique centrale: Quelques axes de réflexion pour une meilleure intégration du secteur pétro-lier dans l'économie nationale," in Rudolf Traub-Merz and Douglas Yates, eds., *Oil Policy in the Gulf of Guinea* (Bonn: Friedrich-Ebert-Stiftung, 2004), 163–75.

8. On maritime boundaries in the Gulf of Guinea, see for example, Tim Daniel, "Maritime Boundaries in the Gulf of Guinea," paper presented at the 2001 ABLOS Conference "Accuracies and Uncertainties in Maritime Boundar-ies and Outer Limits," Monaco, October 2001, www.gmat.unsw.edu.au/ablos/ABLOS01Folder/DANIEL.PDF (accessed 30 August 2009).

9. On the strategic role of African oil and gas and prospects for their use for the development of Africa, see, for example, Michael T. Klare, *Resource Wars: The New Landscape of Global Conflict* (New York: Owl Books, repr. ed. 2002), 217–21; Paul Michael Wihbey and Barry Schutz, eds.,"African Oil: A Priority for U.S. National Security and African Development," *Institute for Advanced Strategic and Political Studies Research Papers in Strategy*, no. 14, May 2002, www.iasps.org/strategic/africatranscript.pdf (accessed 30 August 2009).

10. Thomas Atenga, "Gabon: Apprendre à vivre sans pétrole," *Politique africaine*, 92 (December 2003), 127; Ghazvinian, *Untapped: The Scramble for Africa's Oil*, 116.

11. François Gaulme, "Congo-Brazzaville: La guerre civile et ses conse-quences sur le Gabon," UNHCR Centre for Documentation and Research, *WRITENET Paper*, no. 20/1999, www.unhcr.org (accessed 4 August 2009).

12. On democratization in Gabon in the 1990s, see for example, Atenga, "Gabon: apprendre à vivre sans pétrole," 117–28.

13. Vladimir Katin, "Gabon i Rossiya imeyut mnogo obshchego," *Dipkur'er: Mezdunarodnoe prilozhenie k "Nezavisimoi gazete*," 21 June 2001, world .ng.ru/azimuth/2001-04-19/1_gorbon.html (accessed 4 August 2009).

14. Omar Bongo, *Blanc comme negre: Entretiens de Omar Bongo avec Airy Routier.* (Paris: Editions Grasset, 2001).

15. "Gabon President Still Wants to Run in 2012," *Afrol News*, 24 October 2006, www.afrol.com/articles/22147 (accessed 12 September 2009).

16. "Gabon," *Extractive Industries Transparency Initiative*, eitransparency .org/Gabon (accessed 4 August 2009).

17. Omayra Bermúdez-Lugo, "The Mineral Industry of Gabon [Advance Release]," *2007 Minerals Yearbook, U.S. Geological Survey*, May 2009, minerals.usgs.gov/minerals/pubs/country/2007/myb3-2007-gb.pdf (accessed 9 September 2009).

18. For both positive and negative assessments of the project, see Ghazvinian, *Untapped: The Scramble for Africa's Oil*, 107–8, 113–14.

19. Ghazvinian, *Untapped: The Scramble for Africa's Oil*, 98.

20. For an analysis of the oil boom in Gabon and its consequences, see Douglas A. Yates, *The Rentier State in Africa: Oil Rent Dependency and Neocolonialism in the Republic of Gabon* (Trenton, N.J.: Africa World Press, 1996).

21. Koutassila, "Le syndrome hollandais," 10–14.

22. Philip M. Mobbs, "The Mineral Industry of Congo (Brazzaville) [Advance Release]," *2007 Minerals Yearbook, U.S. Geological Survey*, November 2008, minerals.usgs.gov/minerals/pubs/country/2007/myb3-2007-cf.pdf (accessed 9 September 2009).

23. Ghazvinian, *Untapped: The Scramble for Africa's Oil*, 123–24.

24. "Présentation du C.O.K. Collectif des Originaires du Kouilou," *Congopage.com*, 28 August 2008, www.congopage.com/article/presentation -du-c-o-k (accessed 3 September 2009).

25. Thomas A. Imobighe, "Conflict in the Niger Delta: A Unique Case or a 'Model' for Future Conflicts in Other Oil-Producing Countries," in *Oil Policy in the Gulf of Guinea*, 101–15.

26. The parallel development of Nigeria as a petro-state and its political history is clearly presented in the chapter by Okey Ibeanu and Robin Luckham, "Nigeria: Political Violence, Governance and Corporate Responsibility in a Petro-State," in Mary Kaldor, Terry Lynn Karl, and Yahia Said, eds., *Oil Wars* (London: Pluto Press, 2007), 48–50, table 1.1: "Oil, politics and conflict in Nigeria: a chronology 1953–2005."

27. Maxim Matusevich, "Ideology of Pragmatism: The Biafra War and Nigerian Response to the Soviet Union, 1967–1970," in V. Subbotin and Yuri Potemkin, eds., *Kuda idesh', Afrika? Istoriko-politicheskie etyudy* (Moscow: Institute of African Studies, Russian Academy of Science, 2004), 93–101.

28. Olusegun Obasanjo, "Time to Banish 'Nigerian Way,'" Excerpts of Address by President Olusegun Obasanjo at the Opening of the Special Presidential Retreat on Service Delivery, Abuja, 19–21 March 2004, *Nigeria Monthly*, 1, no. 4 (November 2004), 24.

29. Ibeanu and Luckham, "Nigeria: Political Violence, Governance and Corporate Responsibility in a Petro-State," 43–44.

30. "Nigeria," *Extractive Industries Transparency Initiative*, eitransparency .org/Nigeria (accessed 4 August 2009).

31. "Communique Issued at the End of the First South-South Nigeria Economic Summit Held at Tinapa Business Resort, Calabar, April 22–25, 2009,"

South South Nigeria, 2009, www.southsouthnigeria.org (accessed 9 September 2009).

32. Philip M. Mobbs, "The Mineral Industry of Nigeria [Advance Release]," *2007 Minerals Yearbook, U.S. Geological Survey*, March 2009, minerals.usgs .gov/minerals/pubs/country/2007/myb3-2007-ni.pdf (accessed 9 September 2009).

33. Ibeanu and Luckham, "Nigeria: Political Violence, Governance and Corporate Responsibility in a Petro-State," 41.

34. Based on the Nigerian experience, Leonid Geveling wrote about kleptocracy as a widespread African political phenomenon. See Leonid V. Geveling, *Kleptokratiya* (Moscow: Gumanitarii, 2001).

35. Ghazvinian, *Untapped: The Scramble for Africa's Oil*, 128–29.

36. Philippe Le Billon, "Drilling in Deep Water: Oil, Business and War in Angola," in *Oil Wars*, 100.

37. Le Billon, "Drilling in Deep Water," 101–2.

38. Le Billon, "Drilling in Deep Water," 118.

39. Ghazvinian, *Untapped: The Scramble for Africa's Oil*, 159.

40. "Sergey Vybornov Addresses the World Diamond Council Meeting," *ALROSA*, 11 May 2007, eng.alrosa.ru/eng/news/detail.php?ID=4104 (accessed 30 August 2009). Of course, the opinion of a top executive of a Russian company, which has its own economic interests in Angola, is somewhat biased.

41. Le Billon, "Drilling in Deep Water," 108–9.

42. "Chevron and Angola: Partners through Time," *Chevron*, 2009, www .chevron.com/Documents/Pdf/AngolaBrochureEnglish.pdf (accessed 11 September 2009).

43. Atle Christer Christiansen, "Beyond Petroleum: Can BP Deliver?" (Lysaker, Norway: Fridtjof Nansen Institute, June 2002), *The FNI report* 6/2002, www.fni.no/pdf/FNI-R0602.pdf (accessed 30 August 2009).

44. Job Graça, Statement by Job Graça, Vice-Minister of Finance of Angola at the third plenary conference of the Extractive Industries Transparency Initiative (EITI), Oslo, Norway, October 2006, www.eitioslo.no/Speeches/ Speech+Graca.htm (accessed 9 September 2009). An alternative view is presented in "Angolan Catholic Church Position Statement on the EITI," *PWYP Africa Regional*, 30 September 2006, www.publishwhatyoupay.org/en/ resources/angolan-catholic-church-position-statement-eiti (accessed 1 September 2009).

45. "Chevron and Angola: Partners through Time."

46. For more detail about the problems of Cabinda, see, for example, Ghazvinian, *Untapped: The Scramble for Africa's Oil*, 144–63.

⑨

Conclusion

Oil, Gas, Russia, and the 2008–2009 Economic Crisis

Dmitry Travin

The economic crisis of 2008–2009 dealt a serious blow to the economy of the entire world. Different countries suffered from it in differing degrees. In some places there was a severe decline in GDP. In some countries, sustainable economic growth stopped for a while. And in a relatively small group of countries, the positive dynamic has been preserved, although the growth rate slowed down, as there was a decline in demand on many traditional markets. In 2008–2009, Russia found itself among the first group of countries—those that the crisis hit hardest of all. If over the period of the decade that preceded the crisis, Russian GDP grew by an average of 6–8 percent per year, in January–August 2009 it dropped by 10.2 percent in comparison with the equivalent period in 2008, and the overall decline of GDP during the period of crisis exceeded 8 percent, the worst figures among G20 countries. It is clear that this drastic contrast between the "period of prosperity" and the period of major recession cannot be explained solely by the spread of crisis phenomena from the United States to Russia. The peculiarities of the Russian economy affected the trends of economic development in 2008–2009. And primarily, these peculiarities connected with its oil and gas sector.

The fact that a one-sided structure of the economy persisted in Russia and became one of the major obstacles to its economic development was gradually recognized by almost everyone, including the president of the country, Dmitry Medvedev. In an interview in summer 2009, the president confessed: "I can say openly, I am unhappy with the structure of our economy. . . . What we really have not done to the necessary degree—we have not carried out diversification of the structure of our economy. If the structure of the economy were different, then accordingly there would be effective industries, which provide national wealth in full scale. If labor productivity were different, the technology were different, if energy efficiency were higher, then of course we would have different results. If we worked more actively on the domestic market, and the development of domestic demand, this would also undoubtedly be beneficial. But we entered the crisis with the previous raw materials structure. And as soon as prices on oil and gas declined, of course we started facing problems. The one-sided structure of our economy is expressed in the figures that we have today."[1]

How did the Russian crisis develop, and how did the oil and gas sector of the economy affect economic indicators? Let's start with the harsh statements made by Russian prime minister Vladimir Putin in July 2008. He brutally attacked the owner of the metallurgic company Mechel and accused him of using legal loopholes to reduce tax payments. The fact is that many Russian companies in various sectors of economy actively use similar schemes to minimize taxation.[2] In some cases this does not contradict the law, but the authorities try to use informal methods of influence on taxpayers in order to increase budget revenues. These methods are typically related to behind-the-scene talks and reaching of mutually beneficial agreements. However, sometimes tough measures are also used.

The logic of the steps of the head of government in this case was quite clear. By intimidating one company selectively, he could force other businesses to stop price manipulation, which caused widespread nontransparency of financial operations and de facto tax evasion that used legal loopholes. However, one should remember that in Russia today, the reaction of the stock market to any cases of aggravation of relationships between business and the authorities can be especially painful. Everyone remembers when this sort of aggravation in relationships in 2003 led to the collapse of the major private oil company Yukos and the imprisonment of its owner and the richest businessman in the country, Mikhail Khodorkovsky.[3]

No wonder that the Russian stock market, after the statements made against the company Mechel, immediately fell. However, in this case the Russian authorities did not intend to crash the "guilty company." The initiators of this incident believed that as soon as the company reached an informal agreement with the top leadership of the country on new informal "rules of the game" about payment of taxes, the market would recover. This is also probably how things would have actually happened, if it had not been for the major influence of some other negative factors. The blow to Mechel took place at the very moment when the drastic fall of oil prices on international markets began. By 11 July 2008, the world price of WTI brand oil reached a historically record price of $147.27 per barrel, after which it began to decline.[4] But the problem was that in many ways the rally of oil prices kept the Russian economy going over the previous four years. And even with a relatively small cheapening of oil, Russia becomes less attractive for investors than when oil is rising in price.

In August 2008, to add to the decline of international oil prices and the fears caused by the Mechel affair, the "five days war" between Russia and Georgia on the territory of South Ossetia occurred. Any war is yet another threat for the business climate. If the country is dragged into a lengthy conflict with its neighbors, then the probability of a rise in inflation increases, as well as the risk of the weakening of existing foreign economic ties. In the case of the Russian-Georgian conflict, however, the war did not drag on: it did not seriously affect the Russian economy. The European Union adopted a decision not to take any sanctions against Russia, and this meant that the major export-import flows did not suffer. However, a sober view of the consequences of the war was hindered by the panic caused because of the Mechel affair and increasing problems on the oil market.

One thing led to another, the panic increased, and each investor tried to take his or her capital out of Russia before other investors did, in order to buy dollars and euros at a more acceptable exchange rate. And soon this capital flight was followed by another event, the most important of 2008. The situation on international financial markets worsened drastically in September. The major crisis in the United States and Europe hit banks, mortgages, and the insurance system. The Dow Jones began to fall immensely. And if the leading American index declines, in Russia this is seen as a clear signal to take money out of bonds of private companies and invest them in more reliable assets such as in state and treasury bonds of wealthy countries. In the fourth quarter of 2008, the stock market panic was reflected in the dynamics of industrial production. GDP began to decline. And although on average for 2008, the Russian economic indicators were better than in the United States and the countries of the European Union, it was no longer any secret to anyone that these results were only achieved by the relatively good indicators for the first three quarters.

In order to understand this sudden shift from boom to bust, one should analyze how Russia "flourished" in the decade preceding the crisis. Every year, Russia received a large amount of petrodollars as export revenues. For example, in 2008 alone Russian export grew by more than 40 percent, which exceeded GDP growth by approximately seven times.[5] As it came into Russia, oil money began to spread quickly across the country. The average Russian citizen suddenly discovered at a certain moment that his or her income had increased, but she or he did not see any connection with the favorable situation on the world oil markets. However, in fact this citizen simply received a piece—some quite large, and some rather unfairly small—of the Big Russian Oil Pie. The simplest and most understandable mechanism of the receiving of these pieces of oil rents by the ordinary citizens is the transfer of some part of oil export revenues not only to the Stabilization Fund,[6] but also to the federal and subnational budgets and to the Pension Fund of the Russian Federation. High revenues of the oil sector of the economy also resulted in the high share of the state in consumption. Furthermore, the Russian tax system is oriented toward an extraction of major revenues from oil and gas sector: under favorable market conditions, this sector pays an additional burden—the excise duty on petrol, the subsoil use tax, and the export customs duty. All this money was collected by the fiscal system, and then the government loudly announced yet another increase in pensions and salaries for public sector employees, new social benefits such as the formation of "maternal capital" aimed at solving the problem of low fertility rates, allocation of funds as part of so-called national projects oriented toward the rise of expenditures on public health and education, enormous investments into projects such as the reconstruction of railways, the development of high technologies, construction of stadiums and other facilities for 2014 Winter Olympics in Sochi, and so on. However, petrodollars flowed through the country not only through the budget, but also in other ways. As the "oil oligarchs" received their revenues, they gave numerous bribes to high-ranking officials and politicians, whose assistance was crucial: otherwise the oligarchs would not have gotten where they did. And then the mighty of this world settled accounts with everyone who served them.

First, high salaries were paid to employees of the oil and oil processing industry, the gas sector and employees of service stations, as well as those who serviced pipelines and other transportation facilities carrying oil, petrol, fuel, and respective products. Second, holders of oil and gas export revenues paid off suppliers of equipment for the entire industry, from drilling equipment to service stations. Third, the bosses of the fuel and energy complex bought houses, apartments, and offices in the enormous space from Moscow to the Western Siberian city of Khanty-Mansiisk—the acknowledged major center of the oil and gas industry. After this, with the money received, oil and gas workers, transporters, builders, and so on began to buy consumption goods—food, clothing, cars, furniture, computers, mobile phones, CDs and DVDs, movie tickets, medicine, pulp novels, and travel packages. All the public employees did the same, incidentally (doctors, teachers, professors, librarians, officials, soldiers), as well as employees of both state and private companies, which carry out deliveries on state orders paid from the budget. Even pensioners, despite the fact that their old age is not provided for particularly well by the state in Russia, regularly bought a certain share of the consumption goods listed above. Thus, petrodollars brought in a major rise in demand for the growing consumption sector—light and food industry, trade, services, pharmaceuticals, book publication and printing, and so forth. Employees of all of these sectors, receiving their pieces of the Big Russian Oil Pie, also joined the rally of consumption, increasing demand both for their own products and services and for the above-mentioned petrol, real estate, manufacturing equipment, and so on. As the incomes of major segments of the population increased, cafés, restaurants, sushi bars, bistros, and such began to mushroom because of the rise in mass demand. Accordingly, cooks, waiters, barmen, doormen, and cloakroom attendants suddenly increased their incomes. Also, an expanding business segment provides jobs in the security services, hires cleaners, plumbers, electricians, joiners, and carpenters, and also gives extra jobs to the coercive apparatus of the state, such as traffic police, customs officers, firefighters, and so on.[7] And finally, even if one can imagine that there are any citizens of Russia who do not make any of the above lists of numerous categories of recipients of the pieces of the Big Russian Oil Pie, they were certainly among the family members of recipients.

Can we say that any of the 140 million Russians were left outside this system? It seems rather unlikely. Thus, the complex, highly developed economy of the twenty-first century is ensured by extremely long chains of mutual connections, in which numerous people find themselves in the same system of consumption. If an extra cash supply is suddenly injected into this system due to high oil prices, it will to some degree or another began to flow into various corners, entering all cavities, gaps, and cracks.

The problem was that the unprecedentedly high level of oil prices before the beginning of 2008 economic crisis was determined not only by an increasing demand from the real sector of the economy, but by the speculation bubble. In other words, Russia, on the one hand, earned a lot of money from the expanding consumption of its oil and gas, and on the other, found itself involuntarily involved in the stock market, although the absolute majority of citizens of the country was far away from these developments and did not even imagine its most general features.

Could this have not happened in modern Russia? Alas, a great deal in this story was determined by structural conditions of the oil dependency of the Russian economy. In exporting oil and gas and receiving petrodollars, Russia became addicted, as it were. To a significant degree, the overheated economy was cooled down by the establishment of the Stabilization Fund (which has now been divided into the Reserve Fund and the National Prosperity Fund), which during the period of high oil prices took part of the money, and from 2009 began to cover major gaps due to the insufficient budget revenues. However, there was no way for the Russian economy to move outside the speculation bubble completely. Accordingly, from September 2008, the falling international oil prices hit everyone who had previously benefited from expensive oil in any way. Just as with the favorable situation of the market and huge inflow of petrodollars, demand was spread along a chain from one sector of the economy to another, but since 2008 this demand began to decline and things went in the reverse direction. Oil sector employees stopped buying real estate. Builders, deprived in demand from oil workers, could not consume expensive food as much as they used to. The decline in demand in the food and catering industries left large groups of workers without salaries and other benefits. The decline in demand for various kinds of goods and services also affected the major decline in production. Many Russian citizens suddenly realized that in a market economy, products cannot be produced if no one will pay for them. Also, it is difficult to maintain employment at the previously high level, and also preserve the former amounts of salary: with a major decline in turnover, any enterprise is inevitably forced to cut its expenses.

In October 2008, the GAZ automobile industrial group announced a halt in production of Gazel minibuses. And KamAZ reported that because of the decline in production of dump trucks and crane equipment, the factory would be moving from a six-day to a four-day week. In the agrarian sector, major companies announced the postponement or freezing of major investment projects to build five new elevators and reconstruct ten sugar factories, as well as the development of poultry farms. No wonder that this large-scale curtailment of investment caused the massive decline in demand for construction materials and equipment. In November 2008, the severe decline in production of iron ore and coal had begun in Russia. And the reason was the fall of production in metallurgy: the Novolipetsk metallurgic plant (NLMK) reported that three of its five blast furnaces had stopped work. These results were not surprising, as when manufacturing cars, cranes, and also machines and equipment for various types of enterprises, the market does not need as much metal (and accordingly as much iron ore) as it consumed in the period of economic prosperity. And as metal, machines, coke, or many other goods were not needed, railway transportation also began to decline.[8]

The Russian state budget has also found itself in the same difficult situation as the industrialists, builders, agrarians, and transport workers. In 2008, about half of the budget was filled by oil and gas revenues.[9] However, the major decline of budget revenues did not lead to the drastic reduction of employees in the public sector in Russia, due to the use of funds of the Reserve Fund. Nevertheless, the fact that the state lacks the opportunities to support enterprises that face difficulties has also affected the market conditions. At the initial stage of the crisis, many analysts expected that the state would support the economy more actively, resorting to a cash emission. However, both the government and the Central Bank showed restraint, which caused relatively low levels of inflation, but at the same time it left private business to face the crisis alone. Still, this strategy proved to be relatively successful given the relatively short period of recession: already in the fourth quarter of 2009, the Russian economy began its postcrisis recovery, and the severe decline in major sectors turned into a growth, merely due to international trends of overcoming recession, which contributed to world oil markets. By early 2010, oil prices fluctuated about $70–75 per barrel, which meant that the inflow of export revenues will reheat the Russian economy after the crisis, and major gaps of the federal budget will be filled. However, its midterm prospects are still unclear as yet.

Thus, in summarizing the preliminary results of economic development of Russia during the period of crisis and recession of 2008–2009, one should note that the severity of the decline was to a major degree caused by the nature of the Russian economy, the dominance of the oil and gas sector, and also by the fact that over the course of the previous decade, the huge inflow of petrodollars provided the rise in demand for goods and services of various sectors as well as the rise in the state expenditures. After the crisis, the Russian economy felt the effect of hangover. But whether or not the oil dependency of Russia can be overcome in the foreseeable future remains to be seen.

NOTES

1. Dmitry Medvedev, "Elita na to ona i elita, chtoby bistro obuchat'sya," *Kommersant'*, 5 June 2009.

2. "Zayavlenie Putina obrushilo aktsii Mechela na 45%," Newsru.com, 25 July 2008, www.newsru.com/finance/25jul2008/mechel.html (accessed April 7, 2010).

3. See chapter 5 in this volume.

4. Vladislav Dorofeev and Valeria Bashkirova, eds., *Antikrizisnaya kniga Kommersanta* (Moscow: ID Kommersant', Astrel', 2009), 14.

5. Yegor Gaidar, ed., *Finansovyi krizis v Rossii i mire* (Moscow: Prospekt, 2009), 108.

6. See chapter 6 in this volume.

7. See chapter 3 in this volume.

8. Dorofeev and Bashkirova, *Antikrizisnaya kniga Kommersanta*, 110–23, 173–75.

9 Boris Nemtsov and Vladimir Milov, *Putin i krizis*, February 2009, www.grani.ru/Russia/m.147764.html (accessed 1 February 2010).

Index

About the Contributors

Nikolay Dobronravin is a professor at the Department of World Politics, School of International Relations, St. Petersburg State University. He was a visiting professor at Hamburg University, University of Helsinki, Federal University of Bahia (Brasil) and also taught courses at Washington State University, Zhejiang University, and São Paulo University. He is a specialist on development studies and international relations in Sub-Saharan Africa and Central Asia and published a number of articles and book chapters on these issues.

Vladimir Gel'man is a professor at the Department of Political Science and Sociology, European University at St. Petersburg. He is an author and/or editor of seventeen books, including *Elites and Democratic Development in Russia* (2003), *Making and Breaking Democratic Transitions: The Comparative Politics of Russia's Regions* (2003), and *The Politics of Local Government in Russia* (2004). He was also a visiting professor at the University of Texas at Austin and the Central European University, Budapest, and has published more than a hundred journal articles and book chapters in English and in Russian.

Otar Marganiya is the president of the Center for Modernization Studies at the European University at St. Petersburg and is an advisor to the minister of finance of the Russian Federation. Previously, he taught at the Department of Economics at St. Petersburg State University. With Dmitry Travin, he coauthored a major two-volume study, *Evropeiskaya modernizatsiya* [The European Modernization], which appeared in Russian in 2004. He also served as an editor of several volumes, including *SSSR posle raspada* [Soviet Union: After the Collapse] (2007).

Andrey Scherbak is a research associate at the European University at St. Petersburg. Upon completion of his doctoral dissertation on party politics in Russia, he taught at St. Petersburg Branch of the State University—Higher School of Economics and was a visiting professor at Ohio State University. He published a number of journal articles on post-Soviet politics and political economy.

Dmitry Travin is the academic director of the Center for Modernization Studies at the European University at St. Petersburg. Previously, he served as a deputy editor of the St. Petersburg-based weekly *Delo* and also taught at St. Petersburg State University. His major two-volume study, *Evropeiskaya modernizatsiya* [The European Modernization], coauthored with Otar Marganiya, appeared in Russian in 2004. He also authored numerous books and journal articles in Russian on contemporary political and economic reforms in Russia. In 2008, he received an International Leontief Award "For Contribution to Economic Reforms" (named after Nobel Prize winner Wassily Leontief).

Andrey Zaostrovtsev is a senior research fellow of the Center for Modernization Studies at the European University at St. Petersburg, and associate professor at St. Petersburg University of Economics and Finance. He is a specialist in political economy and public choice theory, and authored more than twenty journal articles and book chapters in Russian and in English. His recent book, *Ekonomicheskii analiz politiki: Kontseptsii teorii obschestvennogo vybora* [Economic Analysis of Politics: Approaches of the Public Choice Theory], appeared in Russian in 2008.

Breinigsville, PA USA
26 July 2010
242395BV00003B/7/P